TABLE OF CONTENTS

Top 20 Test Taking Tips

1. Carefully follow all the test registration procedures
2. Know the test directions, duration, topics, question types, how many questions
3. Setup a flexible study schedule at least 3-4 weeks before test day
4. Study during the time of day you are most alert, relaxed, and stress free
5. Maximize your learning style; visual learner use visual study aids, auditory learner use auditory study aids
6. Focus on your weakest knowledge base
7. Find a study partner to review with and help clarify questions
8. Practice, practice, practice
9. Get a good night's sleep; don't try to cram the night before the test
10. Eat a well balanced meal
11. Know the exact physical location of the testing site; drive the route to the site prior to test day
12. Bring a set of ear plugs; the testing center could be noisy
13. Wear comfortable, loose fitting, layered clothing to the testing center; prepare for it to be either cold or hot during the test
14. Bring at least 2 current forms of ID to the testing center
15. Arrive to the test early; be prepared to wait and be patient
16. Eliminate the obviously wrong answer choices, then guess the first remaining choice
17. Pace yourself; don't rush, but keep working and move on if you get stuck
18. Maintain a positive attitude even if the test is going poorly
19. Keep your first answer unless you are positive it is wrong
20. Check your work, don't make a careless mistake

History, Philosophy, and Methodology of Science

Inquiry

Teaching with the concept of scientific inquiry in mind encourages students to think like scientists rather than merely practice the rote memorization of facts and history. This belief in scientific inquiry puts the burden of learning on students, which is a much different approach than expecting them to simply accept and memorize what they are taught. The standards for science as inquiry are intended to be comprehensive, encompassing a student's K-12 education. More are addressed as students gain knowledge. The National Science Education Standards state that engaging students in inquiry helps them develop the following five skills:

- Understand scientific concepts.
- Appreciate "how we know" what we know in science.
- Understand the nature of science.
- Develop the skills necessary to become independent inquirers about the natural world.
- Develop the skills necessary to use the skills, abilities, and attitudes associated with science.

Abilities that K-4 students should acquire

The six abilities that grades K-4 students should acquire are as follows:

- They should be able to ask questions about objects, organisms, and events in the environment.
- They should be able to devise a simple investigation to answer a question.
- They should be able to use tools such as magnifying glasses, rulers, and balances to gather data and make observations.
- They should be able to use the gathered data and observations to provide an explanation.
- They should be able to talk about, draw pictures, or use another method to communicate the results of an investigation and what they learned.
- With respect to the nature of scientific inquiry and scientists, students should understand that investigations involve formulating questions and answers, using different methods of discovering and disclosing answers, using basic tools, observing, sharing answers, and looking at and understanding others' work.

Abilities that 5-8 students should acquire

The five abilities that grades 5-8 students should acquire are as follows:

- They should be able to reformulate and clarify questions until they can be answered through scientific investigation.
- They should be able to create and carry out a scientific investigation, interpret the data to provide explanations, and use further data to revise explanations.

- They should be able to identify the tools necessary to gather and analyze data. They should be able to use computer hardware and software to store, organize, and gather data.
- They should be able to provide descriptions and explanations, create models, and make predictions based on the body of knowledge they possess.
- They should be able to explain cause and effect relationships using explanations and data from experiments.

Abilities that 9-12 students should acquire

The six abilities that 9-12 students should acquire are as follows:

- They should be able to identify questions and concepts that guide scientific investigation. In other words, they should be able to create a hypothesis and an appropriate experiment to test that hypothesis.
- They should be able to design and conduct a scientific investigation from start to finish. This includes being able to guide the inquiry by choosing the proper technologies and methods, determining variables, selecting an appropriate method for presenting data, and conducting peer reviews.
- They should be able to use technology and mathematics in investigations.
- They should be able to formulate and revise scientific explanations and models.
- They should be able to recognize and analyze alternative explanations. In other words, they should be able to devise other possibilities based on the current body of knowledge.
- They should be able to communicate and defend a scientific argument in both written and oral form.

Scientific knowledge

The National Science Education Standards suggest that science as a whole and its unifying concepts and processes are a way of thought that is taught throughout a student's K-12 education. There are eight areas of content, and all the concepts, procedures, and underlying principles contained within make up the body of scientific knowledge. The areas of content are: unifying concepts and processes in science, science as inquiry, physical science, life science, earth and space science, science and technology, science in personal and social perspectives, and history and nature of science. Specific unifying concepts and processes included in the standards and repeated throughout the content areas are: systems, order, and organization; evidence, models, and explanation; change, constancy, and measurement; evolution and equilibrium; and form and function.

Evolution of scientific knowledge

When one examines the history of scientific knowledge, it is clear that it is constantly evolving. The body of facts, models, theories, and laws grows and changes over time. In other words, one scientific discovery leads to the next. Some advances in science and technology have important and long-lasting effects on science and society. Some discoveries were so alien to the accepted beliefs of the time that not only were they rejected as wrong, but were also considered outright blasphemy. Today, however, many beliefs once considered incorrect have become an ingrained part of scientific knowledge, and have also been the basis of new advances. Examples of advances include: Copernicus's heliocentric view of the universe, Newton's laws of motion and planetary orbits, relativity, geologic time scale, plate tectonics, atomic theory, nuclear physics, biological evolution, germ theory, industrial revolution, molecular biology, information and communication, quantum theory, galactic universe, and medical and health technology.

Facts, hypotheses, theories, models, and laws

A scientific fact is considered an objective and verifiable observation. A scientific theory is a greater body of accepted knowledge, principles, or relationships that might explain a fact. A hypothesis is an educated guess that is not yet proven. It is used to predict the outcome of an experiment in an attempt to solve a problem or answer a question. A law is an explanation of events that always lead to the same outcome. It is a fact that an object falls. The law of gravity explains why an object falls. The theory of relativity, although generally accepted, has been neither proven nor disproved. A model is used to explain something on a smaller scale or in simpler terms to provide an example. It is a representation of an idea that can be used to explain events or applied to new situations to predict outcomes or determine results.

Scientific method

One could argue that scientific knowledge is the sum of all scientific inquiries for truths about the natural world carried out throughout the history of human kind. More simply put, it is thanks to scientific inquiry that we know what we do about the world. Scientists use a number of generally accepted techniques collectively known as the scientific method. The scientific method generally involves carrying out the following steps:

- Identifying a problem or posing a question
- Formulating a hypothesis or an educated guess
- Conducting experiments or tests that will provide a basis to solve the problem or answer the question
- Observing the results of the test
- Drawing conclusions

An important part of the scientific method is using acceptable experimentation techniques to ensure results are not skewed. Objectivity is also important if valid results are to be obtained. Another important part of the scientific method is peer review. It is essential that experiments be performed and data be recorded in such a way that experiments can be reproduced to verify results.

CGS and MKS

The metric system is the accepted standard of measurement in the scientific community. The International System (SI) of Units is a set of measurements (including the metric system) that is almost globally accepted. The United States, Liberia, and Myanmar have not accepted this system. Standardization is important because it allows the results of experiments to be compared and reproduced without the need to laboriously convert measurements. The SI is based partially on the meter-kilogram-second (MKS) system rather

- 7 -

than the centimeter-gram-second (CGS) system. The MKS system considers meters, kilograms, and seconds to be the basic units of measurement, while the CGS system considers centimeters, grams, and seconds to be the basic units of measurement. Under the MKS system, the length of an object would be expressed as 1 meter instead of 100 centimeters, which is how it would be described under the CGS system.

Metric system

Using the metric system is generally accepted as the preferred method for taking measurements. Having a universal standard allows individuals to interpret measurements more easily, regardless of where they are located. The basic units of measurement are: the meter, which measures length; the liter, which measures volume; and the gram, which measures mass. The metric system starts with a base unit and increases or decreases in units of 10. The prefix and the base unit combined are used to indicate an amount. For example, deka is 10 times the base unit. A dekameter is 10 meters; a dekaliter is 10 liters; and a dekagram is 10 grams. The prefix hecto refers to 100 times the base amount; kilo is 1,000 times the base amount. The prefixes that indicate a fraction of the base unit are deci, which is 1/10 of the base unit; centi, which is 1/100 of the base unit; and milli, which is 1/1000 of the base unit.

Metric prefixes for multiples and subdivisions

The prefixes for multiples are as follows: deka (da), 10^1 (deka is the American spelling, but deca is also used); hecto (h), 10^2; kilo (k), 10^3; mega (M), 10^6; giga (G), 10^9; tera (T), 10^{12}; peta (P), 10^{15}; exa (E), 10^{18}; zetta (Z), 10^{21}; and yotta (Y), 10^{24}. The prefixes for subdivisions are as follows: deci (d), 10^{-1}; centi (c), 10^{-2}; milli (m), 10^{-3}; micro (μ), 10^{-6}; nano (n), 10^{-9}; pico (p), 10^{-12}; femto (f), 10^{-15}; atto (a), 10^{-18}; zepto (z), 10^{-21}; and yocto (y), 10^{-24}. The rule of thumb is that prefixes greater than 10^3 are capitalized. These abbreviations do not need a period after them. A decimeter is a tenth of a meter, a deciliter is a tenth of a liter, and a decigram is a tenth of a gram. Pluralization is understood. For example, when referring to 5 mL of water, no "s" needs to be added to the abbreviation.

SI units of measurement

SI uses second(s) to measure time. Fractions of seconds are usually measured in metric terms using prefixes such as millisecond (1/1,000 of a second) or nanosecond (1/1,000,000,000 of a second). Increments of time larger than a second are measured in minutes and hours, which are multiples of 60 and 24. An example of this is a swimmer's time in the 800-meter freestyle being described as 7:32.67, meaning 7 minutes, 32 seconds, and 67 one-hundreds of a second. One second is equal to 1/60 of a minute, 1/3,600 of an hour, and 1/86,400 of a day. Other SI base units are the ampere (A) (used to measure electric current), the kelvin (K) (used to measure thermodynamic temperature), the candela (cd) (used to measure luminous intensity), and the mole (mol) (used to measure the amount of a substance at a molecular level). Meter (m) is used to measure length and kilogram (kg) is used to measure mass.

Significant figures and estimation

The mathematical concept of significant figures or significant digits is often used to determine the accuracy of measurements or the level of confidence one has in a specific measurement. The significant figures of a measurement include all the digits known with certainty plus one estimated or uncertain digit. There are a number of rules for determining which digits are considered "important" or "interesting." They are: all non-zero digits are significant, zeros between digits are significant, and leading and trailing zeros are not significant unless they appear to the right of the non-zero digits in a decimal. For example, in 0.01230 the significant digits are 1230, and this number would be said to be accurate to the hundred-thousandths place. The zero indicates that the amount has actually been measured as 0. Other zeros are considered place holders, and are not important. A decimal point may be placed after zeros to indicate their importance (in 100. for example).

Convertion from decimal notation to scientific notation

Scientific notation is used because values in science can be very large or very small, which makes them unwieldy. A number in decimal notation is 93,000,000. In scientific notation, it is 9.3×10^7. The first number, 9.3, is the coefficient. It is always greater than or equal to 1 and less than 10. This number is followed by a multiplication sign. The base is always 10 in scientific notation. If the number is greater than zero, the exponent is a positive number. If it is less than zero, the exponent is negative. The first digit of the number is followed by a decimal point and then the rest of the number. In this case, the number is 9.3. To get that number, the decimal point was moved seven places from the end of the number, 93,000,000. The number of places, seven, is the exponent.

Lab report

A lab report is an item developed after an experiment that is intended to present the results of a lab experiment. Generally, it should be prepared using a word processor, not hand-written or recorded in a notebook. A lab report should be formally presented. It is intended to persuade others with its acceptance or rejection of a hypothesis and become part of the body of scientific knowledge. It should include a brief but descriptive title and an abstract. The abstract is a summary of the report. It should include a purpose that states the problem that was explored or the question that was answered. It should also include a hypothesis that describes the anticipated results of the experiment. The experiment should include a control and one variable to ensure the results can be interpreted correctly. Observations and results can be presented using written narratives, tables, graphs, and illustrations. The report should also include a summation or conclusion explaining whether the results supported the hypothesis.

Lab notebook

A lab notebook is a record of all pre-lab work and lab work. It differs from a lab report, which is prepared after lab work is completed. A lab notebook is a formal record of lab preparations and what was done. Observational recordings should not be altered, erased, or whited-out to make corrections. Drawing a single line through an entry is sufficient to make changes. Pages should be numbered and should not be torn out. Entries should be made neatly, but don't necessarily have to be complete sentences. Entries should provide detailed information and be recorded in such a way that another person could use them to replicate the experiment. Quantitative data may be recorded in tabular form, and may include calculations made during an experiment. Lab book entries can also include references and research performed before the experiment. Entries may also consist of information about a lab experiment, including the objective or purpose, the procedures, data collected, and the results.

Graphs and charts

Graphs and charts are effective ways to present scientific data such as observations, statistical analyses, and comparisons between dependent variables and independent variables. On a line chart, the independent variable (the one that is being manipulated for the experiment) is represented on the horizontal axis (the x-axis). Any dependent variables (the ones that may change as the independent variable changes) are represented on the y-axis. The points are charted and a line is drawn to connect the points. An XY or scatter plot is often used to plot many points. A "best fit" line is drawn, which allows outliers to be identified more easily. Charts and their axes should have titles. The x and y interval units should be evenly spaced and labeled. Other types of charts are bar charts and histograms, which can be used to compare differences between the data collected for two variables. A pie chart can graphically show the relation of parts to a whole.

Presentation of data

Data collected during a science lab can be organized and presented in any number of ways. While straight narrative is a suitable method for presenting some lab results, it is not a suitable way to present numbers and quantitative measurements. These types of observations can often be better presented with tables and graphs. Data that is presented in tables and organized in rows and columns may also be used to make graphs quite easily. Other methods of presenting data include illustrations, photographs, video, and even audio formats. In a formal report, tables and figures are labeled and referred to by their labels. For example, a picture of a bubbly solution might be labeled Figure 1, Bubbly Solution. It would be referred to in the text in the following way: "The reaction created bubbles 10 mm in size, as shown in Figure 1, Bubbly Solution." Graphs are also labeled as figures. Tables are labeled in a different way. Examples include: Table 1, Results of Statistical Analysis, or Table 2, Data from Lab 2.

Errors

Errors that occur during an experiment can be classified into two categories: random errors and systematic errors. Random errors can result in collected data that does not seem to fit and may be wildly different from the rest of the data, or they may result in data that is indistinguishable from the rest. Random errors are not consistent across the data set. In large data sets, random errors may contribute to the variability of data, but they will not affect the average. Random errors are sometimes referred to as noise. They may be caused by a student's inability to take the same measurement in exactly the same way or by outside factors that are not considered variables, but influence the data. A systematic error will show up consistently across a sample or data set, and may be the result of a flaw in the experiment design. This type of error affects the average, and is also known as bias.

Accident safety measures

Any spills or accidents should be reported to the teacher so that he can determine the safest clean-up method. The student should start to wash off a chemical spilled on the skin while reporting the incident. Some spills may require removal of contaminated clothing and use of the safety shower. Broken glass should be disposed of in a designated container. If someone's clothing catches fire they should walk to the safety shower and use it to extinguish the flames. A fire blanket may be used to smother a lab fire. A fire extinguisher, phone, spill neutralizers, and a first aid box are other types of safety equipment found in the lab. Students should be familiar with routes out of the room and the building in case of fire. Students should use the eye wash station if a chemical gets in the eyes.

Lab safety measures

Students should wear a lab apron and safety goggles. Loose or dangling clothing and jewelry, necklaces, and earrings should not be worn. Those with long hair should tie it back. Care should always be taken not to splash chemicals. Open-toed shoes such as sandals and flip-flops should not be worn, nor should wrist watches. Glasses are preferable to contact lenses since the latter carries a risk of chemicals getting caught between the lens and the eye. Students should always be supervised. The area where the experiment is taking place and the surrounding floor should be free of clutter. Only the lab book and the items necessary for the experiment should be present. There is no smoking, eating, or chewing gum in the lab. Cords should not be allowed to dangle from work stations. There should be no rough-housing in the lab. Hands should be washed after the lab is complete.

Fume hood

Because of the potential safety hazards associated with chemistry lab experiments, such as fire from vapors and the inhalation of toxic fumes, a fume hood should be used in many instances. It carries away vapors from reagents or reactions. A fume hood can reduce exposure to potentially harmful fumes or vapors. Equipment or reactions are placed as far back in the hood as practical to help enhance the collection of the fumes. The glass safety shield automatically closes to the appropriate height, and should be low enough to protect the face and body. The safety shield should only be raised to move equipment in and out of the hood. One should not climb inside a hood or stick one's head inside. All spills should be wiped up immediately and the glass should be cleaned if a splash occurs.

Possible safety hazards

Some specific safety hazards possible in a chemistry lab include:

- Fire: Fire can be caused by volatile solvents such as ether, acetone, and benzene being kept in an open beaker or Erlenmeyer flask. Vapors can creep along the table and ignite if they reach a flame or spark. Solvents should be heated in a hood with a steam bath, not on a hot plate.
- Explosion: Heating or creating a reaction in a closed system can cause an explosion, resulting in flying glass and chemical splashes. The system should be vented to prevent this.
- Chemical and thermal burns: Many mineral acids and alkalis are corrosive to the skin and eyes. Others like acid halides and phenols are corrosive and often toxic.
- Cuts from broken glass.
- Absorption of toxic chemicals such as dimethyl sulfoxide (DMSO) and nitrobenzene through the skin. Inhalation of toxic fumes: Some compounds, such as acetyl chloride, severely irritate membranes in the eyes, nose, throat, and lungs. Others, such as benzyl chloride, cause eye irritation and tears.

- Ingestion of toxic chemicals.

Safety gloves

There are many types of gloves available to help protect the skin from cuts, burns, and chemical splashes. There are many considerations to take into account when choosing a glove. For example, gloves that are highly protective may limit dexterity. Some gloves may not offer appropriate protection against a specific chemical. Other considerations include degradation rating, which indicates how effective a glove is when exposed to chemicals; breakthrough time, which indicates how quickly a chemical breaks through the surface of the glove; and permeation rate, which indicates how quickly chemicals seep through after the initial breakthrough. Disposable latex, vinyl, or nitrile examination gloves are usually appropriate for most circumstances, and offer protection from incidental splashes and contact. Other types of gloves include butyl, neoprene, PVC, PVA, viton, silver shield, and natural rubber. Each offers its own type of protection, but may have drawbacks as well. Double gloving can improve resistance or dexterity in some instances.

Chemical handling and storage

Students should take care when carrying chemicals from one place to another. They should never be taken from the room, tasted, or touched with bare hands. Safety gloves should be worn when appropriate and glove/chemical interactions and glove deterioration should be considered. Hands should always be washed thoroughly after a lab. Potentially hazardous materials intended for use in chemistry, biology, or other science labs should be secured in a safe area where relevant material safety data sheets (MSDS) can be accessed. Chemicals and solutions should be used as directed and labels should be read before handling solutions and chemicals. Extra chemicals should not be returned to their original containers, but should be disposed of as directed by the school district's rules or local ordinances. Local municipalities often have hazardous waste disposal programs. Acids should be stored separately. Flammable liquids should be stored away from acids, bases, and oxidizers.

Bunsen burners

First, loose clothing should be tucked in, long hair should be tied back, and safety goggles and aprons should be worn. Students should be familiar with other safety precautions as well. They should know where the safety shower and eye wash centers are and how to use them. They should also know what to do in case of a fire or accident. Ensure that the Bunsen burner being lit and burners at nearby work stations are turned off before starting. When lighting the burner, strikers should always be used instead of matches. Do not touch the hot barrel. Tongs (never fingers) should be used to hold the material in the flame. To heat liquid, a flask may be set upon wire gauze on a tripod and secured with an iron ring or clamp on a stand. The flame is extinguished by turning off the gas at the source.

Lab animals and dissections

Animals to be used for dissections in a general science, biology, or physiology class should be obtained from a company that provides animals for this purpose. Road kill or decaying animals that a student brings in should not be used. It is possible that such an animal may have a pathogen or a virus, such as rabies, which can be transmitted via the saliva of even a dead animal. Students should use gloves and should not participate if they have open sores or moral objections. It is generally accepted that biological experiments may be performed on lower-order life forms and invertebrates, but not on mammalian vertebrates and birds. No animals should be harmed physiologically. Experimental animals should be kept, cared for, and handled in a safe manner and with compassion. Pathogenic (anything able to cause a disease) substances should not be used in lab experiments.

Lab glassware: flasks, beakers, and pipettes

Two types of flasks commonly used in lab settings are Erlenmeyer flasks and volumetric flasks, which can also be used to accurately measure liquids. Erlenmeyer flasks and beakers can be used for mixing, transporting, and reacting, but are not appropriate for accurate measurements. A pipette can be used to accurately measure small amounts of liquid. Liquid is drawn into the pipette through the bulb and a finger is then quickly placed at the top of the container. The liquid measurement is read exactly at the meniscus. Liquid can be released from the pipette by lifting the finger. There are also plastic disposal pipettes. A repipette is a hand-operated pump that dispenses solutions.

Lab glassware: graduated cylinders and burettes

Graduated cylinders are used for precise measurements and are considered more accurate than flasks or beakers. They are made of either polypropylene (which is shatter-resistant and resistant to chemicals but can not be heated) or polymethylpentene (which is known for its clarity). They are lighter to ship and less fragile than glass. To read a graduated cylinder, it should be placed on a flat surface and read at eye level. The surface of a liquid in a graduated cylinder forms a lens-shaped curve. The measurement should be taken from the bottom of the curve. A ring may be placed at the top of tall, narrow cylinders to help avoid breakage if they are tipped over. A burette, or buret, is a piece of lab glassware used to accurately dispense liquid. It looks similar to a narrow graduated cylinder, but includes a stopcock and tip. It may be filled with a funnel or pipette.

Light microscopes

There are different kinds of microscopes, but optical or light microscopes are the most commonly used in lab settings. Light and lenses are used to magnify and view samples. A specimen or sample is placed on a slide and the slide is placed on a stage with a hole in it. Light passes through the hole and illuminates the sample. The sample is magnified by lenses and viewed through the eyepiece. A simple microscope has one lens, while a typical compound microscope has three lenses. The light source can be room light redirected by a mirror or the microscope can have its own independent light source that passes through a condenser. In this case, there are diaphragms and filters to allow light intensity to be controlled. Optical microscopes also have coarse and fine adjustment knobs.

Other types of microscopes

Other types of microscopes include digital microscopes, which use a camera and a monitor to allow viewing of the sample. No eyepiece or methods for viewing samples directly exist. Scanning electron microscopes (SEMs) provide greater detail of a sample in terms of the surface topography and can produce magnifications much greater than those possible with optical microscopes. The technology of an SEM is quite different from an optical microscope in that it doesn't rely on lenses to magnify objects, but uses samples placed in a chamber. In one type of SEM, a beam of electrons from an electron gun scans and actually interacts with the sample to produce an image.

Balances

Unlike laboratory glassware that measures volume, balances such as triple-beam balances, spring balances, and electronic balances measure mass and force. An electronic balance is the most accurate, followed by a triple-beam balance and then a spring balance. One part of a triple-beam balance is the plate, which is where the item to be weighed is placed. There are also three beams that have hatch marks indicating amounts and hold the weights that rest in the notches. The front beam measures weights between 0 and 10 grams, the middle beam measures weights in 100 gram increments, and the far beam measures weights in 10 gram increments. The sum of the weight of each beam is the total weight of the object. A triple beam balance also includes a set screw to calibrate the equipment and a mark indicating the object and counterweights are in balance. Analytical balances are accurate to within 0.0001 g.

Slide preparation

Wet mount slides designed for use with a light microscope typically require a thin portion of the specimen to be placed on a standard glass slide. A drop of water is added and a cover slip or cover glass is placed on top. Air bubbles and fingerprints can make viewing difficult. Placing the cover slip on at a 45 degree angle and allowing it to drop into place can help avoid the problem of air bubbles. A cover slip should always be used when viewing wet mount slides. The viewer should start with the objective in its lowest position and then fine focus. The microscope should be carried with two hands and stored with the low-power objective in the down position. Lenses should be cleaned with lens paper only. A graticule slide is marked with a grid line, and is useful only for counting or estimating a quantity.

Chromatography

Chromatography refers to a set of laboratory techniques used to separate or analyze mixtures. Mixtures are dissolved in their mobile phases. In the stationary or bonded phase, the desired component is separated from other molecules in the mixture. In chromatography, the analyte is the substance to be separated. Preparative chromatography refers to the type of chromatography that involves purifying a substance for further use rather than further analysis. Analytical chromatography involves analyzing the isolated substance. Other types of chromatography include column, planar, paper, thin layer, displacement, supercritical fluid, affinity, ion exchange, and site exclusion chromatography. Reversed phase, two-dimensional, simulated moving bed, pyrolysis, fast protein, counter current, and chiral are also types of chromatography. Gas chromatography refers to the separation technique in which the mobile phase of a substance is in gas form.

Preparation of materials for classroom

A reagent or reactant is a chemical agent for use in chemical reactions. When preparing for a lab, it should be confirmed that glassware and other equipment has been cleaned and/or sterilized. There should be enough materials, reagents, or other solutions needed for the lab for every group of students completing the experiment. Distilled water should be used instead of tap water when performing lab experiments because distilled water has most of its impurities removed. Other needed apparatus such as funnels, filter paper, balances, Bunsen burners, ring stands, and/or microscopes should also be set up. After the lab, it should be confirmed that sinks, workstations, and any equipment used have been cleaned. If chemicals or specimens need to be kept at a certain temperature by refrigerating them or using another storage method, the temperature should be checked periodically to ensure the sample does not spoil.

Centrifugation

A centrifuge is used to perform centrifugation, which is a process that separates a heterogeneous mixture (one consisting of two or more compounds) of a solid and a liquid by spinning it. Centrifugation uses centrifugal force to separate compounds in a mixture. The solid precipitate settles in the bottom of the test tube and the liquid component of the solution, called the centrifugate, is clear. A well-known application of this process is using a centrifuge to separate blood cells and plasma. The heavier cells settle on the bottom of the test tube and the lighter plasma stays on top. An accessible example of this principle is using a salad spinner to help dry lettuce.

Spectrophotometry

Spectrophotometry involves measuring the amount of visible light absorbed by a colored solution. There are analog and digital spectrometers that measure percent absorbency and percent transmittance. A single beam spectrometer measures relative light intensity. A double beam spectrometer compares light intensity between a reference sample and a test sample. Spectrometers measure the wavelength of light. Spectrometry not only involves working with visible light, but also near-ultraviolet and near-infrared light. A spectrophotometer includes an illumination source. An output wavelength is selected and beamed at the sample, the sample absorbs light, and the detector responds to the light and outputs an analog electronic current in a usable form. A spectrophotometer may require calibration. Some types can be used to identify unknown chemicals.

Electrophoresis, calorimetry, and titration

Electrophoresis is the process whereby molecules are separated using electrical charges. This is possible because particles disbursed in a fluid usually carry electric charges on their surfaces. Molecules are pulled through the fluid toward the positive end if the molecules have a negative charge, and are pulled through the fluid toward the negative end if the molecules have a positive charge. Calorimetry is used to determine the heat released or absorbed in a chemical reaction. Titration helps determine the precise endpoint of a reaction. With this information, the precise quantity of reactant in the titration flask can be determined. A burette is used to deliver the second reactant to the flask and an indicator or pH meter is used to detect the endpoint of the reaction.

Field studies

Field studies may facilitate scientific inquiry in a manner similar to indoor lab experiments. Field studies can be interdisciplinary in nature and can help students learn about any number of scientific concepts and apply many scientific processes. Research projects can be conducted at accessible locations, such as school campuses and local parks, or at more remote locations, including local state and national parks, beaches, mountains, and other places with unique geological properties. Students can practice the general techniques of observation, data collection and organization, collaborative planning, and analysis of experiments. Field studies give students the chance to learn through hands-on applications of scientific processes, such as map making in geography, observation of stratification in geology, observation of life cycles of plants and animals in live and changing biological settings, analysis of water quality in chemistry, and quantitative analysis in math and statistics, just to name a few.

Field study safety concerns

Students should watch out for obvious outdoor hazards. These include poisonous flora and fauna such as poison ivy, poison oak, and sumac. Depending on the region of the United States in which the field study is being conducted, hazards may also include rattlesnakes and black widow or brown recluse spiders. Students should also be made aware of potentially hazardous situations specific to geographic locales, such as great tidal changes, incoming waves, and blow holes at the beach; the chance of becoming lost or disoriented in a nature setting; thunderstorms, sudden rain, snow storms, and flash flooding; steep paths or paths with precarious footing; dilapidated foot bridges; and fast moving streams. Students should also be aware of the possibility of coming into contact with pathogens if, for example, they are conducting an on-campus survey of micro-organisms.

Field study techniques

Field studies allow for great flexibility in the use of traditional and technological methods for making observations and collecting data. For example, a nature study could consist of a simple survey of bird species within a given area. Information could be recorded using still photography or a video camera. This type of activity gives students the chance to use technologies other than computers. Computers could still be used to create a slide show of transferred images or a digital lab report. If a quantitative study of birds was being performed, the simple technique of using a pencil and paper to tabulate the number of birds counted in the field could also be used. Other techniques used during field studies could include collecting specimens for lab study, observing coastal ecosystems and tides, and collecting weather data such as temperature, precipitation amounts, and air pressure in a particular locale.

Contributing individuals to scientific methodology

Charles Robert Darwin (d. 1882)
Best known for contributing to the survival of the fittest through natural selection theory of evolution by observing different species of birds, specifically finches, in various geographic locations. Although the species Darwin looked at were different, he speculated they had a common ancestor. He reasoned that specific traits persisted because they gave the birds a greater chance of surviving and reproducing. He also discovered fossils, noted stratification, dissected marine animals, and interacted with indigenous peoples. He contributed to the fields of biology, marine biology, anthropology, paleontology, geography, and zoology.

Anton van Leeuwenhoek (d. 1723)
Used homemade magnifying glasses to become the first person to observe single-celled organisms. He observed bacteria, yeast, plants, and other microscopic organisms. His observations contributed to the field of microbiology.

Carl Linnaeus (d. 1778)
Created a method to classify plants and animals, which became known as the Linnaean taxonomy. This was an important contribution because it offered a way to organize and therefore study large amounts of data.

Barbara McClintock (d. 1992)
Created the first genetic map for maize and was able to demonstrate basic genetic principles, such as how recombination is an exchange of chromosomal information. She also discovered how transposition flips the switch for traits. Her work contributed to the field of genetics, in particular to areas of study concerned with the structure and function of cells and chromosomes.

Gregor Johann Mendel (d. 1884)
Famous for experimenting with pea plants to observe the occurrence of inherited traits. He eventually became known as the father of genetics.

James Watson and Francis Crick (d. 2004)
Co-discoverers of the structure of deoxyribonucleic acid (DNA), which has a double helix shape. DNA contains the code for genetic information. The discovery of the double helix shape was important because it helped to explain how DNA replicates.

Vocabulary

Mean
The sum of a list of numbers divided by the number of numbers.

Median
The middle number in a list of numbers sorted from least to greatest. If the list has an even number of entries, the median is the smaller of the two in the middle.
Mode
The value that appears most frequently in a data set.

Range
The difference between the highest and lowest numbers, which can be used to determine how spread out data is.

Regression analysis
A method of analyzing sets of data and sets of variables that involves studying how the typical value of the dependent variable changes when any one of the independent variables is varied and the other independent variables remain fixed.

Standard deviation
Measures the variability of a data set and determines the amount of confidence one can have in the conclusions.

Chemistry

Atoms

The atom is one of the most basic units of matter. An atom consists of a central nucleus surrounded by electrons. The nucleus of an atom consists of protons and neutrons. It is positively charged, dense, and heavier than the surrounding electrons. The plural form of nucleus is nuclei. Electrons are atomic particles that are negatively charged and orbit the nucleus of an atom. Along with neutrons, protons make up the nucleus of an atom. The number of protons in the nucleus determines the atomic number of an element. Carbon atoms, for example, have six protons. The atomic number of carbon is 6. The number of protons also indicates the charge of an atom. The number of protons minus the number of electrons indicates the charge of an atom.

Structure of atoms

All matter consists of atoms. Atoms consist of a nucleus and electrons. The nucleus consists of protons and neutrons. The properties of these are measurable; they have mass and an electrical charge. The nucleus is positively charged due to the presence of protons. Electrons are negatively charged and orbit the nucleus. The nucleus has considerably more mass than the surrounding electrons. Atoms can bond together to make molecules. Atoms that have an equal number of protons and electrons are electrically neutral. If the number of protons and electrons in an atom is not equal, the atom has a positive or negative charge and is an ion.

Elements from the periodic table such as hydrogen, carbon, iron, helium, mercury, and oxygen are atoms. Atoms combine to form molecules. For example, two atoms of hydrogen (H) and one atom of oxygen (O) combine to form one molecule of water (H_2O).

Atoms are extremely small. A hydrogen atom is about 5×10^{-8} mm in diameter. According to some estimates, five trillion hydrogen atoms could fit on the head of a pin. Atomic radius refers to the average distance between the nucleus and the outermost electron. Models of atoms that include the proton, nucleus, and electrons typically show the electrons very close to the nucleus and revolving around it, similar to how the Earth orbits the sun. However, another model relates the Earth as the nucleus and its atmosphere as electrons, which is the basis of the term "electron cloud." Another description is that electrons swarm around the nucleus. It should be noted that these atomic models are not to scale. A more accurate representation would be a nucleus with a diameter of about 2 cm in a stadium. The electrons would be in the bleachers. This model is similar to the not-to-scale solar system model.

The atomic number (proton number) of an element refers to the number of protons in the nucleus of an atom. It is a unique identifier. It can be represented as Z. Atoms with a neutral charge have an atomic number that is equal to the number of electrons. Neutrons are the uncharged atomic particles contained within the nucleus. The number of neutrons in a nucleus can be represented as "N." Nucleon refers collectively to the neutrons and protons. An element is matter with one particular type of atom. It can be identified by its atomic number, or the number of protons in its nucleus. There are approximately 117 elements currently known, 94 of which occur naturally on Earth. Elements from the periodic table include hydrogen, carbon, iron, helium, mercury, and oxygen.

An *isotope* is a variation in the number of neutrons in an atom. Carbon, for example, always has the same number of protons (6), but does not always have the same number of neutrons. Its two most common isotopes are carbon-12 and carbon-13. The number after the element names refers to the total number of nucleons in the atom. Carbon's atomic number (Z) is always 6, but carbon-12 has 6 neutrons while carbon-13 has 7. An isotope can also be written by placing the number of nucleons in superscript before the element's symbol (^{13}C).

Mass is a measure of the amount of substance in an object. *Weight* is a measure of the gravitational pull of Earth on an object. *Volume* is a measure of the amount of space occupied. There are many formulas to determine volume. For example, the volume of a cube is the length of one side cubed (a^3) and the volume of a rectangular prism is length times width times height ($l \cdot w \cdot h$). The volume of an irregular shape can be determined by how much water it displaces. *Density* is a measure of the amount of mass per unit volume. The formula to find density is mass divided by volume ($D=m/V$). It is expressed in terms of mass per cubic unit, such as grams per cubic centimeter (g/cm^3). *Specific gravity* is a measure of the ratio of a substance's density compared to the density of water.

Physical vs. chemical properties and changes

Both physical changes and chemical reactions are everyday occurrences. Physical changes do not result in different substances. For example, when water becomes ice it has undergone a physical change, but not a chemical change. It has changed its form, but not its composition. It is still H_2O. Chemical properties are concerned with the constituent particles that make up the physicality of a substance. Chemical properties are apparent when chemical changes occur. The chemical properties of a substance are influenced by its electron configuration, which is determined in part by the number of protons in the nucleus (the atomic number). Carbon, for example, has 6 protons and 6 electrons. It is an element's outermost valence electrons that mainly determine its chemical properties. Chemical reactions may release or consume energy.

Elements, compounds, solutions, and mixtures

Elements are substances that consist of only one type of atom. *Compounds* are substances containing two or more elements. Compounds are formed by chemical reactions and frequently have different properties than the original elements. Compounds are decomposed by a chemical reaction rather than separated by a physical one. *Solutions* are homogeneous mixtures composed of two or more substances that have become one. *Mixtures* contain two or more substances that are combined but have not reacted chemically with each other. Mixtures can be separated using physical methods, while compounds cannot.

Mole

Atomic mass unit (amu) is the smallest unit of mass, and is equal to 1/12 of the mass of the carbon isotope carbon-12. A mole (mol) is a measurement of molecular weight that is equal to the molecule's amu in grams. For example, carbon has an amu of 12, so a mole of carbon weighs 12 grams. One mole is equal to about 6.0221415×10^{23} elementary entities, which are usually atoms or molecules. This amount is also known as the Avogadro constant or Avogadro's number (NA). Another way to say this is that one mole of a substance is the same as one Avogadro's number of that substance. One mole of chlorine, for example, is 6.0221415×10^{23} chlorine atoms. The charge on one mole of electrons is referred to as a Faraday.

Formation of molecules

Electrons in an atom can orbit different levels around the nucleus. They can absorb or release energy, which can change the location of their orbit or even allow them to break free from the atom. The outermost layer is the valence layer, which contains the valence electrons. The valence layer tends to have or share eight electrons. Molecules are formed by a chemical bond between atoms, a bond which occurs at the valence level. Two basic types of bonds are covalent and ionic. A covalent bond is formed when atoms share electrons. An ionic bond is formed when an atom transfers an electron to another atom. A hydrogen bond is a weak bond between a hydrogen atom of one molecule and an electronegative atom (such as nitrogen, oxygen, or fluorine) of another molecule. The Van der Waals force is a weak force between molecules. This type of force is much weaker than actual chemical bonds between atoms.

Electrons

Electrons are subatomic particles that orbit the nucleus at various levels commonly referred to as layers, shells, or clouds. The orbiting electron or electrons account for only a fraction of the atom's mass. They are much smaller than the nucleus, are negatively charged, and exhibit wave-like characteristics. Electrons are part of the lepton family of elementary particles. Electrons can occupy orbits that are varying distances away from the nucleus, and tend to occupy the lowest energy level they can. If an atom has all its electrons in the lowest available positions, it has a stable electron arrangement. The outermost electron shell of an atom in its uncombined state is known as the valence shell. The electrons there are called valence electrons, and it is their number that determines bonding behavior. Atoms tend to react in a manner that will allow them to fill or empty their valence shells.

Chemical bonds involve a negative-positive attraction between an electron or electrons and the nucleus of an atom or nuclei of more than one atom. The attraction keeps the atom cohesive, but also enables the formation of bonds among other atoms and molecules. Each of the four energy levels (or shells) of an atom has a maximum number of electrons they can contain. Each level must be completely filled before electrons can be added to the valence level. The farther away from the nucleus an electron is, the more energy it has. The first shell, or K-shell, can hold a maximum of 2 electrons; the second, the L-shell, can hold 8; the third, the M-shell, can hold 18; the fourth, the N-shell, can hold 32. The shells can also have subshells. Chemical bonds form and break between atoms when atoms gain, lose, or share an electron in the outer valence shell.

Nuclides, isotones, and isobars

A *nuclide* is a more inclusive term than isotope that is related more closely to nuclear properties than composition. Generally, the term nuclide refers to all the atomic nuclei containing a specified number of protons and neutrons, while isotopes are forms of a particular atom that vary in terms of the number of protons and neutrons. In other words, all the isotopes of all the elements are nuclides. *Isotone* refers to nuclides that have the same number of neutrons but a different number of protons. For example, carbon-14, nitrogen-15, and oxygen-16 all have eight neutrons in the nucleus. Therefore, they are all isotones of each other. *Isobar* refers to nuclides that have the same mass number (the same number of nucleons) but differing numbers of protons and neutrons. In other words, isobars have the same total number of protons and neutrons (collectively known as the nucleon) but different numbers of each. For example, the isotopes argon-40 (which has 18 protons and 22 neutrons) and calcium-40 (which has 20 protons and 20 neutrons) are isobars.

Atomic mass and atomic weight

Atomic mass is also known as the mass number. The *atomic mass* is the total number of protons and neutrons in the nucleus of an atom. It is referred to as "A." The atomic mass (A) is equal to the number of protons (Z) plus the number of neutrons (N). This can be represented by the equation $A = Z + N$. The mass of electrons in an atom is basically insignificant because it is so small. *Atomic weight* may sometimes be referred to as "relative atomic mass," but should not be confused with atomic mass. *Atomic weight* is the ratio of the average mass per atom of a sample (which can include various isotopes of an element) to 1/12 of the mass of an atom of carbon-12.

Stable vs. radioactive isotopes

Isotopes that have not been observed to decay are stable, or non-radioactive, isotopes. It is not known whether some stable isotopes may have such long decay times that observing decay is not possible. Currently, 80 elements have one or more stable isotopes. There are 256 known stable isotopes in total. Carbon, for example, has three isotopes. Two (carbon-12 and carbon-13) are stable and one (carbon-14) is radioactive. Radioactive isotopes have unstable nuclei and can undergo spontaneous nuclear reactions, which results in particles or radiation being emitted. It can not be predicted when a specific nucleus will decay, but large groups of identical nuclei decay at predictable rates. Knowledge about rates of decay can be used to estimate the age of materials that contain radioactive isotopes.

Nuclear isomers, allotropes, and quarks

Atomic nuclei are long-lived, have an equal number of protons and neutrons, and differ in energy content. *Nuclear isomers* are excited states of atomic nuclei. Nuclear isomers are different from chemical isomers. *Allotropes* are different structures of an element. Atoms of some elements have the ability to bond to each other in more than one way. This enables an element to have multiple arrangements of atoms, which are known as allotropes. Easily recognizable allotropes of carbon are the diamond and graphite. The carbon atoms of a diamond are bonded in a tetrahedral structure. In graphite, carbon atoms are bonded in hexagonal sheets. *Quarks* are considered basic particles and fundamental components of matter. Various flavors of quarks combine to form hadrons, such as the protons and neutrons of atomic nuclei. The six flavors of quarks are up, down, charm, strange, top, and bottom.

Periodic table

The periodic table groups elements with similar chemical properties together. The grouping of elements is based on atomic structure. It shows periodic trends of physical and chemical properties and identifies families of elements with similar properties. It is a common model for organizing and understanding elements. In the periodic table, each element has its own cell that includes varying amounts of information presented in symbol form about the properties of the element. Cells in the table are arranged in rows (periods) and columns (groups or families). At minimum, a cell includes the symbol for the element and its atomic number. The cell for hydrogen, for example, which appears first in the upper left corner, includes an "H" and a "1" above the letter. Elements are ordered by atomic number, left to right, top to bottom.

In the periodic table, the groups are the columns numbered 1 through 18 that group elements with similar outer electron shell configurations. Since the configuration of the outer electron shell is one of the primary factors affecting an element's chemical properties, elements within the same group have similar chemical properties. Previous naming conventions for groups have included the use of Roman numerals and upper-case letters. Currently, the periodic table groups are: Group 1, alkali metals; Group 2, alkaline earth metals; Groups 3-12, transition metals; Group 13, boron family; Group 14; carbon family; Group 15, pnictogens; Group 16, chalcogens; Group 17, halogens; Group 18, noble gases.

Other information that can be included in each elemental cell includes the atomic weight below the symbol, the element name, colors to organize elements into categories (such as the light pink used for transitional elements and the light blue used for noble gases), colors to indicate the phase of elements (such as red for gas and green for liquid), and line styles around cells to indicate an element's origins (a solid line around the cell indicates a primordial element, a dotted indicates an element created from decay, and no line indicates that the origins have not yet been discovered). Atomic weight is also known as standard atomic weight or relative atomic mass (not atomic mass), and is defined as the ratio of an average mass of atoms of a specific source of an element to 1/12 of the mass of an atom of carbon-12. Uncertainty may also be included in parenthesis after the atomic weight. Instead of atomic weight, artificial elements may list the most stable isotope in brackets.

Relation of periods and blocks to electrons

In the periodic table, there are seven periods (rows), and within each period there are blocks that group elements with the same outer electron subshell (more on this in the next section). The number of electrons in that outer shell determines which group an element belongs to within a given block. Each row's number (1, 2, 3, etc.) corresponds to the highest number electron shell that is in use. For example, row 2 uses only electron shells 1 and 2, while row 7 uses all shells from 1-7.

Trends

Atomic radii will decrease from left to right across a period (row) on the periodic table. In a group (column), there is an increase in the atomic radii of elements from top to bottom. Ionic radii will be smaller than the atomic radii for metals, but the opposite is true for non-metals. From left to right, electronegativity, or an atom's likeliness of taking another atom's electrons, increases. In a group, electronegativity decreases from top to bottom. Ionization energy or the amount of energy needed to get rid of an atom's outermost electron, increases across a period and decreases down a group. Electron affinity will become more negative across a period but will not change much within a group. The melting point decreases from top to bottom in the metal groups and increases from top to bottom in the non-metal groups.

Nuclear fission vs. nuclear fusion

Nuclear fission and *nuclear fusion* are similar in that they occur in the nucleus of an atom, can release great amounts of energy, and result in the formation of different elements (known as nuclear transmutation). They are different in that one breaks apart a nucleus and the other joins nuclei. *Nuclear fission* is the splitting of a large nucleus into smaller pieces. *Nuclear fusion* is the joining of two nuclei, which occurs under extreme temperatures and pressures. Fusion occurs naturally in stars, and is the process responsible for the release of great amounts of energy. When fusion occurs, many atomic nuclei with like charges are joined together, forming a heavier nucleus. When this occurs, energy can be absorbed and/or released.

Formation of compounds

Atoms interact by transferring or sharing the electrons furthest from the nucleus. Known as the outer or valence electrons, they are responsible for the chemical properties of an element. Bonds between atoms are created when electrons are paired up by being transferred or shared. If electrons are transferred from one atom to another, the bond is ionic. If electrons are shared, the bond is covalent. Atoms of the same element may bond together to form molecules or crystalline solids. When two or more different types of atoms bind together chemically, a compound is made. The physical properties of compounds reflect the nature of the interactions among their molecules. These interactions are determined by the structure of the molecule, including the atoms they consist of and the distances and angles between them.

Matter

Matter refers to substances that have mass and occupy space (or volume). The traditional definition of matter describes it as having three states: solid, liquid, and gas. These different states are caused by differences in the distances and angles between molecules or atoms, which result in differences in the energy that binds them. Solid structures are rigid or nearly rigid and have strong bonds. Molecules or atoms of liquids move around and have weak bonds, although they are not weak enough to readily break. Molecules or atoms of gases move almost independently of each other, are typically far apart, and do not form bonds. The current definition of matter describes it as having four states. The fourth is plasma, which is an ionized gas that has some electrons that are described as free because they are not bound to an atom or molecule.

Ions and ionization

Most atoms are neutral since the positive charge of the protons in the nucleus is balanced by the negative charge of the surrounding electrons. Electrons are transferred between atoms when they come into contact with each other. This creates a molecule or atom in which the number of electrons does not equal the number of protons, which gives it a positive or negative charge. A negative ion is created when an atom gains electrons, while a positive ion is created when an atom loses electrons. An ionic bond is formed between ions with opposite charges. The resulting compound is neutral. Ionization refers to the process by which neutral particles are ionized into charged particles. Gases and plasmas can be partially or fully ionized through ionization.

Separation vs. decomposition

Decomposition is considered a chemical reaction whereby a single compound breaks down into component parts or simpler compounds. When a compound or substance separates into these simpler substances, the byproducts are often substances that are different from the original. Decomposition can be viewed as the opposite of combination reactions. Most decomposition reactions are endothermic. Heat needs to be added for the chemical reaction to occur. *Separation* processes can be mechanical or chemical, and usually involve re-organizing a mixture of substances without changing their chemical nature. The separated products may differ from the original mixture in terms of chemical or physical properties. Types of separation processes include filtration, crystallization, distillation, and chromatography. Basically, decomposition breaks down one compound into two or more compounds or substances that are different from the original; separation sorts the substances from the original mixture into like substances.

Chemical reactions

Chemical reactions measured in human time can take place quickly or slowly. They can take fractions of a second or billions of years. The rates of chemical reactions are determined by how frequently reacting atoms and molecules interact. Rates are also influenced by the temperature and various properties (such as shape) of the reacting materials. Catalysts accelerate chemical reactions, while inhibitors decrease reaction rates. Some types of reactions release energy in the form of heat and light. Some types of reactions involve the transfer of either electrons or hydrogen ions between reacting ions, molecules, or atoms. In other reactions, chemical bonds are broken down by heat or light to form reactive radicals with electrons that will readily form new bonds. Processes such as the formation of ozone and greenhouse gases in the atmosphere and the burning and processing of fossil fuels are controlled by radical reactions.

Oxidation/reduction reactions
One way to organize chemical reactions is to sort them into two categories: oxidation/reduction reactions (also called redox reactions) and metathesis reactions (which include acid/base reactions). Oxidation/reduction reactions can involve the transfer of one or more electrons, or they can occur as a result of the transfer of oxygen, hydrogen, or halogen atoms. The species that loses electrons is oxidized and is referred to as the reducing agent. The species that gains electrons is reduced and is referred to as the oxidizing agent. The element undergoing oxidation experiences an increase in its oxidation number, while the element undergoing reduction experiences a decrease in its oxidation number. Single replacement reactions are types of oxidation/reduction reactions. In a single replacement reaction, electrons are transferred from one chemical species to another. The transfer of electrons results in changes in the nature and charge of the species.

Metathesis (acid/base) reactions
Double replacement reactions are metathesis reactions. In a double replacement reaction, the chemical reactants exchange ions but the oxidation state stays the same. One of the indicators of this is the formation of a solid precipitate. In acid/base reactions, an acid is a

compound that can donate a proton, while a base is a compound that can accept a proton. In these types of reactions, the acid and base react to form a salt and water. When the proton is donated, the base becomes water and the remaining ions form a salt. One method of determining whether a reaction is an oxidation/reduction or a metathesis reaction is that the oxidation number of atoms does not change during a metathesis reaction.

Combustion as a chemical reaction

Combustion, or burning, is a sequence of chemical reactions involving fuel and an oxidant that produces heat and sometimes light. There are many types of combustion, such as rapid, slow, complete, turbulent, microgravity, and incomplete. Fuels and oxidants determine the compounds formed by a combustion reaction. For example, when rocket fuel consisting of hydrogen and oxygen combusts, it results in the formation of water vapor. When air and wood burn, resulting compounds include nitrogen, unburned carbon, and carbon compounds. Combustion is an exothermic process, meaning it releases energy. Exothermic energy is commonly released as heat, but can take other forms, such as light, electricity, or sound. In chemistry, *species* is a generic term that can be used to refer to any type of particle, such as atoms, ions, molecules, molecular fragments, or specific forms of elements.

Combination and decomposition reactions

Combination, or *synthesis*, reactions: In a combination reaction, two or more reactants combine to form a single product (A + B → C). These reactions are also called synthesis or addition reactions. An example is burning hydrogen in air to produce water. The equation is $2H_2$ (g) + O_2 (g) → $2H_2O$ (l). Another example is when water and sulfur trioxide react to form sulfuric acid. The equation is H_2O + SO_3 → H_2SO_4. *Decomposition* (or *desynthesis*, *decombination*, or *deconstruction*) reactions: In a decomposition reaction, a reactant is broken down into two or more products (A → B + C). These reactions are also called analysis reactions. Thermal decomposition is caused by heat. Electrolytic decomposition is due to electricity. An example of this type of reaction is the decomposition of water into hydrogen and oxygen gas. The equation is $2H_2O$ → $2H_2$ + O_2.

Isomerization and neutralization reactions

Isomerization, or *rearrangement*, is the process of forming a compound's isomer. Within a compound, bonds are reformed. The reactant and product have the same molecular formula, but different structural formulas and different properties (A → B or A → A'). For example, butane (C_4H_{10}) is a hydrocarbon consisting of four carbon atoms in a straight chain. Heating it to 100° C or higher in the presence of a catalyst forms isobutane (methylpropane), which has a branched-chain structure. Boiling and freezing points are greatly different for butane and isobutane. A rearrangement reaction occurs within the molecule. A *neutralization*, *acid-base*, or *proton transfer* reaction is when one compound acquires H^+ from another. These types of reactions are also usually double displacement reactions. The acid has an H^+ that is transferred to the base and neutralized to form a salt.

Single and double substitution reactions

Single substitution, *displacement*, or *replacement* reactions are when one reactant is displaced by another to form the final product (A + BC → AB + C). Single substitution reactions can be cationic or anionic. When a piece of copper (Cu) is placed into a solution of silver nitrate ($AgNO_3$), the solution turns blue. The copper appears to be replaced with a silvery-white material. The equation is $2AgNO_3$ + Cu → Cu (NO_3)$_2$ + 2Ag. When this reaction takes place, the copper dissolves and the silver in the silver nitrate solution precipitates (becomes a solid), resulting in copper nitrate and silver. Copper and silver have switched

- 25 -

places in the nitrate. *Double displacement, double replacement, substitution, metathesis,* or *ion exchange* reactions are when ions or bonds are exchanged by two compounds to form different compounds (AC + BD → AD + BC). An example of this is that silver nitrate and sodium chloride form two different products (silver chloride and sodium nitrate) when they react. The formula for this reaction is $AgNO_3 + NaCl \rightarrow AgCl + NaNO_3$.

Endothermic vs. exothermic reactions
Endothermic reactions are chemical reactions that absorb heat and exothermic reactions are chemical reactions that release heat. Reactants are the substances that are consumed during a reaction, while products are the substances that are produced or formed. A balanced equation is one that uses reactants, products, and coefficients in such a way that the number of each type of atom (law of conservation of mass) and the total charge remains the same. The reactants are on the left side of the arrow and the products are on the right. The heat difference between endothermic and exothermic reactions is caused by bonds forming and breaking. If more energy is needed to break the reactant bonds than is released when they form, the reaction is endothermic. Heat is absorbed and the environmental temperature decreases. If more energy is released when product bonds form than is needed to break the reactant bonds, the reaction is exothermic. Heat is released and the environmental temperature increases.

In chemistry, the terms exothermic and endothermic are usually used to describe chemical reactions. The terms can also be used more generally to express the characteristics of physical processes. Some exothermic (heat-releasing) processes and reactions are a candle flame, burning sugar, rusting iron, nuclear fission, making ice cubes, condensation of rain from water vapor, forming ion pairs, and mixing water with strong acid, calcium chloride, or anhydrous salt. Some endothermic (heat-releasing) processes or reactions are baking bread, cooking an egg, melting ice cubes, water evaporation, separating pairs of ions, forming a cation (from an atom) in a gas, breaking up a gas atom, mixing water and ammonium nitrate, and melting solid salts. A useful memory aid is that "exo" is close to the word "exit." In these reactions heat goes out, or is released. "Endo" sounds like "in." In these reactions, heat goes in, or is absorbed.

Most abundant elements in the universe and on Earth

Aside from dark energy and dark matter, which are thought to account for all but four percent of the universe, the two most abundant elements in the universe are hydrogen (H) and helium (He). After hydrogen and helium, the most abundant elements are oxygen, neon, nitrogen, carbon, silicon, and magnesium. The most abundant isotopes in the solar system are hydrogen-1 and helium-4. Measurements of the masses of elements in the Earth's crust indicate that oxygen (O), silicon (Si), and aluminum (Al) are the most abundant on Earth. Hydrogen in its plasma state is the most abundant chemical element in stars in their main sequences, but is relatively rare on planet Earth.

Helium atom vs. hydrogen atom
In the periodic table of elements, a period (also known as a row) is organized in such a way that atomic numbers (which indicate the number of protons) increase from left to right. In a single row, the number of electrons in the outermost shell is the same for all elements. In a single row, atomic radii decrease from left to right. In elements with more protons, the electrons are pulled in by the greater nuclear charge and the atoms become smaller because their atomic radii are shorter. Hydrogen and helium are in the same period. The most

common isotope of hydrogen has one proton and one electron, but no neutron. Helium has two electrons and two protons. The higher number of protons exerts a greater force on the electrons, which is why a helium atom is smaller than a hydrogen atom.

Past atomic models and theories

There have been many revisions to theories regarding the structure of atoms and their particles. Part of the challenge in developing an understanding of matter is that atoms and their particles are too small to be seen. It is believed that the first conceptualization of the atom was developed by Democritus in 400 B.C. Some of the more notable models are the solid sphere or billiard ball model postulated by John Dalton, the plum pudding or raisin bun model by J.J. Thomson, the planetary or nuclear model by Ernest Rutherford, the Bohr or orbit model by Niels Bohr, and the electron cloud or quantum mechanical model by Louis de Broglie and Erwin Schrodinger. Rutherford directed the alpha scattering experiment that discounted the plum pudding model. The shortcoming of the Bohr model was the belief that electrons orbited in fixed rather than changing ecliptic orbits.

Cathode ray

The discovery of cathode rays in the late 1800s was basically the discovery of electrons. It was also discovered that electrons carry the negative charge of the atom and that the atom consists of smaller particles. Various scientists used different variations of cathode ray tubes containing no air or varying amounts of air. A cathode ray consists of a cathode, a negative electrode, and an anode, which has a positive charge. Modern cathode ray tubes heat a filament on the cathode end of the tube, which excites the electrons and separates them from their atoms. They travel in straight lines through the tube to the anode and back to the cathode through an electrical wire. The rays are invisible, but early scientists discovered fluorescence when the walls of the glass glowed when electrons hit them. Cathode rays are also known as electron beams.

Spectral lines

Atomic spectral lines indicate change in the electrical level of an atom. This usually occurs when an electron transitions from one orbit to another. During this process, photons are absorbed or emitted. For example, an emission line is formed when an electron transitions to a lower energy level and a photon is emitted. An absorption line is formed when an electron transfers to a higher energy level and a photon is absorbed. A photon is an elementary particle thought to be the basic unit, or quantum, of light. When viewed in comparison to a visible spectrum, an emission line is bright and an absorption line is dark. Spectral lines can be used to help identify atoms and determine the chemical composition of a material. Gas is usually used in spectral analysis.

Nuclear reactions

The particles of an atom's nucleus (the protons and neutrons) are bound together by nuclear force, also known as residual strong force. Unlike chemical reactions, which involve electrons, nuclear reactions occur when two nuclei or nuclear particles collide. This results in the release or absorption of energy and products that are different from the initial particles. The energy released in a nuclear reaction can take various forms, including the release of kinetic energy of the product particles and the emission of very high energy photons known as gamma rays. Some energy may also remain in the nucleus. Radioactivity refers to the particles emitted from nuclei as a result of nuclear instability. There are many nuclear isotopes that are unstable and can spontaneously emit some kind of radiation. The most common types of radiation are alpha, beta, and gamma radiation, but there are several other varieties of radioactive decay.

Radioisotopes, radioactive decay, and radioactivity

Also known as radionuclides or radioactive isotopes, *radioisotopes* are atoms that have an unstable nucleus. This is a nucleus that has excess energy and the potential to make radiation particles within the nucleus (subatomic particles) or undergo radioactive decay, which can result in the emission of gamma rays. Radionuclides may occur naturally, but can also be artificially produced. *Radioactive decay* occurs when an unstable atomic nucleus spontaneously loses energy by emitting ionizing particles and radiation. Decay is a form of energy transfer, as energy is lost. It also results in different products. Before decay there is one type of atom, called the parent nuclide. After decay there are one or more different products, called the daughter nuclide(s). *Radioactivity* refers to particles that are emitted from nuclei as a result of nuclear instability.

Radioactive half-life and radiation

Radioactive half-life is the time it takes for half of the radioactive nuclei in a sample to undergo radioactive decay. Radioactive decay rates are usually expressed in terms of half-lives. The different types of radioactivity lead to different decay paths, which transmute the nuclei into other chemical elements. Decay products (or daughter nuclides) make radioactive dating possible. Decay chains are a series of decays that result in different products. For example, uranium-238 is often found in granite. Its decay chain includes 14 daughter products. It eventually becomes a stable isotope of lead, which is why lead is often found with deposits of uranium ore. Its first half-life is equivalent to the approximate age of the earth, about 4.5 billion years. One of its products is radon, a radioactive gas. *Radiation* is when energy is emitted by one body and absorbed by another. Nuclear weapons, nuclear reactors, and radioactive substances are all examples of things that involve ionizing radiation. Acoustic and electromagnetic radiation are other types of radiation.

Alpha particles, beta particles, and gamma rays

Ionizing radiation is that which can cause an electron to detach from an atom. It occurs in radioactive reactions and comes in three types: alpha (α), beta (β), and gamma (γ). Alpha rays are positive, beta rays are negative, and gamma rays are neutral. Alpha particles are larger than beta particles and can cause severe damage if ingested. Because of their large mass, however, they can be stopped easily. Even paper can protect against this type of radiation. Beta particles can be beta-minus or beta-plus. Beta-minus particles contain an energetic electron, while beta-plus particles are emitted by positrons and can result in gamma photons. Beta particles can be stopped with thin metal. Gamma rays are a type of high energy electromagnetic radiation consisting of photons. Gamma radiation rids the decaying nucleus of excess energy after it has emitted either alpha or beta radiation. Gamma rays can cause serious damage when absorbed by living tissue, and it takes thick lead to stop them. Alpha, beta, and gamma radiation can also have positive applications.

Radioactive waste

Radioactive waste is a waste product that is considered dangerous because of either low levels or high levels of radioactivity. Radioactive waste could include discarded clothing that was used as protection against radiation or decay products of substances used to create electricity through nuclear fission. Small amounts of radioactive material can be ingested as a method of tracing how the body distributes certain elements. Other radioactive materials are used as light sources because they glow when heated. Uncontrolled radiation or even small amounts of radioactive material can cause sickness and cancer in humans. Gamma wave radiation is fast moving radiation that can cause cancer and damage genetic information by crashing into DNA molecules or other cells. Low-level radiation also occurs naturally. When related to everyday occurrences, radiation is measured in millirems per hour (mrem/hr). Humans can be exposed to radiation from stone used to build houses, cosmic rays from space, x-rays and other medical devices, and nuclear energy products.

Thermodynamics

Thermodynamics refers to a branch of physics that studies the conversion of energy into work and heat. It is especially concerned with variables such as temperature, volume, and pressure. Thermodynamic equilibrium refers to objects that have the same temperature because heat is transferred between them to reach equilibrium. *Open systems* are capable of interacting with a surrounding environment and can exchange heat, work (energy), and matter outside their system boundaries. A *closed system* can exchange heat and work, but not matter. An *isolated system* cannot exchange heat, work, or matter with its surroundings. Its total energy and mass stay the same. In physics, *surrounding environment* refers to everything outside a thermodynamic system (system). The terms "surroundings" and "environment" are also used. The term "boundary" refers to the division between the system and its surroundings.

Basic laws of thermodynamics
The laws of thermodynamics are generalized principles dealing with energy and heat.
- The zeroth law of thermodynamics states that two objects in thermodynamic equilibrium with a third object are also in equilibrium with each other. Being in thermodynamic equilibrium basically means that different objects are at the same temperature.
- The first law deals with conservation of energy. It states that neither mass nor energy can be destroyed; only converted from one form to another.
- The second law states that the entropy (the amount of energy in a system that is no longer available for work or the amount of disorder in a system) of an isolated system can only increase. The second law also states that heat is not transferred from a lower-temperature system to a higher-temperature one unless additional work is done.
- The third law of thermodynamics states that as temperature approaches absolute zero, entropy approaches a constant minimum. It also states that a system cannot be cooled to absolute zero.

Heat is the transfer of energy from a body or system as a result of thermal contact. Heat consists of random motion and the vibration of atoms, molecules, and ions. The higher the temperature is, the greater the atomic or molecular motion will be. *Energy* is the capacity to do work. *Work* is the quantity of energy transferred by one system to another due to

- 29 -

changes in a system that is the result of external forces, or macroscopic variables. Another way to put this is that work is the amount of energy that must be transferred to overcome a force. Lifting an object in the air is an example of work. The opposing force that must be overcome is gravity. Work is measured in joules (J). The rate at which work is performed is known as power. *Thermal energy* is the energy present in a system due to temperature.

Thermal contact

Thermal contact refers to energy transferred to a body by a means other than work. A system in thermal contact with another can exchange energy with it through the process of heat transfer. Thermal contact does not necessarily involve direct physical contact. Heat is energy that can be transferred from one body or system to another without work being done. Everything tends to become less organized and less useful over time (entropy). In all energy transfers, therefore, the overall result is that the heat is spread out so that objects are in thermodynamic equilibrium and the heat can no longer be transferred without additional work.

Concepts related to the first law of thermodynamics

The laws of thermodynamics state that energy can be exchanged between physical systems as heat or work, and that systems are affected by their surroundings. It can be said that the total amount of energy in the universe is constant. The first law is mainly concerned with the conservation of energy and related concepts, which include the statement that energy can only be transferred or converted, not created or destroyed. The formula used to represent the first law is $\Delta U = Q - W$, where ΔU is the change in total internal energy of a system, Q is the heat added to the system, and W is the work done by the system. Energy can be transferred by conduction, convection, radiation, mass transfer, and other processes such as collisions in chemical and nuclear reactions. As transfers occur, the matter involved becomes less ordered and less useful. This tendency towards disorder is also referred to as entropy.

Types of energy

Some discussions of energy consider only two types of energy: kinetic energy (the energy of motion) and potential energy (which depends on relative position or orientation). There are, however, other types of energy. Electromagnetic waves, for example, are a type of energy contained by a field. Another type of potential energy is electrical energy, which is the energy it takes to pull apart positive and negative electrical charges. Chemical energy refers to the manner in which atoms form into molecules, and this energy can be released or absorbed when molecules regroup. Solar energy comes in the form of visible light and non-visible light, such as infrared and ultraviolet rays. Sound energy refers to the energy in sound waves.

Examples
Electric to mechanical: Ceiling fan

Chemical to heat: A familiar example of a chemical to heat energy transformation is the internal combustion engine, which transforms the chemical energy (a type of potential energy) of gas and oxygen into heat. This heat is transformed into propulsive energy, which is kinetic. Lighting a match and burning coal are also examples of chemical to heat energy transformations.

Chemical to light: Phosphorescence and luminescence (which allow objects to glow in the dark) occur because energy is absorbed by a substance (charged) and light is re-emitted comparatively slowly. This process is different from the one involved with glow sticks. They glow due to chemiluminescence, in which an excited state is created by a chemical reaction and transferred to another molecule.

Heat to electricity: Examples include thermoelectric, geothermal, and ocean thermal.

Nuclear to heat: Examples include nuclear reactors and power plants.

Mechanical to sound: Playing a violin or almost any instrument

Sound to electric: Microphone

Light to electric: Solar panels

Electric to light: Light bulbs

Heat to mechanical: An example of a heat to mechanical energy transformation is a steam engine, such as the type used on a steam locomotive. A heat source such as coal is used to boil water. The steam produced turns a shaft, which eventually turns the wheels.

Kinetic to potential and potential to kinetic: A pendulum swinging is an example of both a kinetic to potential and a potential to kinetic energy transformation. When a pendulum is moved from its center point (the point at which it is closest to the ground) to the highest point before it returns, it is an example of a kinetic to potential transformation. When it swings from its highest point toward the center, it is considered a potential to kinetic transformation. The sum of the potential and kinetic energy is known as the total mechanical energy.

Potential to kinetic: Stretching a rubber band gives it potential energy. That potential energy becomes kinetic energy when the rubber band is released.

Heat vs. temperature
Heat is energy transfer (other than direct work) from one body or system to another due to thermal contact. Everything tends to become less organized and less orderly over time (entropy). In all energy transfers, therefore, the overall result is that the energy is spread out uniformly. This transfer of heat energy from hotter to cooler objects is accomplished by conduction, radiation, or convection. Temperature is a measurement of an object's stored heat energy. More specifically, temperature is the average kinetic energy of an object's particles. When the temperature of an object increases and its atoms move faster, kinetic energy also increases. Temperature is not energy since it changes and is not conserved. Thermometers are used to measure temperature.

Temperature scales
There are three main scales for measuring temperature. Celsius uses the base reference points of water freezing at 0 degrees and boiling at 100 degrees. Fahrenheit uses the base reference points of water freezing at 32 degrees and boiling at 212 degrees. Celsius and Fahrenheit are both relative temperature scales since they use water as their reference point. The Kelvin temperature scale is an absolute temperature scale. Its zero mark

corresponds to absolute zero. Water's freezing and boiling points are 273.15 Kelvin and 373.15 Kelvin, respectively. Where Celsius and Fahrenheit are measured is degrees, Kelvin does not use degree terminology.

- Converting Celsius to Fahrenheit: $°F = \frac{9}{5}°C + 32$
- Converting Fahrenheit to Celsius: $°C = \frac{5}{9}(°F - 32)$
- Converting Celsius to Kelvin: $K = °C + 273.15$
- Converting Kelvin to Celsius: $°C = K - 273.15$

Heat capacity and specific heat capacity

Heat capacity, also known as *thermal mass*, refers to the amount of heat energy required to raise the temperature of an object, and is measured in Joules per Kelvin or Joules per degree Celsius. The equation for relating heat energy to heat capacity is $Q = C\Delta T$, where Q is the heat energy transferred, C is the heat capacity of the body, and ΔT is the change in the object's temperature. *Specific heat capacity*, also known as *specific heat*, is the heat capacity per unit mass. Every element and compound has its own specific heat. For example, it takes different amounts of heat energy to raise the temperature of the same amounts of magnesium and lead by one degree. The equation for relating heat energy to specific heat capacity is $Q = mc\Delta T$, where m represents the mass of the object, and c represents its specific heat capacity.

Convection and radiation

Convection refers to heat transfer that occurs through the movement or circulation of fluids (liquids or gases). Some of the fluid becomes or is hotter than the surrounding fluid, and is less dense. Heat is transferred away from the source of the heat to a cooler, denser area. Examples of convection are boiling water and the movement of warm and cold air currents in the atmosphere and the ocean. Forced convection occurs in convection ovens, where a fan helps circulate hot air. Radiation is heat transfer that occurs through the emission of electromagnetic waves, which carry energy away from the emitting object. All objects with temperatures above absolute zero radiate heat.

Latent heat refers to the amount of heat required for a substance to undergo a phase (state) change (from a liquid to a solid, for example).

Second law of thermodynamics

The second law of thermodynamics explains how energy can be used. In particular, it states that heat will not transfer spontaneously from a cold object to a hot object. Another way to say this is that heat transfers occur from higher temperatures to lower temperatures. Also covered under this law is the concept that systems not under the influence of external forces tend to become more disordered over time. This type of disorder can be expressed in terms of entropy. Another principle covered under this law is that it is impossible to make a heat engine that can extract heat and convert it all to useful work. A thermal bottleneck occurs in machines that convert energy to heat and then use it to do work. These types of machines are less efficient than ones that are solely mechanical.

Calorie is the amount of energy it takes to raise the temperature of a gram of water by one degree Celsius. A kilocalorie refers to the amount of energy it takes to raise the temperature of a kilogram of water by one degree Celsius. A calorie is equal to 4.184 joules. *Calorimeter* is a measurement device with a thermometer in which chemical or physical processes take place. The resulting change in temperature and the heat capacity can then be determined. Specific heat capacities have already been identified for many materials, and can be viewed in table form. *BTU* stands for British thermal unit. It is a measurement of the amount of energy it takes to raise the temperature of a pound of water by one degree Fahrenheit. A BTU is equal to 252 calories or 1.054 kilojoules (kJ).

Conduction is a form of heat transfer that occurs at the molecular level. It is the result of molecular agitation that occurs within an object, body, or material while the material stays motionless. An example of this is when a frying pan is placed on a hot burner. At first, the handle is not hot. As the pan becomes hotter due to conduction, the handle eventually gets hot too. In this example, energy is being transferred down the handle toward the colder end because the higher speed particles collide with and transfer energy to the slower ones. When this happens, the original material becomes cooler and the second material becomes hotter until equilibrium is reached. Thermal conduction can also occur between two substances such as a cup of hot coffee and the colder surface it is placed on. Heat is transferred, but matter is not.

Conductor is a material that provides little resistance to heat transfer between its particles. *Insulator* is a material that provides resistance to heat transfer between its particles. When studying atoms at a microscopic level, it can be seen that some materials such as metals have properties that allow electrons to flow easily. Metals are good conductors of electricity because their valence electrons are loosely held in a network of atoms. This is because the valence shells of metal atoms have weak attractions to their nuclei. This results in a "sea of electrons," and electrons can flow between atoms with little resistance. In insulating materials such as glass, they hardly flow at all. In between materials can be called semiconducting materials, and have intermediate conducting behavior. At low temperatures, some materials become superconductors and offer no resistance to the flow of electrons. Thermal conductivity refers to a material's capacity to conduct heat.

Conservation of matter and atomic theory

Atomic theory is concerned with the characteristics and properties of atoms that make up matter. It deals with matter on a microscopic level as opposed to a macroscopic level. Atomic theory, for instance, discusses the kinetic motion of atoms in order to explain the properties of macroscopic quantities of matter. John Dalton (1766-1844) is credited with making many contributions to the field of atomic theory that are still considered valid. This includes the notion that all matter consists of atoms and that atoms are indestructible. In other words, atoms can be neither created nor destroyed. This is also the theory behind the conservation of matter, which explains why chemical reactions do not result in any detectable gains or losses in matter. This holds true for chemical reactions and smaller scale processes. When dealing with large amounts of energy, however, atoms can be destroyed by nuclear reactions. This can happen in particle colliders or atom smashers.

Conservation of mass number and charge in nuclear reactions

Mass number is the sum of neutrons and protons in the nucleus (A = N + Z). The conservation of mass number is a concept related to nuclear reactions. Two conditions are required to balance a nuclear reaction. They are conservation of mass number and conservation of nuclear charge. In a nuclear equation, the mass numbers should be equal on each side of the arrow. In this type of equation, the mass number is in superscript in front of the element and the atomic number is in subscript. The total number of nucleons is the same even though the product elements are different. For example, when a specific isotope of uranium decays into thorium and helium, the original mass number of uranium is 238. After the reaction, the mass number of thorium is 234 and the mass number of helium is 4 (238 = 234 + 4). The mass number is the same on both sides of the equation.

Example of using the alpha decay of radon for conservation of mass number

The alpha decay of radon (Rn) to polonium (Po), which is part of the uranium-238 decay chain, is a good example of conservation of mass number. Two protons and two neutrons are lost when a nucleus emits an alpha particle, meaning the mass number will be four less and the atomic number (Z), protons, will be 2 less. When the atomic number (Z) and mass number (A) are diagrammed in a formula, the mass number is in superscript in front of the symbol for the element and the atomic number is in subscript. When Rn, with a mass number of 222 and an atomic number of 86, emits an alpha particle, it loses four from its mass number. It becomes polonium, which has a mass number of 218 and an atomic number of 84. Since an alpha particle with two protons and two neutrons is also a result of the reaction, the mass number is conserved.

Atomic radius and ionic radius

Atomic size is typically measured in Angstroms (A) or picometers, where 1 Angstrom is equal to 10^{-10} of a meter, or 100 picometers (pm). The atomic radius of a chemical element refers to the distance from the nucleus to the boundary of an electron cloud or half the distance between two bonded nuclei. It may also refer to an isolated atom, but this can be confusing since atoms can share electrons, electron clouds can overlap, and electrons may be in motion. The trend across a period is for the atomic radius to decrease since as the atomic number (number of protons) increases across a row, electrons tend to be added in the same outermost shell, which increases nuclear charge and contracts the atom. The ionic radius is based upon nuclei when the ions are in a crystal lattice, meaning the atoms are organized in a specific manner.

Electronegativity

Electronegativity is a measure of how capable an atom is of attracting a pair of bonding electrons. It refers to the fact that one atom exerts slightly more force in a bond than another, creating a dipole. If the electronegative difference between two atoms is small, the atoms will form a polar covalent bond. If the difference is large, the atoms will form an ionic bond. When there is no electronegativity, a pure nonpolar covalent bond is formed. Electronegativity can be discussed as a trend in the periodic table. Fluorine (F) has the greatest electronegativity, and elements to the left and below fluorine have lower levels of electronegativity. This property of elements is often measured using the Pauling scale, which ranges from 4.0 (fluorine) to 0.7 (francium). Elements with high electronegativity are highly reactive because they can capture electrons. The symbols δ^+ (delta plus) and δ^- (delta minus) stand for fractional charges.

Oxidation state vs. oxidation number

Oxidation state and oxidation number are usually the same number. Even though they have different meanings, they are frequently used interchangeably. Oxidation numbers are

Roman numerals in parentheses that are used as part of the naming scheme for inorganic compounds. Oxidation state refers to the hypothetical charge on an atom if all of its bonds are 100 percent ionic. They are integers that can occasionally be fractional numbers. Oxidation state is increased through oxidation (loss of electrons) and decreased through reduction (gain of electrons). The number for an oxidation state refers to a single atom or ion, and is a way to keep track of electrons. When using Lewis diagrams, shared electrons are generally assigned to the more electronegative element. In bonds involving two atoms of the same element, electrons are split between them. Lone pairs of electrons are assigned to the atom they are with.

Determining oxidation state
Rules for calculating oxidation state include the one that states that the oxidation state is 0 for atoms in elemental form (only one kind of atom is present and its charge is 0). For example, both S_8 and Fe have an oxidation state of 0. For a monatomic ion, the oxidation state is equal to its charge. For example, the oxidation state is -2 for S^{2-} and +3 for Al^{3+}. For all Group 1A (alkali) metals, the oxidation state is +1. It is +2 for all Group 2A (alkaline earth) metals unless they are in elemental form. Hydrogen has an oxidation state of +1 when it is bonded to a nonmetal. It can be -1 when bonded to a metal. Oxygen almost always has an oxidation state of -2, but in peroxides it is -1. There are other exceptions as well. The oxidation state for fluorine is always -1. In a neutral compound, the sum of all atoms or ions must equal zero. In a polyatomic ion, its charge is equal to the sum of all oxidation state numbers.

Ionization energy, electron affinity, and polar bond

Ionization energy is the energy required for an electron to free itself from the grip of its neutral atom. Ionization energy increases across a row. Groups on the left of the table have fewer valence electrons and noble gases have the maximum number of valence electrons (a filled outer shell). Ionization energy can be measured in kilojoules (kJ) per mole or electron volts (eV) per atom (1 kJ/mol = 0.010364 eV/atom). Elements with low ionization energies are highly reactive because they can easily give up electrons. *Electron affinity* is a way to measure the change in energy when a negative ion is formed by adding an electron to a neutral atom. *Polar bond* refers to a covalent type of bond with a separation of charge. One end is negative and the other is positive. The hydrogen-oxygen bond in water is one example of a polar bond.

Electron shells

There are seven electron shells. One is closest to the nucleus and seven is the farthest away. Electron shells can also be identified with the letters K, L, M, N, O, P, and Q. Traditionally, there were four subshells identified by the first letter of their descriptive name: s (sharp), p (principal), d (diffuse), and f (fundamental). The maximum number of electrons for each subshell is as follows: s is 2, p is 6, d is 10, and f is 14. Every shell has an s subshell, the second shell and those above also have a p subshell, the third shell and those above also have a d subshell, and so on. Each subshell contains atomic orbitals, which describes the wave-like characteristics of an electron or a pair of electrons expressed as two angles and the distance from the nucleus. Atomic orbital is a concept used to express the likelihood of an electron's position in accordance with the idea of wave-particle duality.

Electron configuration is a trend whereby electrons fill shells and subshells in an element in a particular order and with a particular number of electrons. The chemical properties of the elements reflect their electron configurations. Energy levels (shells) do not have to be completely filled before the next one begins to be filled. A example of electron configuration notation is $1s^2 2s^2 2p^5$, where the first number is the row (period), or shell. The letter refers to the subshell of the shell, and the number in superscript is the number of electrons in the subshell. A common shorthand method for electron configuration notation is to use a noble gas (in a bracket) to abbreviate the shells that elements have in common. For example, the electron configuration for neon is $1s^2 2s^2 2p^6$. The configuration for phosphorus is $1s^2 2s^2 2p^6 3s^2 3p^3$, which can be written as $[Ne]3s^2 3p^3$. Subshells are filled in the following manner: 1s, 2s, 2p, 3s, 3p, 4s, 3d, 4p, 5s, 4d, 5p, 6s, 4f, 5d, 6p, 7s, 5f, 6d, and 7p.

Aufbau principle states that the electrons of an atom occupy quantum levels or orbitals starting at the lowest energy level and proceeding to the highest. Each orbital can only contain a maximum of two paired electrons that have opposite spins. *Valence shell* is the highest occupied electron shell, and contains the valence electrons. *IUPAC* stands for International Union of Pure and Applied Chemistry. *Alloy* is a mixture of elements that have metal properties. The original elements do not necessarily have to be metals. *Stoichiometry* refers to measuring the relationship between reactants and products that form compounds or are involved in chemical reactions. It relates to the law of conservation of mass, which states that matter can not be created, even during a chemical reaction. The *Pauli exclusion principle* states that no more than two electrons can be in the same quantum state in one energy level. This affects how electrons are configured.

Lewis formulas and Kekulé diagrams

Lewis formulas show the bonding or nonbonding tendency of specific pairs of valence electrons. Lewis dot diagrams use dots to represent valence electrons. Dots are paired around an atom. When an atom forms a covalent bond with another atom, the elements share the dots as they would electrons. Double and triple bonds are indicated with additional adjacent dots. Methane (CH_4), for instance, would be shown as a C with 2 dots above, below, and to the right and left and an H next to each set of dots. In structural formulas, the dots are single lines. Like Lewis dot diagrams, Kekulé diagrams are two-dimensional representations of chemical compounds. Covalent bonds are shown as lines between elements. Double and triple bonds are shown as two or three lines and unbonded valence electrons are shown as dots.

Gases

Kinetic theory of gases
The kinetic theory of gases assumes that gas molecules are small compared to the distances between them and that they are in constant random motion. The attractive and repulsive forces between gas molecules are negligible. Their kinetic energy does not change with time as long as the temperature remains the same. The higher the temperature is, the greater the motion will be. As the temperature of a gas increases, so does the kinetic energy of the molecules. In other words, gas will occupy a greater volume as the temperature is increased and a lesser volume as the temperature is decreased. In addition, the same amount of gas will occupy a greater volume as the temperature increases, but pressure remains constant. At any given temperature, gas molecules have the same average kinetic energy. The ideal gas law is derived from the kinetic theory of gases.

Molar mass, Charles's law, and Boyle's law

Molar mass refers to the mass of one mole of a substance (element or compound), usually measured in grams per mole (g/mol). This differs from molecular mass in that molecular mass is the mass of one molecule of a substance relative to the atomic mass unit (amu). Charles's law states that gases expand when they are heated. It is also known as the law of volumes. Boyle's law states that gases contract when pressure is applied to them. It also states that if temperature remains constant, the relationship between absolute pressure and volume is inversely proportional. When one increases, the other decreases. Considered a specialized case of the ideal gas law, Boyle's law is sometimes known as the Boyle-Mariotte law.

Ideal gas law

The ideal gas law is used to explain the properties of a gas under ideal pressure, volume, and temperature conditions. It is best suited for describing monatomic gases (gases in which atoms are not bound together) and gases at high temperatures and low pressures. It is not well-suited for instances in which a gas or its components are close to their condensation point. All collisions are perfectly elastic and there are no intermolecular attractive forces at work. The ideal gas law is a way to explain and measure the macroscopic properties of matter. It can be derived from the kinetic theory of gases, which deals with the microscopic properties of matter. The equation for the ideal gas law is $PV = nRT$, where "P" is absolute pressure, "V" is absolute volume, and "T" is absolute temperature. "R" refers to the universal gas constant, which is 8.3145 J/mol Kelvin, and "n" is the number of moles.

Inorganic vs. organic molecules

The terms inorganic and organic have become less useful over time as their definitions have changed. Historically, inorganic molecules were defined as those of a mineral nature that were not created by biological processes. Organic molecules were defined as those that were produced biologically by a "life process" or "vital force." It was then discovered that organic compounds could be synthesized without a life process. Currently, molecules containing carbon are considered organic. Carbon is largely responsible for creating biological diversity, and is more capable than all other elements of forming large, complex, and diverse molecules of an organic nature. Carbon often completes its valence shell by sharing electrons with other atoms in four covalent bonds, which is also known as tetravalence.

Organic compounds

Two of the main characteristics of organic compounds are that they include carbon and are formed by covalent bonds. Carbon can form long chains, double and triple bonds, and rings. While inorganic compounds tend to have high melting points, organic compounds tend to melt at temperatures below 300° C. They also tend to boil, sublimate, and decompose below this temperature. Unlike inorganic compounds, they are not very water soluble. Organic molecules are organized into functional groups based on their specific atoms, which helps determine how they will react chemically. A few groups are alkanes, nitro, alkenes, sulfides, amines, and carbolic acids. The hydroxyl group (-OH) consists of alcohols. These molecules are polar, which increases their solubility. By some estimates, there are more than 16 million organic compounds.

Properties of water

The important properties of water (H_2O) are high polarity, hydrogen bonding, cohesiveness, adhesiveness, high specific heat, high latent heat, and high heat of vaporization. It is essential to life as we know it, as water is one of the main if not the main constituent of many living things. Water is a liquid at room temperature. The high specific heat of water means it resists the breaking of its hydrogen bonds and resists heat and motion, which is why it has a relatively high boiling point and high vaporization point. It also resists temperature change. Water is peculiar in that its solid state floats in its liquid state. Most substances are denser in their solid forms. Water is cohesive, which means it is attracted to itself. It is also adhesive, which means it readily attracts other molecules. If water tends to adhere to another substance, the substance is said to be hydrophilic. Water makes a good solvent. Substances, particularly those with polar ions and molecules, readily dissolve in water.

Inorganic compounds

The main trait of inorganic compounds is that they lack carbon. Inorganic compounds include mineral salts, metals and alloys, non-metallic compounds such as phosphorus, and metal complexes. A metal complex has a central atom (or ion) bonded to surrounding ligands (molecules or anions). The ligands sacrifice the donor atoms (in the form of at least one pair of electrons) to the central atom. Many inorganic compounds are ionic, meaning they form ionic bonds rather than share electrons. They may have high melting points because of this. They may also be colorful, but this is not an absolute identifier of an inorganic compound. Salts, which are inorganic compounds, are an example of inorganic bonding of cations and anions. Some examples of salts are magnesium chloride ($MgCl_2$) and sodium oxide (Na_2O). Oxides, carbonates, sulfates, and halides are classes of inorganic compounds. They are typically poor conductors, are very water soluble, and crystallize easily. Minerals and silicates are also inorganic compounds.

Reading a molecular formula

Elements are represented in upper case letters. If there is no subscript, it indicates there is only one atom of the element. Otherwise, the subscript indicates the number of atoms. In molecular formulas, elements are organized according to the Hill system. Carbon is first, hydrogen comes next, and the remaining elements are listed in alphabetical order. If there is no carbon, all elements are listed alphabetically. There are a couple of exceptions to these rules. First, oxygen is usually listed last in oxides. Second, in ionic compounds the positive ion is listed first, followed by the negative ion. In CO_2, for example, C indicates 1 atom of carbon and O_2 indicates 2 atoms of oxygen. The compound is carbon dioxide. The formula for ammonia (an ionic compound) is NH_3, which is one atom of nitrogen and three of hydrogen. H_2O is two atoms of hydrogen and one of oxygen. Sugar is $C_6H_{12}O_6$, which is 6 atoms of carbon, 12 of hydrogen, and 6 of oxygen.

Nomenclature for organic compounds

Nomenclature refers to the manner in which a compound is named. First, it must be determined whether the compound is ionic (formed through electron transfer between cations and anions) or molecular (formed through electron sharing between molecules). When dealing with an ionic compound, the name is determined using the standard naming conventions for ionic compounds. This involves indicating the positive element first (the charge must be defined when there is more than one option for the valency) followed by the negative element plus the appropriate suffix. The rules for naming a molecular compound are as follows: write elements in order of increasing group number and determine the prefix by determining the number of atoms. Exclude mono for the first atom. The name for CO_2, for example, is carbon dioxide. The end of oxygen is dropped and "ide" is added to make oxide, and the prefix "di" is used to indicate there are two atoms of oxygen.

Binary ionic compounds start with a metal or ammonium cation, often from opposite sides of the periodic table. In the case of polyatomic ions, the positive ion is written first. Some polyatomic ions include hydroxide (OH^-), which consists of one atom of oxygen and one of hydrogen with a charge of -1; nitrate (NO_3^-); ammonium (NH_4^+); and sulfate (SO_4^{-2}). Negative ions are usually nonmetals or polyatomic. If they are monatomic, the suffix "-ide" is used. Organic compounds begin with a C and contain a large number of Hs and some Os. Me Eat Peanut Butter is an acronym that can be used to remember the order of prefixes for compounds containing 1 to 4 carbons. The first letters of the words correspond to meth-, eth-, prop-, and but-. There are three basic hydrocarbon suffixes. -Ane is used for alkanes, single bonds, and saturated compounds. -Ene is used for alkenes, double bonds, and unsaturated compounds. -Yne is used for alkynes, triple bonds, and unsaturated compounds. Alkanes are considered the simplest organic molecules. They contain only hydrogen and carbon molecules joined by single bonds. Examples of carbon chain names include methane (1 carbon), heptane (7 carbons), octane (8 carbons), and nonane (9 carbons).

Chemical equations

Chemical equations describe chemical reactions. The reactants are on the left side before the arrow and the products are on the right side after the arrow. The arrow indicates the reaction or change. The coefficient, or stoichiometric coefficient, is the number before the element, and indicates the ratio of reactants to products in terms of moles. The equation for the formation of water from hydrogen and oxygen, for example, is $2H_2$ (g) + O_2 (g) → $2H_2O$ (l). The 2 preceding hydrogen and water is the coefficient, which means there are 2 moles of hydrogen and 2 of water. There is 1 mole of oxygen, which does not have to be indicated with the number 1. In parentheses, g stands for gas, l stands for liquid, s stands for solid, and aq stands for aqueous solution (a substance dissolved in water). Charges are shown in superscript for individual ions, but not for ionic compounds. Polyatomic ions are separated by parentheses so the ion will not be confused with the number of ions.

An unbalanced equation is one that does not follow the law of conservation of mass, which states that matter can only be changed, not created. If an equation is unbalanced, the numbers of atoms indicated by the stoichiometric coefficients on each side of the arrow will not be equal. Start by writing the formulas for each species in the reaction. Count the atoms on each side and determine if the number is equal. Coefficients must be whole numbers. Fractional amounts, such as half a molecule, are not possible. Equations can be balanced by multiplying the coefficients by a constant that will produce the smallest possible whole number coefficient. H_2 + O_2 → H_2O is an example of an unbalanced equation. The balanced equation is $2H_2$ + O_2 → $2H_2O$, which indicates that it takes two moles of hydrogen and one of oxygen to produce two moles of water.

Bond enthalpy

Bond enthalpy refers to the amount of energy it takes to break a chemical bond, and can also be viewed as the amount of energy being stored by a bond. It is usually expressed using kJ/mol. Enthalpy is influenced by the molecular environment, so exact enthalpy changes and listed enthalpies may be averages. In most cases, stronger bonds are created by shorter bond lengths. For example, in a bromine to bromine bond, the enthalpy is 193 kJ/mol and the bond length is 0.228 nm. In a chlorine to chlorine bond, the enthalpy is 243kJ/mol and the bond length is 0.199 nm. Enthalpy is indicated using the symbol H. The formation of bonds is considered exothermic, while the breaking of bonds is endothermic. Carbon forms four bonds, oxygen forms two, nitrogen forms three, and hydrogen forms one.

Example of freezing point in compounds

Identify which one of the following compounds would have the lowest freezing point:
    $C_6H_{12}O_6$
    $Al(NO_3)_3$
    $MgCl_2$
    KBr.

The melting point of a compound is the temperature at which its solid and liquid forms exist in equilibrium. The freezing point of a compound is the temperature at which a compound changes from a liquid to a solid. Generally, a compound's melting and freezing points are the same. Freezing point is a colligative property in that it is affected by the number of particles in a compound. If compounds are in an aqueous solution, the concentration of ions in the solution affects the freezing point. The freezing point for a solution is lower than for a pure solvent. An example of this is that the freezing point for sea water is lower than the freezing point for fresh water because it contains a salt. $C_6H_{12}O_6$ is the functional group of hexose, a group of organic compounds. The other three are ionic compounds and salts. $Al(NO_3)_3$ is aluminum nitrate, $MgCl_2$ is magnesium chloride, and KBr is potassium bromide. Breaking down the salts in an aqueous solution leads to $Al(NO_3)_3$. It has about four ions and therefore has the lowest freezing point.

Crystals

The crystalline structure of crystals is also known as a lattice. Crystal particles have symmetrical arrangements. Solidification may result in the formation of a single crystal or a group of crystals, which is known as a polycrystalline structure. The symmetry of a crystal is used to determine its classification. Although they are organized, structured, and symmetrical, crystals are imperfect and can have defects. Some may also have specific electrical properties. Crystal systems are grouped in accordance with their axial systems (there are three axes). The unique systems of crystals are cubic, hexagonal, rhombohedral, orthorhombic, monoclinic, and triclinic. Crystals in the cubic system are the most symmetric. The unit cell is the spatial arrangement of atoms. The spacing between unit cells is known as the lattice parameters. Salts form in cubic crystals. Common table salt (NaCl), for instance, forms a cubic lattice through ionic bonding. Rapid evaporation of a salt water solution results in small crystals, while slower evaporation leads to larger crystals.

The two kinds of crystals, or crystalline solids, are liquid and solid. A crystal is considered to be a well-organized, repeating configuration of atoms, ions, or molecules. The strong attractive forces between oppositely-charged ions are responsible for the repeating patterns in solid crystals. These arrangements of repeating patterns can occur as a liquid cools to form a solid, as is seen with cubes of salt or ice. The three-dimensional crystal lattice pattern of a solid is lost when it melts into a liquid. However, this may only be lost in one or two dimensions, so some of the crystalline properties may remain. Crystalline structures occur across all classes of materials and form from all types of bonding. Salt is an example of a crystal formed with ionic bonds. A diamond is formed with covalent bonds. The majority of naturally occurring and artificially prepared solids have crystalline structures. Solids that do not are called amorphous solids because they have random arrangements.

Binary compounds

Binary compounds refer to compounds that contain only two elements. They can be ionic or covalent. Binary ionic compounds are formed by cations (metallic positive ions) and anions (nonmetal negative ions). Ionic compounds are not molecules. The suffix "ide" is used if there is one anion, as in the case of cuprous oxide, for example. Another example is that fluorine is an element, while fluoride is the negative ion of fluorine. The binary compound barium fluoride would be written as BaF_2. This is because one barium ion has a charge of +2 and one fluoride ion has a charge of -1, so it would take two fluoride ions to balance out the one barium ion. If there is no charge symbol, it is assumed that the charge is 1. The suffixes "ate" or "ite" are used when there is more than one anion, as in the case of mercurous nitrate, for example. A ternary compound is one formed of three elements.

Using naming systems for acids and binary molecular compounds

The four naming systems are for acids, organic compounds, binary ionic compounds, and binary molecular compounds. General rules are as follows:
- Acids: Compounds that start with H and contain only one other element (except H_2O) use "hydro-," the "element," and "-ic." HCl, for instance, would be hydrochloric acid. A compound consisting of H and a polyatomic ion with the suffix "-ate" is named using the "element" and "-ic." H_2SO_4, for instance, would be sulfuric acid. Similarly, a compound consisting of H and a polyatomic ion with the suffix "-ite" is named using the "element" and "-ous." H_2SO_3, for example, would be sulfurous acid.
- Binary molecular compounds: These start with a nonmetal other than H or C and contain a combination of nonmetals in close proximity on the periodic table. These compounds use the "-ide" suffix. The prefix is based on the subscript found in the formula, and may be mono-, di-, tri-, tetra-, penta-, hexa-, hepta-, octa-, nona-, deca-, undeca-, dodeca-, etc.

Oxidation numbers

Oxidation numbers are Roman numerals used in the stock naming system to identify inorganic compounds. The Roman numerals can be placed in superscript or parentheses to the right of the element symbol or name [FeIII or iron(III)]. The classic system uses the Latin root name of the element. The root takes the suffix "ous" for the lower oxidation state and "ic" for the higher oxidation state. For example, ferrous sulphate is $Fe(SO_4)_3$ and ferric sulphate is $Fe_2(SO_4)_3$. Other classic names are cuprum for copper, stannum for tin, and plumbum for lead. The stock system uses Roman numerals in parentheses after the element to indicate the ionization (the charge on the ion), which is an important piece of information for ionic compounds. Cu_2O would be copper(I) oxide under the stock naming system and cuprous oxide under the classic naming system, while $Hg_2(NO_3)_2$ would be mercury(I) nitrate under the stock naming system and mercurous nitrate under the classic naming system. Mercury(II) nitrate could also be called mercuric nitrate.

Hydrogen bonds

Hydrogen bonds are weaker than covalent and ionic bonds, and refer to the type of attraction in an electronegative atom such as oxygen, fluorine, or nitrogen. Hydrogen bonds can form within a single molecule or between molecules. A water molecule is polar, meaning it is partially positively charged on one end (the hydrogen end) and partially negatively charged on the other (the oxygen end). This is because the hydrogen atoms are arranged around the oxygen atom in a close tetrahedron. Hydrogen is oxidized (its number of electrons is reduced) when it bonds with oxygen to form water. Hydrogen bonds tend not only to be weak, but also short-lived. They also tend to be numerous. Hydrogen bonds give water many of its important properties, including its high specific heat and high heat of vaporization, its solvent qualities, its adhesiveness and cohesiveness, its hydrophobic qualities, and its ability to float in its solid form. Hydrogen bonds are also an important component of proteins, nucleic acids, and DNA.

Intermolecular forces

Intermolecular forces are weaker than ionic and covalent bonds. They occur between stable molecules or functional groups of macromolecules. Macromolecules are large molecules that are usually created by polymerization and sometimes distinguished by their lack of covalent bonds. London dispersion force, dipole-dipole interactions, and hydrogen bonding are all examples of intermolecular forces. London dispersion force is also known as instantaneous dipole-induced dipole force because the force is caused by a change in dipole (a separation of the positive and negative charges in an atom). These forces are weak and the attractions are quickly formed and broken. An electron from one atom affects another atom, resulting in a force that dissipates as soon as an electron moves. Dipole-dipole (Keesom) interactions occur within atoms that are already covalently bonded and have permanent dipoles. These atoms have a different amount of electronegativity (attraction of electrons). One atom attracts another, electrostatic forces are generated, and molecules align to increase this attraction.

Solutions

A solution is a homogeneous mixture. A mixture is two or more different substances that are mixed together, but not combined chemically. Homogeneous mixtures are those that are uniform in their composition. Solutions consist of a solute (the substance that is dissolved) and a solvent (the substance that does the dissolving). An example is sugar water. The solvent is the water and the solute is the sugar. The intermolecular attraction between the solvent and the solute is called solvation. Hydration refers to solutions in which water is the solvent. Solutions are formed when the forces of the molecules of the solute and the solvent are as strong as the individual molecular forces of the solute and the solvent. An example is that salt (NaCl) dissolves in water to create a solution. The Na^+ and the Cl^- ions in salt interact with the molecules of water and vice versa to overcome the individual molecular forces of the solute and the solvent.

Polar vs. nonpolar solutes and solvents

For solvation to occur, bonds of similar strength must be broken and formed. Nonpolar substances are usually soluble in nonpolar solvents. Ionic and polar matter is usually soluble in polar solvents. Water is a polar solvent. Oil is nonpolar. Therefore, the saying "oil and water don't mix" is quite true. Heptane (C_7H_{16}) is another nonpolar liquid that is said to be immiscible in water, meaning it can't combine with water. The hydrogen bonds of the water molecules are stronger than the London dispersion forces of the heptane. Polar molecules such as NH_3 (ammonia), SO_2 (sulfur dioxide), and H_2S (hydrogen sulfide) are termed hydrophilic, meaning they readily combine with water. Nonpolar molecules, including the noble gases and other gases such as He (helium), Ne (neon), and CO_2 (carbon dioxide) are termed hydrophobic, meaning they repel or do not readily combine with water. One way to remember this is that "like dissolves like." Polar solvents dissolve polar solutes, while nonpolar solvents dissolve nonpolar solutes.

Effect of temperature and pressure on solubility

Solids tend to dissolve faster when the temperature is increased. Higher temperatures help break bonds through an increase in kinetic energy. Solubility tends to increase for solids being dissolved in water as the temperature approaches 100 °C, but at higher temperatures ionic solutes tend to become less soluble. Gases tend to be less soluble at higher temperatures. When solutions are saturated at high temperatures, the solute will precipitate (return to solid form) and "fall out of the solution" as the solution cools. Melting points can be lowered by using a solvent such as salt on icy roads, which lowers the freezing point of ice. Adding salt to water when making ice cream also lowers the melting point of the water. A solution's melting point is usually lower than the melting point of the solvent alone. Pressure has little effect on the solubility of liquid solutions. In gas solutions, an increase in pressure increases solubility, and vice versa.

Molarity, molality, and colligative properties

The concentration of a solution is measured in terms of molarity. One molar (M) is equal to a quantity of moles of solute per liter of solution. Adding one mole of a substance to one liter of solution would most likely result in a molarity greater than one. The amount of substance should be measured into a small amount of solution, and then more solution should be added to reach a volume of one liter to ensure accuracy. Molality refers to the concentration or ratio of moles of solute per kilogram of solvent. Colligative properties refer to how a solvent acts when it becomes a solution. Colligative properties are determined by the number of solute molecules rather than their exact characteristics. Some examples of colligative properties are that a solution's osmotic pressure and boiling point increase and its melting point decreases when the amount of solute is increased. As the amount of solute is increased, vapor will decrease above the solution when it is composed of a solid, nonvolatile solute dissolved in a liquid.

A syrup is a solution of water and sugar. A brine is a solution of table salt, or sodium chloride (NaCl), and water. A saline solution is a sterilized concentration of sodium chloride in water. A seltzer is a solution of carbon dioxide in water. The term *dilute* is used when there is less solute. Adding more solvent is known as diluting a solution, as is removing a portion of the solute. Concentrated is the term used when there is more solute. Adding more solute makes a solution more concentrated, as does removing a portion of the solvent.

Properties of solutions include:
- they have a maximum particle size of one nm
- they do not separate when allowed to stand or when poured through a fiber filter
- they are clear and do not scatter light
- their boiling points increase while their melting points decrease when the amount of solute is increased.

A *mixture* is a combination of two or more substances that are not bonded. *Suspensions* are mixtures of heterogeneous materials. Particles are usually larger than those found in true solutions. Dirt mixed vigorously with water is an example of a suspension. The dirt is temporarily suspended in water, but the two separate once the mixing is ceased. A mixture of large (1 nm to 500 nm) particles is called a *colloidal suspension*. The particles are termed dispersants and the dispersing medium is similar to the solvent in a solution. Sol refers to a liquid or a solid that also has solids dispersed through it, such as milk or gelatin. An aerosol spray is a colloid suspension of gas and the solid or liquid being dispersed. An *emulsion* refers to a liquid or a solid that has a liquid dispersed through it. A *foam* is a liquid that has gas dispersed through it.

Electrolytes and electrolysis

Electrolyte refers to a substance that is ionized in water. Strong electrolytes are completely ionized and are good conductors of electricity. Salts are examples of strong electrolytes. Compounds that dissolve in water without completely ionizing are weak electrolytes. Acids and bases are examples of weak electrolytes. Nonelectrolytes are those that dissolve with no ionization. *Electrolysis* refers to the decomposition of a substance by electric current. For example, when electric current is passed through melted NaCl (sodium chloride), sodium (Na), a metal, and chlorine gas (Cl_2) are formed. The formula for solutions is CV=n, where "V" is volume measured in liters, "C" is molarity, and "n" is the number of moles of solute.

Define calorimeter, endergonic, exergonic, Gibbs free energy, and enthalpy.

Calorimeter is a device that measures heat. It may be used to measure the heat generated by a chemical reaction, state change, or solution formation. When using a calorimeter and the medium in which the reaction took place (not the reaction itself) gains heat, it would indicate an exothermic reaction. The heat left the reaction and entered the medium, and the difference in heat was what was measured with the calorimeter. Endergonic is a chemical reaction in which it takes more energy to instigate the reaction than is produced by it. Exergonic is a chemical reaction in which the net amount of Gibbs free energy is less than zero. Gibbs free energy is a value that is similar to the available energy or maximum work of a closed system. Enthalpy is a measure of heat content in a system. It is usually assumed that the system is closed and the pressure is constant. Enthalpy is represented by the symbol H. The heat of a reaction is the difference between the heat stored in the reactants and in the products. It is represented by ΔH.

Effect of temperature on reaction rate

The collision theory states that for a chemical reaction to occur, atoms or molecules have to collide with each other with a certain amount of energy. A certain amount of energy is required to breach the activation barrier. Heating a mixture will raise the energy levels of the molecules and the rate of reaction (the time it takes for a reaction to complete). Generally, the rate of reaction is doubled for every 10 degrees Celsius temperature increase.

However, the increase needed to double a reaction rate increases as the temperature climbs. This is due to the increase in collision frequency that occurs as the temperature increases. Other factors that can affect the rate of reaction are surface area, concentration, pressure, and the presence of a catalyst.

Effects of catalysts on reactions

Catalysts, substances that help change the rate of reaction without changing their form, can increase reaction rate by decreasing the number of steps it takes to form products. The mass of the catalyst should be the same at the beginning of the reaction as it is at the end. The activation energy is the minimum amount required to get a reaction started. Activation energy causes particles to collide with sufficient energy to start the reaction. A catalyst enables more particles to react, which lowers the activation energy. Examples of catalysts in reactions are manganese oxide (MnO_2) in the decomposition of hydrogen peroxide, iron in the manufacture of ammonia using the Haber process, and concentrate of sulfuric acid in the nitration of benzene. Maxwell-Boltzmann distribution refers to a graph or plot showing the energies or speeds of particles or gas molecules in a system.

Catalysts can be *heterogeneous* or *homogeneous*. The catalyst in a heterogeneous reaction is in a different phase than the reactants. Heterogeneous catalysis usually involves a solid catalyst and liquid or gas reactants. The reactant (or reactants) is adsorbed onto the surface of the catalyst. The reactant's adsorption on the catalyst is temporary, and helps facilitate the interaction of the reactants. Some bonds may also weaken. When the reactants collide, new bonds are formed. The products (or soon to be products) desorb from the catalyst's surface and more reactants may adsorb on the surface. Some metals make better catalysts than others. Silver does not form strong enough bonds, while the bonds formed by tungsten are too strong. Neither is a good catalyst. Platinum and nickel are good catalysts because the adsorption bonds are strong enough to temporarily hold the reactants, but also weak enough to allow them to desorb.

Homogeneous catalysis is a reaction in which the catalysts are in the same phase as the reactants. Catalysts and reactants, for example, may all be in gas or liquid form. Electrocatalysts are metal-containing catalysts used in fuel cells to increase half reaction rates. For example, nanoparticles of platinum or carbon particles can be used to increase the rate at which oxygen undergoes a reduction reaction to produce water. Organocatalysis involves the use of non-metal catalysts such as enzymes rather than the typically used transition metals. Autocatalysis refers to a reaction that is catalyzed by one of its products. The Haber (Haber-Bosch) process uses an iron catalyst with nitrogen and hydrogen gas as the reactants to form ammonia. This is an example of heterogeneous catalysis. The process is important because fertilizer is generated from ammonia. Before the Haber process, there was not a way to make use of the abundance of nitrogen in the atmosphere to produce ammonia on a large scale.

Ultraviolet light breaks O_2 into two very reactive oxygen atoms with unpaired electrons, which are known as free radicals. A free radical of oxygen pairs with another oxygen molecule to form ozone (O_3). Ultraviolet light also breaks ozone (O_3) into O_2 and a free radical of oxygen. This process usually acts as an ultraviolet light filter for the planet. Other free radical catalysts are produced by natural phenomena such as volcanic eruptions and by human activities. When these enter the atmosphere, they disrupt the normal cycle by breaking down ozone so it cannot absorb more ultraviolet radiation. One such catalyst is the chlorine in chlorofluorocarbons (CFCs). CFCs were used as aerosols and refrigerants. When a CFC like CF_2Cl_2 is broken down in the atmosphere, chlorine free radicals are produced. These act as catalysts to break down ozone. Whether a chlorine free radical reacts with an ozone or oxygen molecule, it is able to react again.

Acids and bases

Three different theories related to the classification of acids and bases are the *Arrhenius theory*, the *Bronsted-Lowry theory*, and the *Lewis theory*. The *Arrhenius acid-base theory* states that substances that can ionize to form positive hydrogen ions (H^+) or hydronium ions in an aqueous solution are acids and substances that produce hydroxide ions (OH^-) are bases. The *Bronsted-Lowry theory* states that substances that can act as a proton donor are acids and those that can act as a proton acceptor are bases. The *Lewis theory* states that acids are electron-pair acceptors and bases are electron-pair donors. When combined, acids and bases neutralize each other's properties and produce a salt. The H^+ cation of the acid combines with the OH^- anion of the base to form water. The cation of the base and the anion of the acid form a salt compound. An example is that hydrochloric acid and sodium hydroxide react to form table salt. The equation for the reaction is $HCl + NaOH \rightarrow H_2O + NaCl$.

When they are dissolved in aqueous solutions, some properties of *acids* are that they conduct electricity, change blue litmus paper to red, have a sour taste, react with bases to neutralize them, and react with active metals to free hydrogen. A weak acid is one that does not donate all of its protons or disassociate completely. Strong acids include hydrochloric, hydriodic, hydrobromic, perchloric, nitric, and sulfuric. They ionize completely. Superacids are those that are stronger than 100 percent sulfuric acid. They include fluoroantimonic, magic, and perchloric acids. Acids can be used in pickling, a process used to remove rust and corrosion from metals. They are also used as catalysts in the processing of minerals and the production of salts and fertilizers. Phosphoric acid (H_3PO_4) is added to sodas and other acids are added to foods as preservatives or to add taste.

When they are dissolved in aqueous solutions, some properties of *bases* are that they conduct electricity, change red litmus paper to blue, feel slippery, and react with acids to neutralize their properties. A weak base is one that does not completely ionize in an aqueous solution, and usually has a low pH. Strong bases can free protons in very weak acids. Examples of strong bases are hydroxide compounds such as potassium, barium, and lithium hydroxides. Most are in the first and second groups of the periodic table. A superbase is extremely strong compared to sodium hydroxide and cannot be kept in an aqueous solution. Superbases are organized into organic, organometallic, and inorganic classes. Bases are used as insoluble catalysts in heterogeneous reactions and as catalysts in hydrogenation.

Some properties of salts are that they are formed from acid base reactions, are ionic compounds consisting of metallic and nonmetallic ions, dissociate in water, and are comprised of tightly bonded ions. Some common salts are sodium chloride (NaCl), sodium bisulfate, potassium dichromate ($K_2Cr_2O_7$), and calcium chloride ($CaCl_2$). Calcium chloride is used as a drying agent, and may be used to absorb moisture when freezing mixtures. Potassium nitrate (KNO_3) is used to make fertilizer and in the manufacture of explosives. Sodium nitrate ($NaNO_3$) is also used in the making of fertilizer. Baking soda (sodium bicarbonate) is a salt, as are Epsom salts [magnesium sulfate ($MgSO_4$)]. Salt and water can react to form a base and an acid. This is called a hydrolysis reaction.

A buffer is a solution whose pH remains relatively constant when a small amount of an acid or a base is added. It is usually made of a weak acid and its conjugate base (proton receiver) or one of its soluble salts. It can also be made of a weak base and its conjugate acid (proton donor) or one of its salts. A constant pH is necessary in living cells because some living things can only live within a certain pH range. If that pH changes, the cells could die. Blood is an example of a buffer. A pKa is a measure of acid dissociation or the acid dissociation constant. Buffer solutions can help keep enzymes at the correct pH. They are also used in the fermentation process, in dyeing fabrics, and in the calibration of pH meters. An example of a buffer is HC_2H_3O (a weak acid) and $NaC_2H_3O_2$ (a salt containing the $C_2H_3O_2^-$ ion).

The potential of hydrogen (pH) is a measurement of the concentration of hydrogen ions in a substance in terms of the number of moles of H^+ per liter of solution. A lower pH indicates a higher H^+ concentration, while a higher pH indicates a lower H^+ concentration. Pure water has a neutral pH, which is 7. Anything with a pH lower than water (less than 7) is considered acidic. Anything with a pH higher than water (greater than 7) is a base. Drain cleaner, soap, baking soda, ammonia, egg whites, and sea water are common bases. Urine, stomach acid, citric acid, vinegar, hydrochloric acid, and battery acid are acids. A pH indicator is a substance that acts as a detector of hydrogen or hydronium ions. It is halochromic, meaning it changes color to indicate that hydrogen or hydronium ions have been detected.

Preparing dilute sulfuric acid

When using water to prepare a solution of dilute sulfuric acid, the acid should be added to the water. Water and sulfuric acid cause an exothermic reaction, and can cause splattering if water is added to sulfuric acid. The water is less dense and can float on top of the acid. Heat can be produced rapidly during this reaction. Techniques to deal with this include using cold water and putting the mixing container within a larger container filled with ice cubes and cold water. Other lab safety procedures should also be followed. Sulfuric acid can easily cause burns. Immiscible is a substance that cannot be blended or used to form a homogeneous substance. It will stay separated or will separate into layers. The antonym of immiscible is miscible, which refers to a substance that can be mixed.

Physics

Theory of relativity

Albert Einstein proposed two theories of relativity: the general theory of relativity (1916) and the special theory of relativity (1905). Special relativity is based on two basic premises. The first is that the laws of physics are the same for all observers in uniform motion relative to one another. This is also known as the principle of relativity. The second is that the speed of light in a vacuum is also the same for all observers and their relative motion or the motion of the source of the light does not affect this. General relativity is the generally accepted explanation of gravity as a property of space and time, or space-time. Einstein was born in Germany in 1879 and received the Nobel Prize in Physics in 1921. He died in April of 1955.

Static electricity and electric current

In an atom, the charge of an electron is generally -1, the charge of a proton is +1, and a neutron has no charge. When atoms have equal numbers of electrons and protons, their net charge is zero. Molecules also often have a net charge of zero for a similar reason: the number of negatively charged atoms, or anions (pronounced "an-eye-ons") equals the number of positively charged atoms, or cations (pronounced "cat-eye-ons"). Static electricity occurs when the net electric charge is non-zero, motionless, and produces an electrostatic discharge in two objects brought together. The objects' charges are changed to achieve a balance. Polarization is when there is a zero net charge that is unevenly distributed, which leads to a bound charge. The motion of charged particles in a given direction is known as electric current. It does not produce a net loss or gain of charge.

Insulators are materials that prevent the movement of electrical charges, while conductors are materials that allow the movement of electrical charges. This is because conductive materials have free electrons that can move through the entire volume of the conductor. This allows an external charge to change the charge distribution in the material. In induction, a neutral conductive material, such as a sphere, can become charged by a positively or negatively charged object, such as a rod. The charged object is placed close to the material without touching it. This produces a force on the free electrons, which will either be attracted to or repelled by the rod, polarizing (or separating) the charge. The sphere's electrons will flow into or out of it when touched by a ground. The sphere is now charged. The charge will be opposite that of the charging rod.

Circuit refers to the movement of electric charge along a path between areas of high electric potential and areas of low electric potential. A *circuit breaker* stops the flow of an electric charge through a circuit by creating a break in the path. A fuse also creates a break. *Resistance* refers to the hindrance to the flow of an electric charge. Resistance is measured in Ohms. Ohms law is $I = V/R$, where "I" is current measured in amps, "V" is potential difference in volts, and "R" is resistance. A *resistor* is a device used in a circuit that opposes the flow of an electric charge. A *transistor* is a device made of a semiconductive material that can amplify or switch an electric charge. A *semiconductor* is a material with conductivity between an insulator and a conductor. These materials replaced earlier electric devices such as vacuum tubes. A *solid state device* is used in modern circuits, solid state devices are solid materials in which the charge carriers, or electrons, are contained entirely within the material. Examples include transistors, microprocessors, integrated circuits, light-emitting diodes (LEDs), and liquid-crystal displays (LCDs).

Movement of electric charge along a path between areas of high electric potential and low electric potential, with a resistor or load device between them, is the definition of a *simple circuit*. It is a closed conducting path between the high and low potential points, such as the positive and negative terminals on a battery. One example of a circuit is the flow from one terminal of a car battery to the other. The electrolyte solution of water and sulfuric acid provides work in chemical form to start the flow. A frequently used classroom example of circuits involves using a D cell (1.5 V) battery, a small light bulb, and a piece of copper wire to create a circuit to light the bulb.

Short circuit refers to a low-resistance connection between two nodes of an electrical circuit, which results in an excessive electric current, or overcurrent. For example, a D cell battery with no load (such as a light bulb within the circuit) would result in a high rate of charge flow between terminals. This could cause unwanted or unintended high temperatures or rapid energy loss. Other short circuit circumstances could lead to circuit damage, fire, or explosion. Because of the risks, circuit breakers or fuses placed within a circuit are used as safety features to prevent overcurrent. Once a fault is detected, the circuit breaker acts like a switch to interrupt flow. It can be reset once the condition is corrected. A fuse has a component that melts, which interrupts the flow of charges. Fuses differ from breakers in that fuses are one-time interrupters that must be replaced before the circuit can be restored.

Models that can be used to explain the flow of electric current, potential, and circuits include water, gravity, and roller coasters. For example, just as gravity is a force and a mass can have a potential for energy based on its location, so can a charge within an electrical field. Just as a force is required to move an object uphill, a force is also required to move a charge from a low to high potential. Another example is water. Water does not flow when it is level. If it is lifted to a point and then placed on a downward path, it will flow. A roller coaster car requires work to be performed to transport it to a point where it has potential energy (the top of a hill). Once there, gravity provides the force for it to flow (move) downward. If either path is broken, the flow or movement stops or is not completed.

As they relate to electric current, series circuits are circuits in which there is only one path through which electrons can flow. If a load in this type of circuit is removed, disabled, or switched off, the circuit is open and electricity does not flow. A parallel circuit is one in which there is more than one path through which electrons can travel. In a series circuit, the same current flows through all components. In a parallel circuit, on the other hand, the same voltage exists across all parallel paths, though the current may be vastly different among them. An example of a series circuit is a string of old-fashioned Christmas tree lights. If one bulb breaks or comes loose, the entire string will not work.

Measured in watts, electric *power* refers to the rate at which electrical energy is transferred by an electric circuit. It can be calculated using Joule's law: $P = V*I$, where "P" is power, "V" is the potential difference (in volts) and "I" is current (in amps). Power can be generated, transmitted, and converted into various forms of light. A *watt* is the unit used to measure power. One watt is equal to one joule of energy per second. A *transformer* is a device that uses induction to transfer current from one circuit to another. Two wound coils act as a pair of inductors. Voltage can be modified to be transferred to another circuit (as in transmission lines) or to a load, such as an electrical device plugged into a socket.

Dielectric refers to a nonconducting substance of electric current that can usually sustain an electric field or maintain polarization. It differs from an insulator, which is typically defined as a material used to prevent the flow of current. An *electroscope* is an instrument used to detect a charge on another object. One somewhat low-tech type is the gold foil electroscope. It includes a conducting part connected to thin leaves of gold or aluminum foil which separate when a charged object is touched with the conducting part. The reason for this separation is that like charges repel each other. Electroscopes require high levels of voltage and are used with high voltage sources, such as static electricity and electrostatic machines. An electroscope cannot be used to determine whether a charge is positive or negative. A *Van de Graaff generator*, typically composed of a hollow metal ball and belt, is used to produce static electricity or high-voltage electricity with a low current.

Direct current (DC) is the flow of an electric charge in one direction. Batteries and solar cells typically use direct current. *Alternating current* (AC) is current that periodically reverses direction. AC is typically used in houses and other buildings. A diode is an electronic device used to conduct electric current in one direction. The process of conduction in one direction is known as rectification. A rectifier is used to convert alternating current to direct current. Diodes are also used to remove modulation from radio signals. An inverter is the opposite of a rectifier in that it converts direct current to alternating current. Electromotive force (emf) is what causes electrons to move when there is potential difference between two points (voltage). Devices that can provide emf include batteries, voltaic cells, thermoelectric devices, solar cells, electrical generators, transformers, and Van de Graaff generators.

Electric charges
The attractive force between the electrons and the nucleus is called the electric force. A positive (+) charge or a negative (-) charge creates a field of sorts in the empty space around it, which is known as an electric field. The direction of a positive charge is away from it and the direction of a negative charge is towards it. An electron within the force of the field is pulled towards a positive charge because an electron has a negative charge. A particle with a positive charge is pushed away, or repelled, by another positive charge. Like charges repel each other and opposite charges attract. Lines of force show the paths of charges. Electric force between two objects is directly proportional to the product of the charge magnitudes and inversely proportional to the square of the distance between the two objects. Electric charge is measured with the unit Coulomb (C). It is the amount of charge moved in one second by a steady current of one ampere ($1C = 1A \times 1s$).

Charging by conduction is similar to charging by induction, except that the material transferring the charge actually touches the material receiving the charge. A negatively or positively charged object is touched to an object with a neutral charge. Electrons will either flow into or out of the neutral object and it will become charged. Insulators cannot be used to conduct charges. Charging by conduction can also be called charging by contact. The law of conservation of charge states that the total number of units before and after a charging process remains the same. No electrons have been created. They have just been moved around. The removal of a charge on an object by conduction is called grounding.

Electric potential, or electrostatic potential or voltage, is an expression of potential energy per unit of charge. It is measured in volts (V) as a scalar quantity. The formula used is V = E/Q, where V is voltage, E is electrical potential energy, and Q is the charge. Voltage is typically discussed in the context of electric potential difference between two points in a circuit. Voltage can also be thought of as a measure of the rate at which energy is drawn from a source in order to produce a flow of electric charge.

Electric current is the sustained flow of electrons that are part of an electric charge moving along a path in a circuit. This differs from a static electric charge, which is a constant non-moving charge rather than a continuous flow. The rate of flow of electric charge is expressed using the ampere (amp or A) and can be measured using an ammeter. A current of 1 ampere means that 1 coulomb of charge passes through a given area every second. Electric charges typically only move from areas of high electric potential to areas of low electric potential. To get charges to flow into a high potential area, you must to connect it to an area of higher potential, by introducing a battery or other voltage source.

Ohm's law

Electric currents experience resistance as they travel through a circuit. Different objects have different levels of resistance. The ohm (Ω) is the measurement unit of electric resistance. The symbol is the Greek letter omega. Ohm's Law, which is expressed as I = V/R, states that current flow (I, measured in amps) through an object is equal to the potential difference from one side to the other (V, measured in volts) divided by resistance (R, measured in ohms). An object with a higher resistance will have a lower current flow through it given the same potential difference.

Magnets

A magnet is a piece of metal, such as iron, steel, or magnetite (lodestone) that can affect another substance within its field of force that has like characteristics. Magnets can either attract or repel other substances. Magnets have two poles: north and south. Like poles repel and opposite poles (pairs of north and south) attract. The magnetic field is a set of invisible lines representing the paths of attraction and repulsion. Magnetism can occur naturally, or ferromagnetic materials can be magnetized. Certain matter that is magnetized can retain its magnetic properties indefinitely and become a permanent magnet. Other matter can lose its magnetic properties. For example, an iron nail can be temporarily magnetized by stroking it repeatedly in the same direction using one pole of another magnet. Once magnetized, it can attract or repel other magnetically inclined materials, such as paper clips. Dropping the nail repeatedly will cause it to lose its charge.

Magnetic fields

A magnetic field can be formed not only by a magnetic material, but also by electric current flowing through a wire. When a coiled wire is attached to the two ends of a battery, for example, an electromagnet can be formed by inserting a ferromagnetic material such as an iron bar within the coil. When electric current flows through the wire, the bar becomes a magnet. If there is no current, the magnetism is lost. A magnetic domain occurs when the magnetic fields of atoms are grouped and aligned. These groups form what can be thought of as miniature magnets within a material. This is what happens when an object like an iron nail is temporarily magnetized. Prior to magnetization, the organization of atoms and their various polarities are somewhat random with respect to where the north and south poles are pointing. After magnetization, a significant percentage of the poles are lined up in one direction, which is what causes the magnetic force exerted by the material.

The motions of subatomic structures (nuclei and electrons) produce a magnetic field. It is the direction of the spin and orbit that indicate the direction of the field. The strength of a magnetic field is known as the magnetic moment. As electrons spin and orbit a nucleus, they produce a magnetic field. Pairs of electrons that spin and orbit in opposite directions cancel each other out, creating a net magnetic field of zero. Materials that have an unpaired electron are magnetic. Those with a weak attractive force are referred to as paramagnetic materials, while ferromagnetic materials have a strong attractive force. A diamagnetic material has electrons that are paired, and therefore does not typically have a magnetic moment. There are, however, some diamagnetic materials that have a weak magnetic field.

Electromagnetic spectrum

The electromagnetic spectrum is defined by frequency (f) and wavelength (λ). Frequency is typically measured in hertz and wavelength is usually measured in meters. Because light travels at a fairly constant speed, frequency is inversely proportional to wavelength, a relationship expressed by the formula $f = c/\lambda$, where c is the speed of light (about 300 million meters per second). Frequency multiplied by wavelength equals the speed of the wave; for electromagnetic waves, this is the speed of light, with some variance for the medium in which it is traveling. Electromagnetic waves include (from largest to smallest wavelength) radio waves, microwaves, infrared radiation (radiant heat), visible light, ultraviolet radiation, x-rays, and gamma rays. The energy of electromagnetic waves is carried in packets that have a magnitude inversely proportional to the wavelength. Radio waves have a range of wavelengths, from about 10^{-3} to 10^5 meters, while their frequencies range from about 10^3 to 10^{11} Hz.

Electromagnetic dipole

Two types of dipoles in physics are the electric dipole and the magnetic dipole. They both refer to the phenomenon of polarization of opposite charges, charges which cancel each other out. In other words, a dipole refers to a pairing of a positively-charged pole and a negatively-charged pole. The dipole is usually visualized using lines of force in a field, which are familiar patterns associated with magnetic bars and the magnetic field that surrounds Earth. The permanent bar magnet has an intrinsic magnetic dipole moment. The dipole moment is a way to measure or quantify the phenomenon. It is a vector quantity, meaning it has a direction. The term electric dipole refers to the separation of a pair of positive and negative charges of roughly equal magnitude. It usually occurs at a close distance.

Electric motor

An electric motor converts electric energy into mechanical energy. Energy can be provided by an AC or DC source. The power provided has many practical applications. The basic premise of a motor is that the electric current passing through a wire or coil creates a magnetic field that opposes the poles of a permanent magnet. The repelling forces between one pole of the electromagnet and the opposing pole of the fixed magnet cause the coil to move about ½ a turn. As it approaches the pole of like attraction, the coil would normally stop moving. In a motor, however, the current is reversed at this time, which reverses the poles and again forces rotation. In a DC motor, a switch or commuter can be used to reverse the charge. In an AC motor, the charge alternates on its own. The coil is attached to a shaft that is rotated, which provides the mechanical energy necessary to do work.

Electric motor vs. generator

An electrical generator is the opposite of a motor in that it transforms magnetic force into electrical energy. Like a motor, however, it uses an electromagnetic field and a permanent magnet to achieve electromagnetic induction. Generators do not create electricity, but rather convert mechanical energy into electric energy. Smaller gas generators are used as backup or primary power sources of electricity for equipment, homes, and other small-scale applications. Larger generators may use mechanical energy from many different sources, including water, steam, wind, compressed air, or even a hand crank. The current does not flow through the bird because it and the wire have the same electric potential. Therefore, there is no reason for current to move from the wire to the bird. If the bird touched something else in addition to the wire and became grounded, the electrons would flow through the bird and electrocute it.

Electrical force

Electrical force is a universal force that exists between any two electrically charged objects. Opposite charges attract one another and like charges repel one another. The magnitude of the force is directly proportional to the magnitude of the charges (q)and inversely proportional to the square of the distance (r) between the two objects:

$$F = kq_1q_2/r^2, \text{ where } k = 9 \times 10^9 \text{ N-m}^2/\text{C}^2$$

Magnetic forces operate on a similar principle.

Waves

Waves have energy and can transfer energy when they interact with matter. Although waves transfer energy, they do not transport matter. They are a disturbance of matter that transfers energy from one particle to an adjacent particle. There are many types of waves, including sound, seismic, water, light, micro, and radio waves. The two basic categories of waves are mechanical and electromagnetic. Mechanical waves are those that transmit energy through matter. Electromagnetic waves can transmit energy through a vacuum. A transverse wave provides a good illustration of the features of a wave, which include crests, troughs, amplitude, and wavelength.

Waves are divided into types based on the direction of particle motion in a medium and the direction of wave propagation.
- *Longitudinal waves*: These are waves that travel in the same direction as the particle movement. They are sometimes called pressure, compressional, or density waves. Longitudinal sound waves are the easiest to produce and have the highest speed. A longitudinal wave consists of compressions and rarefactions, such as those seen by extending and collapsing a Slinky toy.
- *Shear* or *transverse waves*: These types of waves move perpendicular to the direction of the particle movement. For example, if the particles in a medium move up and down, a transverse wave will move forward. Transverse waves are possible only in solids and are slower than longitudinal waves.
- *Surface (circular) waves*: These waves travel at the surface of a material and move in elliptical orbits. They are a little slower than shear waves.

- *Plate waves*: These waves move in elliptical orbits and only occur in very thin pieces of material.

Waves can be in phase or out of phase, which is similar to the concept of being in sync or out of sync. For example, if two separate waves originate from the same point and the peaks (crests) and valleys (troughs) are exactly aligned, they are said to be in phase. If the peak of a wave aligns with the valley of another wave, they are out of phase. When waves are in phase their displacement is doubled. If they are out of phase they cancel each other out. If they are somewhere in between being completely in phase and completely out of phase, the wave interaction is a wave that is the sum of the amplitudes of all points along the wave. If waves originate from different points, the amplitude of particle displacement is the combined sum of the particle displacement amplitude of each individual wave.

When waves traveling in the same medium interact, it is known as wave interference. While a single wave generally remains the same in terms of waveform, frequency, amplitude, and wavelength, several waves traveling through particles in a medium take on a more complicated appearance after they interact. The final properties of a wave are dependent on many factors, such as the points of origin of waves and whether they are in phase, out of phase, or somewhere in between. Constructive interference refers to what happens when two crests or two troughs of a wave meet. The resulting amplitude of the crest or trough is doubled. Destructive interference is what happens when the crest of one wave and the trough of another that are the same shape meet. When this occurs, the two waves cancel each other out. An example of destructive interference is when two unlike sound waves reduce the volume of the sound.

Waveforms refer to the shapes and forms of waves as they are depicted on graphs. Forms include sinusoidal, square, triangle, and sawtooth. Sinusoidal refers to a waveform in which the amplitude (displacement from the rest position) is proportional to the sine (side opposite of angle/hypotenuse) of a variable such as time. Square, triangle, and sawtooth waveforms are nonsinusoidal, and are usually based on formulas. Square waves are used to depict digital information. Pulse waves, also known as rectangular waves, are a nonsinusoidal form similar to square waves, and are found in synthesizer programming. Triangle waves, like square waves, only have odd harmonics. The harmonic of a wave is the integer multiple of a base frequency. Sawtooth waves have both even and odd harmonics, and produce a sound particularly suited for synthesizing bowed string instruments.

Frequency is a measure of how often particles in a medium vibrate when a wave passes through the medium with respect to a certain point or node. Usually measured in Hertz (Hz), frequency might refer to cycles per second, vibrations per second, or waves per second. One Hz is equal to one cycle per second. Period is a measure of how long it takes to complete a cycle. It is the inverse of frequency; where frequency is measure in cycles per second, period can be thought of as seconds per cycle, though it is measured in units of time only. Speed refers to how fast or slow a wave travels. It is measured in terms of distance divided by time. While frequency is measured in terms of cycles per second, speed might be measured in terms of meters per second.

Amplitude is the maximum amount of displacement of a particle in a medium from its rest position, and corresponds to the amount of energy carried by the wave. High-energy waves have greater amplitudes; low energy waves have lesser amplitudes. Amplitude is a measure of a wave's strength. *Rest position*, also called *equilibrium*, is the point at which there is neither positive nor negative displacement. *Crest*, also called the *peak*, is the point at which a wave's positive or upward displacement from the rest position is at its maximum. *Trough*, also called a *valley*, is the point at which a wave's negative or downward displacement from the rest position is at its maximum. A wavelength is one complete wave cycle. It could be measured from crest to crest, trough to trough, rest position to rest position, or any point of a wave to the corresponding point on the next wave.

Sound

Sound is a pressure disturbance that moves through a medium in the form of mechanical waves, which transfer energy from one particle to the next. Sound requires a medium to travel through, such as air, water, or other matter since it is the vibrations that transfer energy to adjacent particles, not the actual movement of particles over a great distance. Sound is transferred through the movement of atomic particles, which can be atoms or molecules. Waves of sound energy move outward in all directions from the source. Sound waves consist of compressions (particles are forced together) and rarefactions (particles move farther apart and their density decreases). A wavelength consists of one compression and one rarefaction. Different sounds have different wavelengths. Sound is a form of kinetic energy.

Pitch is the quality of sound determined by frequency. For example, a musical note can be tuned to a specific frequency. A, for instance, has a frequency of 440 Hz, which is a higher frequency than middle C. Humans can detect frequencies between about 20 Hz to 20,000 Hz. *Loudness* is a human's perception of sound intensity. *Sound intensity* is measured as the sound power per unit area, and can be expressed in decibels. *Timbre* is a human's perception of the type or quality of sound. *Oscillation* is a measurement, usually of time, against a basic value, equilibrium, or rest point.

When light waves pass from water to air, the frequency stays the same even though the speed and wavelength increase. This is because frequency is equal to speed (velocity) divided by wavelength ($f = v/\lambda$). In this case, there are two different mediums (water and air), which have different refractive indexes. Air has a smaller refractive index. The smaller the refractive index, the faster light moves through the medium. The refractive index of a medium can affect the speed and direction of travel of transmitted light. In air, both the speed and wavelength of the light increase, but the frequency (the number of cycles in a given unit of time) is the same. The speed of a wave is equal to its frequency times its wavelength ($v = f * \lambda$). Nodes of a wave are the points at which the amplitude is at its minimum. Wavelength is measured as the distance between nodes.

The *Doppler effect* refers to the effect the relative motion of the source of the wave and the location of the observer has on waves. The Doppler effect is easily observable in sound waves. What a person hears when a train approaches or a car honking its horn passes by are examples of the Doppler effect. The pitch of the sound is different not because the emitted frequency has changed, but because the received frequency has changed. The frequency is higher (as is the pitch) as the train approaches, the same as emitted just as it passes, and lower as the train moves away. This is because the wavelength changes. The Doppler effect can occur when an observer is stationary, and can also occur when two trains approach and pass each other. Electromagnetic waves are also affected in this manner. The motion of the medium can also affect the wave. For waves that do not travel in a medium, such as light waves, it is the difference in velocity that determines the outcome.

Optics

Geometric optics uses the concept of rays to determine how light will propagate. Ray diagrams can illustrate the path of light through a lens. Different types of lenses refract light, either convergently or divergently, to form images. After passing through a lens, rays converge at a focal point. Collimated rays are nearly parallel, and can be thought of as having no focal point. There are many types and combinations of lenses. Convergent lenses, also called positive lenses, are thicker in the middle and thinner at the edges. Rays are focused to a point. Divergent lenses, also called negative lenses, are thicker at the ends and thinner in the middle. Rays are spread apart, or diverged. A convex lens is bowed outward, either at one vertical surface or both. A convex lens with two convex surfaces may also be termed biconvex or double convex. A concave lens is bowed inward, while a planar lens is flat.

A rainbow is another example of the separation of light. Instead of a prism, the water molecules act as the separator, relying on both refraction and reflection. Rainbows include the colors of the visible light spectrum: red, orange, yellow, green, blue, indigo, and violet, which can be remembered using the acronym Roy G. Biv. The observer is at the center of the rainbow with the sun at his back, but only an arc of the rainbow circle is visible from the ground. Soap bubbles consist of a thin layer of soap with both an inside and outside surface. Light is reflected from both surfaces at once, and this causes interference. In this case of interference, some wavelengths cancel each other out and others are reinforced.

Light

Light is the portion of the electromagnetic spectrum that is visible because of its ability to stimulate the retina. It is absorbed and emitted by electrons, atoms, and molecules that move from one energy level to another. Visible light interacts with matter through molecular electron excitation (which occurs in the human retina) and through plasma oscillations (which occur in metals). Visible light is between ultraviolet and infrared light on the spectrum. The wavelengths of visible light cover a range from 380 nm (violet) to 760 nm (red). Different wavelengths correspond to different colors.

When light waves encounter an object, they are either reflected, transmitted, or absorbed. If the light is reflected from the surface of the object, the angle at which it contacts the surface will be the same as the angle at which it leaves, on the other side of the perpendicular. If the ray of light is perpendicular to the surface, it will be reflected back in the direction from which it came. When light is transmitted through the object, its direction may be altered upon entering the object. This is known as refraction. When light waves are refracted, or bent, an image can appear distorted. The degree to which the light is refracted depends on the speed at which light travels in the object. Light that is neither reflected nor transmitted will be absorbed by the surface and stored as heat energy. Nearly all instances of light hitting an object will involve a combination of two or even all three of these.

The human brain interprets or perceives visible light, which is emitted from the sun and other stars, as color. For example, when the entire wavelength reaches the retina, the brain perceives the color white. When no part of the wavelength reaches the retina, the brain perceives the color black. The particular color of an object depends upon what is absorbed and what is transmitted or reflected. For example, a leaf consists of chlorophyll molecules, the atoms of which absorb all wavelengths of the visible light spectrum except for green, which is why a leaf appears green. Certain wavelengths of visible light can be absorbed when they interact with matter. Wavelengths that are not absorbed can be transmitted by transparent materials or reflected by opaque materials.

The various properties of light have numerous real life applications. For example, polarized sunglasses have lenses that help reduce glare, while non-polarized sunglasses reduce the total amount of light that reaches the eyes. Polarized lenses consist of a chemical film of molecules aligned in parallel. This allows the lenses to block wavelengths of light that are intense, horizontal, and reflected from smooth, flat surfaces. The "fiber" in fiber optics refers to a tube or pipe that channels light. Because of the composition of the fiber, light can be transmitted greater distances before losing the signal. The fiber consists of a core, cladding, and a coating. Fibers are bundled, allowing for the transmission of large amounts of data.

Motion

Motion is a change in the location of an object, and is the result of an unbalanced net force acting on the object. Understanding motion requires the understanding of three basic quantities: displacement, velocity, and acceleration. When something moves from one place to another, it has undergone *displacement*. Displacement along a straight line is a very simple example of a vector quantity. If an object travels from position $x = -5$ cm to $x = 5$ cm, it has undergone a displacement of 10 cm. If it traverses the same path in the opposite direction, its displacement is -10 cm. A vector that spans the object's displacement in the direction of travel is known as a displacement vector.

Gravitational force is a universal force that causes every object to exert a force on every other object. The gravitational force between two objects can be described by the formula, $F = Gm_1m_2/r^2$, where m_1 and m_2 are the masses of two objects, r is the distance between them, and G is the gravitational constant, $G = 6.672 \times 10^{-11}$ N-m^2/kg^2. In order for this force to have a noticeable effect, one or both of the objects must be extremely large, so the equation is generally only used in problems involving planetary bodies. For problems involving objects on the earth being affected by earth's gravitational pull, the force of gravity is simply calculated as $F = mg$, where g is 9.81 m/s^2 toward the ground.

Newton's first law
An object at rest or in motion will remain at rest or in motion unless acted upon by an external force.

This phenomenon is commonly referred to as inertia, the tendency of a body to remain in its present state of motion. In order for the body's state of motion to change, it must be acted on by an unbalanced force.

Newton's second law
An object's acceleration is directly proportional to the net force acting on the object, and inversely proportional to the object's mass.

It is generally written in equation form $F = ma$, where F is the net force acting on a body, m is the mass of the body, and a is its acceleration. Note that since the mass is always a positive quantity, the acceleration is always in the same direction as the force.

Newton's third law

For every force, there is an equal and opposite force.

When a hammer strikes a nail, the nail hits the hammer just as hard. If we consider two objects, *A* and *B*, then we may express any contact between these two bodies with the equation $F_{AB} = -F_{BA}$, where the order of the subscripts denotes which body is exerting the force. At first glance, this law might seem to forbid any movement at all since every force is being countered with an equal opposite force, but these equal opposite forces are acting on different bodies with different masses, so they will not cancel each other out.

Velocity and acceleration

There are two types of velocity to consider: *average velocity* and *instantaneous velocity*. Unless an object has a constant velocity or we are explicitly given an equation for the velocity, finding the instantaneous velocity of an object requires the use of calculus. If we want to calculate the *average velocity* of an object, we need to know two things: the displacement, or the distance it has covered, and the time it took to cover this distance. The formula for average velocity is simply the distance traveled divided by the time required. In other words, the average velocity is equal to the change in position divided by the change in time. Average velocity is a vector and will always point in the same direction as the displacement vector (since time is a scalar and always positive). *Acceleration* is the change in the velocity of an object. Typically, the acceleration will be a constant value. Like position and velocity, acceleration is a vector quantity and will therefore have both magnitude and direction.

When an object is thrown upward the acceleration throughout its flight is 9.8 meters per second squared (m/s^2) downward. This is Earth's gravity (g) close to its surface. It is the acceleration of all objects when there is no resistance, such as that of air. If an object is held stationary, there is no work performed. This is because the formula for work performed is equal to the force times distance, or displacement ($W = F * d[\cos\Theta]$). Displacement is a vector measurement, and there must be displacement for work to be done. If an object is being held up, forces are at work, but are canceling each other out. No work is being done.

Work

Work can be thought of as the amount of energy expended in accomplishing some goal. The simplest equation for mechanical work (*W*) is $W = Fd$, where *F* is the force exerted and *d* is the displacement of the object on which the force is exerted. This equation requires that the force be applied in the same direction as the displacement. If this is not the case, then the work may be calculated as $W = Fd \cos(\theta)$, where θ is the angle between the force and displacement vectors. If force and displacement have the same direction, then work is positive; if they are in opposite directions, then work is negative; and if they are perpendicular, the work done by the force is zero.

Mechanics

Mechanics is the study of matter and motion, and the topics related to matter and motion, such as force, energy, and work. Discussions of mechanics will often include the concepts of vectors and scalars. Vectors are quantities with both magnitude and direction, while scalars have only magnitude. Scalar quantities include length, area, volume, mass, density, energy, work, and power. Vector quantities include displacement, velocity, acceleration, momentum, and force.

Calculating the amount of work being done

If a man pushes a block horizontally across a surface with a constant force of 10 N for a distance of 20 m, the work done by the man is 200 N-m or 200 J. If instead the block is sliding and the man tries to slow its progress by pushing against it, his work done is -200 J, since he is pushing in the direction opposite the motion. If the man pushes vertically downward on the block while it slides, his work done is zero, since his force vector is perpendicular to the displacement vector of the block.

Affect of mass

The weight of an object is the force of gravity on the object, and may be defined as the mass times the acceleration of gravity: $w = mg$. Mass is the amount of matter an object contains. When an object falls, it will accelerate at the same speed regardless of its mass, provided that gravity is the only force working on the object. Where mass can come into play is when there is significant air resistance. The force due to air resistance is a function of the object's size, shape, and velocity, but not mass. Thus, the air resistance force on two identically sized and shaped objects of different masses will be the same, but the heavier object will not be as affected, since it requires a greater force to overcome its momentum.

Simple machines

Simple machines include the inclined plane, lever, wheel and axle, and pulley. These simple machines have no internal source of energy. More complex or compound machines can be formed from them. Simple machines provide a force known as a mechanical advantage and make it easier to accomplish a task. The inclined plane enables a force less than the object's weight to be used to push an object to a greater height. A lever enables a multiplication of force. The wheel and axle allows for movement with less resistance. Single or double pulleys allows for easier direction of force. The wedge and screw are forms of the inclined plane. A wedge turns a smaller force working over a greater distance into a larger force. The screw is similar to an incline that is wrapped around a shaft.

Inclined plane

A certain amount of work is required to move an object. The amount cannot be reduced, but by changing the way the work is performed a mechanical advantage can be gained. A certain amount of work is required to raise an object to a given vertical height. By getting to a given height at an angle, the effort required is reduced, but the distance that must be traveled to reach a given height is increased. An example of this is walking up a hill. One may take a direct, shorter, but steeper route, or one may take a more meandering, longer route that requires less effort. Examples of wedges include doorstops, axes, plows, zippers, and can openers.

Levers

A lever consists of a bar or plank and a pivot point or fulcrum. Work is performed by the bar, which swings at the pivot point to redirect the force. There are three types of levers: first, second, and third class. Examples of a first-class lever include balances, see-saws, nail extractors, and scissors (which also use wedges). In a second-class lever the fulcrum is placed at one end of the bar and the work is performed at the other end. The weight or load to be moved is in between. The closer to the fulcrum the weight is, the easier it is to move.

Force is increased, but the distance it is moved is decreased. Examples include pry bars, bottle openers, nutcrackers, and wheelbarrows. In a third-class lever the fulcrum is at one end and the positions of the weight and the location where the work is performed are reversed. Examples include fishing rods, hammers, and tweezers.

<u>Wheels and axles</u>
The center of a wheel and axle can be likened to a fulcrum on a rotating lever. As it turns, the wheel moves a greater distance than the axle, but with less force. Obvious examples of the wheel and axle are the wheels of a car, but this type of simple machine can also be used to exert a greater force. For instance, a person can turn the handles of a winch to exert a greater force at the turning axle to move an object. Other examples include steering wheels, wrenches, faucets, waterwheels, windmills, gears, and belts. Gears work together to change a force. The four basic types of gears are spur, rack and pinion, bevel, and worm gears. The larger gear turns slower than the smaller, but exerts a greater force. Gears at angles can be used to change the direction of forces.

<u>Pulley</u>
A single pulley consists of a rope or line that is run around a wheel. This allows force to be directed in a downward motion to lift an object. This does not decrease the force required, just changes its direction. The load is moved the same distance as the rope pulling it. When a combination pulley is used, such as a double pulley, the weight is moved half the distance of the rope pulling it. In this way, the work effort is doubled. Pulleys are never 100% efficient because of friction. Examples of pulleys include cranes, chain hoists, block and tackles, and elevators.

Friction

Friction is a force that arises as a resistance to motion where two surfaces are in contact. The maximum magnitude of the frictional force (f)can be calculated as $f = F_c\mu$, where F_c is the contact force between the two objects and μ is a coefficient of friction based on the surfaces' material composition. Two types of friction are static and kinetic. To illustrate these concepts, imagine a book resting on a table. The force of its weight (W) is equal and opposite to the force of the table on the book, or the normal force (N). If we exert a small force (F) on the book, attempting to push it to one side, a frictional force (f) would arise, equal and opposite to our force. At this point, it is a *static frictional force* because the book is not moving. If we increase our force on the book, we will eventually cause it to move. At this point, the frictional force opposing us will be a *kinetic frictional force*. Generally, the kinetic frictional force is lower than static frictional force (because the frictional coefficient for static friction is larger), which means that the amount of force needed to maintain the movement of the book will be less than what was needed to start it moving.

A glass rod and a plastic rod can illustrate the concept of static electricity due to friction. Both start with no charge. A glass rod rubbed with silk produces a positive charge, while a plastic rod rubbed with fur produces a negative charge. The electron affinity of a material is a property that helps determine how easily it can be charged by friction. Materials can be sorted by their affinity for electrons into a triboelectric series. Materials with greater affinities include celluloid, sulfur, and rubber. Materials with lower affinities include glass, rabbit fur, and asbestos. In the example of a glass rod and a plastic one, the glass rod rubbed with silk acquires a positive charge because glass has a lower affinity for electrons than silk. The electrons flow to the silk, leaving the rod with fewer electrons and a positive charge.

When a plastic rod is rubbed with fur, electrons flow to the rod and result in a negative charge.

Kinetic and potential energy

The two types of energy most important in mechanics are potential and kinetic energy. Potential energy is the amount of energy an object has stored within itself because of its position or orientation. There are many types of potential energy, but the most common is gravitational potential energy. It is the energy that an object has because of its height (h) above the ground. It can be calculated as $PE = mgh$, where m is the object's mass and g is the acceleration of gravity. Kinetic energy is the energy of an object in motion, and is calculated as $KE = mv^2/2$, where v is the magnitude of its velocity. When an object is dropped, its potential energy is converted into kinetic energy as it falls. These two equations can be used to calculate the velocity of an object at any point in its fall.

Floating object

A key determiner as to whether an object will float or sink in water is its density. The general rule is that if an object is less dense than water, it floats; if it is denser than water, it sinks. The density of an object is equal to its mass divided by its volume ($d = m/v$). It is important to note the difference between an object's density and a material's density. Water has a density of one gram per cubic centimeter, while steel has a density approximately eight times that. Despite having a much higher material density, an object made of steel may still float. A hollow steel sphere, for instance, will float easily because the density of the object includes the air contained within the sphere. An object may also float only in certain orientations. An ocean liner that is placed in the water upside down, for instance, may not remain afloat. An object will float only if it can displace a mass of water equal to its own mass.

Archimedes's principle states that a buoyant (upward) force on a submerged object is equal to the weight of the liquid displaced by the object. Water has a density of one gram per cubic centimeter. Anything that floats in water has a lower effective density, and anything that sinks has a higher effective density. This principle of buoyancy can also be used to calculate the volume of an irregularly shaped object. The mass of the object (m) minus its apparent mass in the water (m_a) divided by the density of water (ρ_w), gives the object's volume: $V = (m-m_a)/\rho_w$.

Biology

Cells in living organisms

The functions of plant and animal cells vary greatly, and the functions of different cells within a single organism can also be vastly different. Animal and plant cells are similar in structure in that they are eukaryotic, which means they contain a nucleus. The nucleus is a round structure that controls the activities of the cell and contains chromosomes. Both types of cells have cell membranes, cytoplasm, vacuoles, and other structures. The main difference between the two is that plant cells have a cell wall made of cellulose that can handle high levels of pressure within the cell, which can occur when liquid enters a plant cell. Plant cells have chloroplasts that are used during the process of photosynthesis, which is the conversion of sunlight into food. Plant cells usually have one large vacuole, whereas animal cells can have many smaller ones. Plant cells have a regular shape, while the shapes of animal cell can vary.

Nuclear parts of a cell

Nucleus (pl. nuclei): This is a small structure that contains the chromosomes and regulates the DNA of a cell. The nucleus is the defining structure of eukaryotic cells, and all eukaryotic cells have a nucleus. The nucleus is responsible for the passing on of genetic traits between generations. The nucleus contains a nuclear envelope, nucleoplasm, a nucleolus, nuclear pores, chromatin, and ribosomes.

Chromosomes: These are highly condensed, threadlike rods of DNA. Short for deoxyribonucleic acid, DNA is the genetic material that stores information about the plant or animal.
Chromatin: This consists of the DNA and protein that make up chromosomes.
Nucleolus (nucleole): This structure contained within the nucleus consists of protein. It is small, round, does not have a membrane, is involved in protein synthesis, and synthesizes and stores RNA (ribonucleic acid).

Nuclear envelope: This encloses the structures of the nucleus. It consists of inner and outer membranes made of lipids.

Nuclear pores: These are involved in the exchange of material between the nucleus and the cytoplasm.

Nucleoplasm: This is the liquid within the nucleus, and is similar to cytoplasm.

Cell structure

Ribosomes: Ribosomes are involved in synthesizing proteins from amino acids. They are numerous, making up about one quarter of the cell. Some cells contain thousands of ribosome. Some are mobile and some are embedded in the rough endoplasmic reticulum.

Golgi complex (Golgi apparatus): This is involved in synthesizing materials such as proteins that are transported out of the cell. It is located near the nucleus and consists of layers of membranes.

Vacuoles: These are sacs used for storage, digestion, and waste removal. There is one large vacuole in plant cells. Animal cells have small, sometimes numerous vacuoles.

Vesicle: This is a small organelle within a cell. It has a membrane and performs varying functions, including moving materials within a cell.
Cytoskeleton: This consists of microtubules that help shape and support the cell.

Microtubules: These are part of the cytoskeleton and help support the cell. They are made of protein.

Cytosol: This is the liquid material in the cell. It is mostly water, but also contains some floating molecules.

Cytoplasm: This is a general term that refers to cytosol and the substructures (organelles) found within the plasma membrane, but not within the nucleus.

Cell membrane (plasma membrane): This defines the cell by acting as a barrier. It helps keeps cytoplasm in and substances located outside the cell out. It also determines what is allowed to enter and exit the cell.

Endoplasmic reticulum: The two types of endoplasmic reticulum are rough (has ribosomes on the surface) and smooth (does not have ribosomes on the surface). It is a tubular network that comprises the transport system of a cell. It is fused to the nuclear membrane and extends through the cytoplasm to the cell membrane.

Mitochondrion (pl. mitochondria): These cell structures vary in terms of size and quantity. Some cells may have one mitochondrion, while others have thousands. This structure performs various functions such as generating ATP, and is also involved in cell growth and death. Mitochondria contain their own DNA that is separate from that contained in the nucleus.

Plant cell structure

Cell wall: Made of cellulose and composed of numerous layers, the cell wall provides plants with a sturdy barrier that can hold fluid within the cell. The cell wall surrounds the cell membrane.

Chloroplast: This is a specialized organelle that plant cells use for photosynthesis, which is the process plants use to create food energy from sunlight. Chloroplasts contain chlorophyll, which has a green color.

Plastid: This is a membrane-bound organelle found in plant cells that is used to make chemical compounds and store food. It can also contain pigments used during photosynthesis. Plastids can develop into more specialized structures such as chloroplasts, chromoplasts (make and hold yellow and orange pigments), amyloplasts (store starch), and leucoplasts (lack pigments, but can become differentiated).

Plasmodesmata (sing. plasmodesma): These are channels between the cell walls of plant cells that allow for transport between cells.

Animal cell structure

Centrosome: This is comprised of the pair of centrioles located at right angles to each other and surrounded by protein. The centrosome is involved in mitosis and the cell cycle.

Centriole: These are cylinder-shaped structures near the nucleus that are involved in cellular division. Each cylinder consists of nine groups of three microtubules. Centrioles occur in pairs.

Lysosome: This digests proteins, lipids, and carbohydrates, and also transports undigested substances to the cell membrane so they can be removed. The shape of a lysosome depends on the material being transported.

Cilia (singular: cilium): These are appendages extending from the surface of the cell, the movement of which causes the cell to move. They can also result in fluid being moved by the cell.
Flagella: These are tail-like structures on cells that use whip-like movements to help the cell move. They are similar to cilia, but are usually longer and not as numerous. A cell usually only has one or a few flagella.

Lipid, organelle, RNA, polymer, monomer, nucleotides, and nucleoid

Lipids take many forms and have varying functions, such as storing energy and acting as a building block of cell membranes. Lipids are produced by anabolysis.

Organelle: This is a general term that refers to an organ or smaller structure within a cell. Membrane-bound organelles are found in eukaryotic cells.

RNA: RNA is short for ribonucleic acid, which is a type of molecule that consists of a long chain (polymer) of nucleotide units.

Polymer: This is a compound of large molecules formed by repeating monomers.

Monomer: A monomer is a small molecule. It is a single compound that forms chemical bonds with other monomers to make a polymer.

Nucleotides: These are molecules that combine to form DNA and RNA. They can be easily stained to make them more visible.

Nucleoid: This is the nucleus-like, irregularly-shaped mass of DNA that contains the chromatin in a prokaryotic cell.

Eukaryotic and prokaryotic cells

The main difference between eukaryotic and prokaryotic cells is that eukaryotic cells have a nucleus and prokaryotic cells do not. Eukaryotic cells are considered more complex, while prokaryotic cells are smaller and simpler. Eukaryotic cells have membrane-bound organelles that perform various functions and contribute to the complexity of these types of cells. Prokaryotic cells do not contain membrane-bound organelles. In prokaryotic cells, the genetic material (DNA) is not contained within a membrane-bound nucleus. Instead, it aggregates in the cytoplasm in a nucleoid. In eukaryotic cells, DNA is mostly contained in chromosomes in the nucleus, although there is some DNA in mitochondria and chloroplasts. Prokaryotic cells usually divide by binary fission and are haploid. Eukaryotic cells divide by mitosis and are diploid. Prokaryotic structures include plasmids, ribosomes, cytoplasm, a cytoskeleton, granules of nutritional substances, a plasma membrane, flagella, and a few others. They are single-celled organisms. Bacteria are prokaryotic cells.

Plant and animal cell differences

Plant cells can be much larger than animal cells, ranging from 10 to 100 micrometers. Animal cells are 10 to 30 micrometers in size. Plant cells can have much larger vacuoles that occupy a large portion of the cell. They also have cell walls, which are thick barriers consisting of protein and sugars. Animal cells lack cell walls. Chloroplasts in plants that perform photosynthesis absorb sunlight and convert it into energy. Mitochondria produce energy from food in animal cells. Plant and animal cells are both eukaryotic, meaning they contain a nucleus. Both plant and animal cells duplicate genetic material, separate it, and then divide in half to reproduce. Plant cells build a cell plate between the two new cells, while animal cells make a cleavage furrow and pinch in half. Microtubules are components of the cytoskeleton in both plant and animal cells. Microtubule organizing centers (MTOCs) make microtubules in plant cells, while centrioles make microtubules in animal cells.

Mitochondria functions

Four functions of mitochondria are: the production of cell energy, cell signaling (how communications are carried out within a cell, cellular differentiation (the process whereby a non-differentiated cell becomes transformed into a cell with a more specialized purpose), and cell cycle and growth regulation (the process whereby the cell gets ready to reproduce and reproduces). Mitochondria are numerous in eukaryotic cells. There may be hundreds or even thousands of mitochondria in a single cell. Mitochondria can be involved in many functions, their main one being supplying the cell with energy. Mitochondria consist of an inner and outer membrane. The inner membrane encloses the matrix, which contains the mitochondrial DNA (mtDNA) and ribosomes. Between the inner and outer membranes are folds (cristae). Chemical reactions occur here that release energy, control water levels in cells, and recycle and create proteins and fats. Aerobic respiration also occurs in the mitochondria.

Cellular respiration

Cellular respiration refers to a set of metabolic reactions that convert chemical bonds into energy stored in the form of ATP. Respiration includes many oxidation and reduction reactions that occur thanks to the electron transport system within the cell. Oxidation is a loss of electrons and reduction is a gain of electrons. Electrons in C-H (carbon/hydrogen) and C-C (carbon/carbon) bonds are donated to oxygen atoms. Processes involved in cellular respiration include glycolysis, the Krebs cycle, the electron transport chain, and chemiosmosis. The two forms of respiration are aerobic and anaerobic. Aerobic respiration is very common, and oxygen is the final electron acceptor. In anaerobic respiration, the final electron acceptor is not oxygen. Aerobic respiration results in more ATP than anaerobic respiration. Fermentation is another process by which energy is converted.

Photosynthesis

Photosynthesis is the conversion of sunlight into energy in plant cells, and also occurs in some types of bacteria and protists. Carbon dioxide and water are converted into glucose during photosynthesis, and light is required during this process. Cyanobacteria are thought to be the descendants of the first organisms to use photosynthesis about 3.5 billion years ago. Photosynthesis is a form of cellular respiration. It occurs in chloroplasts that use thylakoids, which are structures in the membrane that contain light reaction chemicals. Chlorophyll is a pigment that absorbs light. During the process, water is used and oxygen is released. The equation for the chemical reaction that occurs during photosynthesis is $6H_2O + 6CO_2 \rightarrow C_6H_{12}O_6 + 6O_2$. During photosynthesis, six molecules of water and six molecules of carbon dioxide react to form one molecule of sugar and six molecules of oxygen.

Cell transport mechanisms

Active transport mechanisms include exocytosis and endocytosis. Active transport involves transferring substances from areas of lower concentration to areas of higher concentration. Active transport requires energy in the form of ATP. Endocytosis is the ingestion of large particles into a cell, and can be categorized as phagocytosis (ingestion of a particle), pinocytosis (ingestion of a liquid), or receptor mediated. Endocytosis occurs when a substance is too large to cross a cell membrane. Endocytosis is a process by which eukaryotes ingest food particles. During phagocytosis, cell eating vesicles used during ingestion are quickly formed and unformed. Pinocytosis is also known as cell drinking. Exocytosis is the opposite of endocytosis. It is the expulsion or discharge of substances from a cell. A lysosome digests particles with enzymes, and can be expelled through exocytosis. A vacuole containing the substance to be expelled attaches to the cell membrane and expels the substance.

Passive transport mechanisms

Transport mechanisms allow for the movement of substances through membranes. Passive transport mechanisms include simple and facilitated diffusion and osmosis. They do not require energy from the cell. Diffusion is when particles are transported from areas of higher concentration to areas of lower concentration. When equilibrium is reached, diffusion stops. Examples are gas exchange (carbon dioxide and oxygen) during photosynthesis and the transport of oxygen from air to blood and from blood to tissue. Facilitated diffusion is when specific molecules are transported by a specific carrier protein. Carrier proteins vary in terms of size, shape, and charge. Glucose and amino acids are examples of substances transported by carrier proteins. Osmosis is the diffusion of water through a semi-permeable membrane from an area of higher concentration to one of lower concentration. Examples of osmosis include the absorption of water by plant roots and the alimentary canal. Plants lose and gain water through osmosis. A plant cell that swells because of water retention is said to be turgid.

Cell cycle

The term cell cycle refers to the process by which a cell reproduces, which involves cell growth, the duplication of genetic material, and cell division. Complex organisms with many cells use the cell cycle to replace cells as they lose their functionality and wear out. The entire cell cycle in animal cells can take 24 hours. The time required varies among different cell types. Human skin cells, for example, are constantly reproducing. Some other cells only divide infrequently. Once neurons are mature, they do not grow or divide. The two ways that cells can reproduce are through meiosis and mitosis. When cells replicate through mitosis, the "daughter cell" is an exact replica of the parent cell. When cells divide through meiosis, the daughter cells have different genetic coding than the parent cell. Meiosis only happens in specialized reproductive cells called gametes.

Cell division

Cell division is performed in organisms so they can grow and replace cells that are old, worn out, or damaged.

Chromatids: During cell division, the DNA is replicated, and chromatids are the two identical replicated pieces of chromosome that are joined at the centromere to form an "X."

Gametes: These are cells used by organisms to reproduce sexually. Gametes in humans are haploid, meaning they contain only half of the organism's genetic information (23 chromosomes). Other human cells contain all 46 chromosomes.

Haploid/diploid: Haploid means there is one set of chromosomes. Diploid means there are two sets of chromosomes (one set from each parent).
Cytokinesis: This is the splitting of a cell (including the cytoplasm) into two cells. Some believe this occurs following telophase. Others say it occurs from anaphase, as the cell begins to furrow, through telophase, when the cell actually splits into two.

Homeostasis, gene expression, transcription, translation, and cellular differentiation

Homeostasis: This describes the ability and tendency of an organism, cell, or body to adjust to environmental changes to maintain equilibrium.

Gene expression: This refers to the use of information in a gene, usually during the processes of transcription and translation, that result in a protein product.

Transcription: This refers to the synthesis of RNA. Information is provided by DNA.

Translation: This is the decoding of mRNA (messenger RNA) used in the fabrication of protein. It occurs after transcription.

Cellular differentiation: This is the process by which a less specialized cell becomes a more specialized cell.

Size: The size of the nucleus in a eukaryotic cell is about 6 micrometers (μm). It occupies about 10 percent of the cell. A chloroplast is about 1 μm. Plant and animal cell sizes range from about 10 µm to 100 µm, while the sizes of bacteria range from about 1 µm to 10 µm. Atoms have a size of about 0.1 µm.

Meiosis

Meiosis has the same phases as mitosis, but they happen twice. In addition, different events occur during some phases of meiosis than mitosis. The events that occur during the first phase of meiosis are interphase (I), prophase (I), metaphase (I), anaphase (I), telophase (I), and cytokinesis (I). During this first phase of meiosis, chromosomes cross over, genetic material is exchanged, and tetrads of four chromatids are formed. The nuclear membrane dissolves. Homologous pairs of chromatids are separated and travel to different poles. At this point, there has been one cell division resulting in two cells. Each cell goes through a second cell division, which consists of prophase (II), metaphase (II), anaphase (II), telophase (II), and cytokinesis (II). The result is four daughter cells with different sets of chromosomes. The daughter cells are haploid, which means they contain half the genetic material of the parent cell. The second phase of meiosis is similar to the process of mitosis. Meiosis encourages genetic diversity.

Mitosis

Interphase: The cell prepares for division by replicating its genetic and cytoplasmic material. Interphase can be further divided into G_1, S, and G_2.

Prophase: The chromatin thickens into chromosomes and the nuclear membrane begins to disintegrate. Pairs of centrioles move to opposite sides of the cell and spindle fibers begin to form. The mitotic spindle, formed from cytoskeleton parts, moves chromosomes around within the cell.

Metaphase: The spindle moves to the center of the cell and chromosome pairs align along the center of the spindle structure.
Anaphase: The pairs of chromosomes, called sisters, begin to pull apart, and may bend. When they are separated, they are called daughter chromosomes. Grooves appear in the cell membrane.

Telophase: The spindle disintegrates, the nuclear membranes reform, and the chromosomes revert to chromatin. In animal cells, the membrane is pinched. In plant cells, a new cell wall begins to form.

Cytokinesis: This is the physical splitting of the cell (including the cytoplasm) into two cells. Some believe this occurs following telophase. Others say it occurs from anaphase, as the cell begins to furrow, through telophase, when the cell actually splits into two.

Cancerous cells

In cancerous cells, the DNA or gene structure is disrupted. Abnormal numbers of chromosomes can develop. Cancer cells can have defective Krebs cycles, and get most of their energy from glycolysis rather than the Krebs cycle. Normal cells get about 70% of their energy from the Krebs cycle and about 20% from glycolysis. In addition, normal cells usually use oxygen during energy production, while cancer cells mainly produce energy without using oxygen. Cancerous cells lack a blood vessel system and use amino acids to construct it, while normal cells have a built-in blood vessel system. Cancer cells over populate and are very active, making more demands on system resources. The enzymes and hormones involved with cancer cells tend to be overactive or underactive, which can lead to other problems.

Cell theory

The basic tenets of cell theory are that all living things are made up of cells and that cell are the basic units of life. Cell theory has evolved over time and is subject to interpretation. The development of cell theory is attributed to Matthias Schleiden and Theodor Schwann, who developed the theory in the early 1800s. Early cell theory was comprised of four statements: all organisms (living things) are made of cells; new cells are formed from pre-existing cells; all cells are similar; and cells are the most basic units of life. Other concepts related to classic and modern cell theory include statements such as: cells provide the basic units of functionality and structure in living things; cells are both distinct stand-alone units and basic building blocks; energy flow occurs within cells; cells contain genetic information in the form of DNA; and all cells consist of mostly the same chemicals.

Enzymes

Enzymes can be divided into six classes: oxidoreductase, transferase, hydrolase, lyase, isomerase, and ligase. These classes end with the suffix "ase," which is true of most enzymes. Each enzyme catalyzes a chemical reaction. Oxidoreductase enzymes catalyze oxidation reduction (redox) reactions, during which hydrogen and oxygen are gained or lost. Examples include cytochrome oxidase, lactate, and dehydrogenase. Transferase enzymes catalyze the transfer of functional groups, such as the amino or phosphate group. Examples include acetate kinase and alanine deaminase. Hydrolase enzymes break chemical bonds by using water. Examples include lipase and sucrase. Lyase enzymes break chemical bonds or remove groups of atoms without using water. Examples include oxalate decarboxylase and isocitrate lyase. Isomerase enzymes catalyze the rearrangement of atoms within a molecule. Examples include glucose-phosphate isomerase and alanine racemase. Ligase enzymes join two molecules by forming a bond between atoms. Examples of ligases are acetyl-CoA synthetase and DNA ligase.

Metabolism, macromolecules, metabolic pathways, anabolic and catabolic reactions

Metabolism is all of the chemical reactions that take place within a living organism. These chemical changes convert nutrients to energy and macromolecules. Macromolecules are large and complex, and play an important role in cell structure and function. Metabolic pathways refer to a series of reactions in which the product of one reaction is the substrate for the next. These pathways are dependent upon enzymes that act as catalysts. An anabolic reaction is one that builds larger and more complex molecules (macromolecules) from smaller ones. Catabolic reactions are the opposite. Larger molecules are broken down into smaller, simpler molecules. Catabolic reactions release energy, while anabolic ones require energy. The four basic organic macromolecules produced by anabolic reactions are carbohydrates (polysaccharides), nucleic acids, proteins, and lipids. The four basic building blocks involved in catabolic reactions are monosaccharides (glucose), amino acids, fatty acids (glycerol), and nucleotides.

Catabolism

Catabolism is the biosynthetic process by which macromolecules are broken down into smaller molecules. During this process, both energy and molecules that are used in anabolic processes are produced. Hydrolysis is a process used in catabolism. The four main groups of molecules produced through catabolism are monosaccharides (glucose), amino acids, fatty acids (glycerol), and nucleotides. Carbohydrates (polysaccharides) are broken down into sugars or glucose. It is the oxidation of carbohydrates that provides the cells with most of their energy. Glucose can be further broken down by respiration or fermentation by glycolysis. The first step of glycolysis breaks down pyruvic acid with the byproducts of NADH and ATP. Pyruvic acid can then be used in the Krebs cycle or in fermentation. Glycolysis occurs in the cytoplasm of eukaryotic cells. Fatty acids are long chains that are oxidized to acetyl-CoA, which provides energy to cells. Nucleic acids consist of nucleotides. Nucleotide triphosphates such as ATP carry energy. They also release energy when their bonds are broken.

Anabolism

Anabolism is a form of biosynthesis. It usually involves a series of steps, or pathways, where the product of one reaction is used in the next. Anabolism uses smaller molecules to build carbohydrates (polysaccharides), nucleic acids, amino acids and proteins, and lipids. Energy is used and stored during this process. Anabolic reactions can form a variety of macromolecules. An example of polysaccharide biosynthesis in animals and bacteria is glycolysis, the formation of glycogen from glucose with covalent bonds. Examples of nucleic acid synthesis include the formation of DNA, RNA, ATP, and other macromolecules. It can be achieved by either the pentose phosphate or Entner Doudoroff pathways. Protein biosynthesis uses amino acids, which are intermediate products of the Krebs cycle. Lipid biosynthesis uses fatty acids, which are formed from acetyl CoA (coenzyme A) during the Krebs cycle, and glycerol, which is derived from dihydroxyacetone phosphate and glycolysis.

Proteins

Proteins are macromolecules formed from amino acids. They are polypeptides, which consist of many (10 to 100) peptides linked together. The peptide connections are the result of condensation reactions. A condensation reaction results in a loss of water when two molecules are joined together. A hydrolysis reaction is the opposite of a condensation reaction. During hydrolysis, water is added. -H is added to one of the smaller molecules and OH is added to another molecule being formed. A peptide is a compound of two or more amino acids. Amino acids are formed by the partial hydrolysis of protein, which forms an amide bond. This partial hydrolysis involves an amine group and a carboxylic acid. In the carbon chain of amino acids, there is a carboxylic acid group (-COOH), an amine group (-NH_2), a central carbon atom between them with an attached hydrogen, and an attached "R" group (side chain), which is different for different amino acids. It is the "R" group that determines the properties of the protein.

Types of proteins

Alkyl: This is a nonpolar group that forms hydrophobic amino acids. Amino acids include glycine with a single hydrogen atom R group, alanine with a methyl R group, and valine with an isopropyl R group. Leucine and isoleucine also have alkyl side chains.

Hydroxyl: This is a polar group that forms hydrophilic amino acids such as serine and threonine.
Sulfur: Amino acids in this group include cysteine and methionine.

Carboxylic acid: In proteins belonging to this group, a second carboxylic acid group is attached as the R group. This acid group is polar and can be negatively charged when the acidic proton attaches to a water molecule, which leaves a negatively charged carboxylate ion. Proteins that belong to this group include aspartic acid and glutamic acid.

Amide: The formula for amides is $-CONH_2$. Proteins belonging to this group include glutamine and asparagine.
Amino: This group includes lysine, arginine, and histidine. The double-bonded nitrogen atom can take a proton to become positively charged.

Aromatic: This group has a ring structure, and includes the proteins phenylalanine, tyrosine, and tryptophan. Tyrosine is polar, while tryptophan and phenylalanine are nonpolar.

Looped: This group includes praline. Because it is nonpolar, it forms a ring rather than a chain.

Chemiosmosis and enzymes

Chemiosmosis is a process by which energy is made available for ADP to form ATP. When electrons move down the electron transport chain, the energy pumps protons to one side of a membrane. The equilibrium is disrupted at this point because the concentration gradient where the protons have gathered is greater than the concentration gradient on the other side of the membrane. The protons diffuse through the membrane as a result. The energy of this process fuels phosphorylation.

Enzymes act as catalysts by lowering the activation energy necessary for a reaction. They are proteins, have specific functions, are often globular and 3-D in form, and have names that end in "-ase." An enzyme has an active site where a substrate attaches and products are formed and released. Most enzymes also need a non-protein coenzyme that attaches to the enzyme to form the active site.

Nucleic acids

Nucleic acids are macromolecules that are composed of nucleotides. Hydrolysis is a reaction in which water is broken down into hydrogen cations (H or H^+) and hydroxide anions (OH or OH^-). This is part of the process by which nucleic acids are broken down by enzymes to produce shorter strings of RNA and DNA (oligonucleotides). Oligonucleotides are broken down into smaller sugar nitrogenous units called nucleosides. These can be digested by cells since the sugar is divided from the nitrogenous base. This, in turn, leads to the formation of the five types of nitrogenous bases, sugars, and the preliminary substances involved in the synthesis of new RNA and DNA. DNA and RNA have a double helix shape.

Macromolecular nucleic acid polymers, such as RNA and DNA, are formed from nucleotides, which are monomeric units joined by phosphodiester bonds. Cells require energy in the form of ATP to synthesize proteins from amino acids and replicate DNA. Nitrogen fixation is used to synthesize nucleotides for DNA and amino acids for proteins. Nitrogen fixation uses the enzyme nitrogenase in the reduction of dinitrogen gas (N_2) to ammonia (NH_3). Nucleic acids store information and energy and are also important catalysts. It is the RNA that catalyzes the transfer of DNA genetic information into protein coded information. ATP is an RNA nucleotide. Nucleotides are used to form the nucleic acids. Nucleotides are made of a five carbon sugar, such as ribose or deoxyribose, a nitrogenous base, and one or more phosphates. Nucleotides consisting of more than one phosphate can also store energy in their bonds.

Lipids

Carbohydrates, proteins, and nucleic acids are groups of macromolecules that are polymers. Lipids are not long polymers with high molecular weights. They are hydrophobic, meaning they do not bond well with water or mix well with water solutions. Lipids have numerous C-H bonds. In this way, they are similar to hydrocarbons (substances consisting only of carbon and hydrogen).The major roles of lipids include energy storage and structural functions. Examples of lipids include fats, phospholipids, steroids, and waxes. Fats are made of long chains of fatty acids (three fatty acids bound to a glycerol). Fatty acids are chains with reduced carbon at one end and a carboxylic acid group at the other. An example is soap, which contains the sodium salts of free fatty acids. Phospholipids are lipids that have a phosphate group rather than a fatty acid. Glycerides are another type of lipid. Examples of glycerides are fat and oil. Glycerides are formed from fatty acids and glycerol (a type of alcohol).

Catabolization of macromolecules

Amino acids are catabolized either during glycolysis or during the Krebs cycle. First, they are broken down into substances that can be catabolized. Processes used to break down amino acids include transamination, which is the transfer of NH_2 (amine), decarboxylation, which is the loss of -COOH groups, and dehydrogenation of H_2. While sugars like glucose from carbohydrates usually begin to be broken down by glycolysis at the beginning of the cycle, eventually going through the Krebs cycle and then the electron transport chain, proteins get broken down into amino acids and have many different entry points into the cycles. Carbohydrates are responsible for providing energy. They are involved in the metabolic energy cycles of photosynthesis and respiration. Structurally, carbohydrates usually take the form of some variation of CH_2O. In respiration, glucose is completely dismantled, but is only partially broken up during fermentation. Lipids get broken down into glycerol for glycolysis and fatty acids enter at the Krebs cycle.

Glycolysis

In glycolysis, glucose is converted into pyruvate and energy stored in ATP bonds is released. Glycolysis can involve various pathways. Various intermediates are produced that are used in other processes, and the pyruvic acid produced by glycolysis can be further used for respiration by the Krebs cycle or in fermentation. Glycolysis occurs in both aerobic and anaerobic organisms. Oxidation of molecules produces reduced coenzymes, such as NADH. The coenzymes relocate hydrogens to the electron transport chain. The proton is transported through the cell membrane and the electron is transported down the chain by proteins. At the end of the chain, water is formed when the final acceptor releases two electrons that combine with oxygen. The protons are pumped back into the cell or organelle by the ATP synthase enzyme, which uses energy produced to add a phosphate to ADP to form ATP. The proton motive force is produced by the protons being moved across the membrane.

Intermediaries of glycolysis

Glycolysis can involve different metabolic pathways. The following 10 steps are based on the Embden-Meyerhof pathway, in which glucose is the starting product and pyruvic acid is the final product. Two molecules of ATP and two of NADH are the products of this process. To start, enzymes utilize ATP to form glucose-6-phosphate. The glucose-6 is converted to fructose-6-phosphate. Another ATP molecule and an enzyme are used to convert fructose-6-phosphate to fructose-1,6-disphosphate. Both dihydroxyacetone phosphate (DHAP) and glyceraldehyde-3-phosphate are formed from fructose-1,6-disphosphate. It is during the preceding reactions that energy is conserved or gained. NAD conversions to NADH molecules and phosphate influx result in 1,3-diphosphoglceric acid. Then, two ADP molecules are phosphorized into ATP molecules, resulting in 3-phosphoglyceric acid, which reforms into 2-phosphoglyceric acid. At this point, water is produced as a product and phosphoenolpyruvic acid is formed. Another set of ADP molecules are phosphorized into ATP molecules. Pyruvic acid is the end result.

Glycolic pathways

Glycolysis is a general term for the conversion of glucose into pyruvate.

Embden-Meyerhof pathway: This is a type of glycolysis in which one molecule of glucose becomes two ATP and two NADH molecules. Pyruvic acid (two pyruvate molecules) is the end product.

Entner-Doudoroff pathway: This is a type of glycolysis in which one glucose molecule forms into one molecule of ATP and two of NADPH, which are used for other reactions. The end product is two pyruvate molecules.

Pentose Phosphate pathway: Also known as the hexose monophosphate shunt, this is a type of glycolysis in which one glucose molecule produces one ATP and two NADPH molecules. Five carbon sugars are metabolized during this reaction. Glucose is broken down into ribose, ribulose, and xylose, which are used during glycolysis and during the Calvin (or Calvin-Benson) cycle to create nucleotides, nucleic acids, and amino acids.

Monosaccharides, disaccharides, starches

The simple sugars can be grouped into monosaccharides (glucose, fructose, and sucrose) and disaccharides. These are both types of carbohydrates. Monosaccharides have one monomer of sugar and disaccharides have two. Monosaccharides (CH_2O) have one carbon for every water molecule. Aldose and ketose are monosaccharides with a carbonyl (=O, double bonded oxygen to carbon) functional group. The difference between aldose and ketose is that the carbonyl group in aldose is connected at an end carbon and the carbonyl group in ketose is connected at a middle carbon. Glucose is a monosaccharide containing six carbons, making it a hexose and an aldose. A disaccharide is formed from two monosaccharides with a glycosidic link. Examples include two glucoses forming a maltose, a glucose and a galactose forming a lactose, and a glucose and a fructose forming a sucrose. A starch is a polysaccharide consisting only of glucose monomers. Examples are amylose, amylopectin, and glycogen.

Krebs cycle

The Krebs cycle is also called the citric acid cycle or the tricarboxylic acid cycle (TCA). It is a catabolic pathway in which the bonds of glucose and occasionally fats or lipids are broken down and reformed into ATP. It is a respiration process that uses oxygen and produces carbon dioxide, water, and ATP. Cells require energy from ATP to synthesize proteins from amino acids and replicate DNA. The cycle is acetyl CoA, citric acid, isocitric acid, ketoglutaric acid (products are amino acids and CO_2), succinyl CoA, succinic acid, fumaric acid, malic acid, and oxaloacetic acid. One of the products of the Krebs cycle is NADH, which is then used in the electron chain transport system to manufacture ATP. From glycolysis, pyruvate is oxidized in a step linking to the Krebs cycle. After the Krebs cycle, NADH and succinate are oxidized in the electron transport chain.

Fermentation

Fermentation is an anaerobic reaction in which glucose is only partially broken down. It releases energy through the oxidation of sugars or other types of organic molecules. Oxygen is sometimes involved, but not always. It is different from respiration in that it uses neither the Krebs cycle nor the electron transport chain and the final electron acceptor is an organic molecule. It uses substrate-level phosphorylation to form ATP. NAD^+ is reduced to NADH and NADH further reduces pyruvic acid to various end products. Fermentation can lead to excess waste products and is less efficient than aerobic respiration. Homolactic fermentation refers to lactic acid fermentation in which the sugars are converted to lactic acid only (there is one end product). In heterolactic fermentation, the sugars are converted to a range of products.

Electron transport chain

The electron transport chain is part of phosphorylation, whereby electrons are transported from enzyme to enzyme until they reach a final acceptor. The electron transport chain includes a series of oxidizing and reducing molecules involved in the release of energy. In redox reactions, electrons are removed from a substrate (oxidative) and H^+ (protons) can also be simultaneously removed. A substrate gains electrons during reduction. For example, when glucose is oxidated, electrons are lost and energy is released. There are enzymes in the membranes of mitochondria. The electrons are carried from one enzyme to another by a co-enzyme. Protons are also released to the other side of the membrane. For example, FAD and $FADH_2$ are used in oxidative phosphorylation. FAD is reduced to $FADH_2$. Electrons are stored there and then sent onward, and the $FADH_2$ becomes FAD again. In aerobic respiration, the final electron acceptor is O_2. In anaerobic respiration, it is something other than O_2.

Homeostasis and feedback loops

Homeostasis is the ability and tendency of an organism, cell, or body to adjust to environmental changes to maintain equilibrium. One way an organism, such as a human body, can maintain homeostasis is through the release of hormones. Some hormones work in pairs. When a condition reaches an upper limit, a hormone is released to correct the condition. When a condition reaches the other end of the spectrum, another hormone is released. Hormones that work in this way are termed antagonistic. Insulin and glucagon are a pair of antagonistic hormones that help regulate the level of glucagon in the blood. Positive feedback loops actually tend to destabilize systems by increasing changes. A negative feedback loop acts to make a system more stable by buffering changes.

Examples of fermentation

Examples of organisms (fermentors) and their products include lactic acid fermentation, whereby streptococcus and lactobacillus bacteria form an end product of lactic acid. Lactic acid can be broken down by propionibacterium freudenreichii into propionic acid and carbon dioxide. This process is involved in making Swiss cheese. Yeast (saccharomyces) and some bacteria produce ethanol during alcohol fermentation, which is commonly used in baking bread and brewing alcohol. Carbon dioxide is also a product of alcohol fermentation. Alcohol fermentation is also involved in making beer. The starter is a malt extract, the fermentor is Saccharomyces cerevisiae, and the end product is ethanol. Citric acid is used as a flavoring. It starts as molasses, which is fermented by aspergillus (a fungus). Lactic acid is found as an end product of fermentation in cheese, yogurt, rye bread, and other foods.

Examples of homeostasis

The hormones insulin and glucagon (an antagonistic pair of hormones) are involved in negative feedback loops in the liver's control of blood sugar levels. Alpha cells secrete glucagon when the concentration of blood glucose decreases. Glucagon is broken down and fatty acids and amino acids are converted to glucose. Once there is more glucose, glucagon secretion is reduced. Beta cells secrete insulin when the concentration of blood glucose increases. This leads to the liver absorbing glucose. Glucose is converted to glycogen, and fat and the concentration of glucose decrease. Insulin production is then reduced. Hormones work in other ways aside from antagonistically. For example, follicle stimulating hormone (FSH) increases the production of estrogen. Once estrogen reaches a certain level, it suppresses FSH production. In some cases, a single hormone can increase or decrease the level of a substance.

DNA

Chromosomes consist of genes, which are single units of genetic information. Genes are made up of deoxyribonucleic acid (DNA). DNA is a nucleic acid located in the cell nucleus. There is also DNA in the mitochondria. DNA replicates to pass on genetic information. The DNA in almost all cells is the same. It is also involved in the biosynthesis of proteins. The model or structure of DNA is described as a double helix. A helix is a curve, and a double helix is two congruent curves connected by horizontal members. The model can be likened to a spiral staircase. It is right-handed. The British scientist Rosalind Elsie Franklin is credited with taking the x-ray diffraction image in 1952 that was used by Francis Crick and

James Watson to formulate the double-helix model of DNA and speculate about its important role in carrying and transferring genetic information.

DNA structure

DNA has a double helix shape, resembles a twisted ladder, and is compact. It consists of nucleotides. Nucleotides consist of a five-carbon sugar (pentose), a phosphate group, and a nitrogenous base. Two bases pair up to form the rungs of the ladder. The "side rails" or backbone consists of the covalently bonded sugar and phosphate. The bases are attached to each other with hydrogen bonds, which are easily dismantled so replication can occur. Each base is attached to a phosphate and to a sugar. There are four types of nitrogenous bases: adenine (A), guanine (G), cytosine (C), and thymine (T). There are about 3 billion bases in human DNA. The bases are mostly the same in everybody, but their order is different. It is the order of these bases that creates diversity in people. Adenine (A) pairs with thymine (T), and cytosine (C) pairs with guanine (G).

DNA replication

Pairs of chromosomes are composed of DNA, which is tightly wound to conserve space. When replication starts, it unwinds. The steps in DNA replication are controlled by enzymes. The enzyme helicase instigates the deforming of hydrogen bonds between the bases to split the two strands. The splitting starts at the A-T bases (adenine and thymine) as there are only two hydrogen bonds. The cytosine-guanine base pair has three bonds. The term "origin of replication" is used to refer to where the splitting starts. The portion of the DNA that is unwound to be replicated is called the replication fork. Each strand of DNA is transcribed by an mRNA. It copies the DNA onto itself, base by base, in a complementary manner. The exception is that uracil replaces thymine.

Types of DNA replication

Semiconservative: DNA replication is considered semiconservative because the two replicated copies of DNA each have one strand of the original parent DNA, or half of the original genetic material.

Antiparallel replication: This refers to the fact that during DNA replication, the nucleotides (A, C, G, T, and U) on leading and lagging strands run in opposite directions. RNA synthesis is said to occur in a $5' \rightarrow 3'$ (five prime to three prime) direction. That means that the phosphate group of the nucleotide that is being added to the chain, which is $5'$, is attached to the end of the chain at the end of a hydroxyl group, which is $3'$.

Base pairing: This explains how RNA transcribes DNA in an inverted fashion. C on DNA is inserted as a G on RNA, and A on DNA becomes U on RNA.

Functions of proteins in DNA replication

Many proteins are involved in the replication of DNA, and each has a specific function. Helicase is a protein that facilitates the unwinding of the double helix structure of DNA. Single strand binding (SSB) proteins attach themselves to each strand to prevent the DNA strands from joining back together. After DNA is unwound, there are leading and lagging strands. The leading strand is synthesized continuously and the lagging strand is

- 76 -

synthesized in Okazaki fragments. Primase, an RNA polymerase (catalyzing enzyme), acts as a starting point for replication by forming short strands, or primers, of RNA. The DNA clamp, or sliding clamp, helps prevent DNA polymerase from coming apart from the strand. DNA polymerase helps form the DNA strand by linking nucleotides. As the process progresses, RNase H removes the primers. DNA ligase then links the existing shorter strands into a longer strand.

Types of RNA

RNA acts as a helper to DNA and carries out a number of other functions. Types of RNA include ribosomal RNA (rRNA), transfer RNA (tRNA), and messenger RNA (mRNA). Viruses can use RNA to carry their genetic material to DNA. Ribosomal RNA is not believed to have changed much over time. For this reason, it can be used to study relationships in organisms. Messenger RNA carries a copy of a strand of DNA and transports it from the nucleus to the cytoplasm. Transcription is the process whereby DNA uses RNA in transcription. DNA unwinds itself and serves as a template while RNA is being assembled. The DNA molecules are copied to RNA. Translation is the process whereby ribosomes use transcribed RNA to put together the needed protein. Transfer RNA is a molecule that helps in the translation process, and is found in the cytoplasm. Ribosomal RNA is in the ribosomes.

Differences between RNA and DNA

RNA and DNA differ in terms of structure and function. RNA has a different sugar than DNA. It has ribose rather than deoxyribose sugar. The RNA nitrogenous bases are adenine (A), guanine (G), cytosine (C), and uracil (U). Uracil is found only in RNA and thymine in found only in DNA. RNA consists of a single strand and DNA has two strands. If straightened out, DNA has two side rails. RNA only has one "backbone," or strand of sugar and phosphate group components. RNA uses the fully hydroxylated sugar pentose, which includes an extra oxygen compared to deoxyribose, which is the sugar used by DNA. RNA supports the functions carried out by DNA. It aids in gene expression, replication, and transportation.

Nucleotides and ester bonds

The five bases in DNA and RNA can be categorized as either pyrimidine or purine according to their structure. The pyrimidine bases include cytosine, thymine, and uracil. They are six-sided and have a single ring shape. The purine bases are adenine and guanine, which consist of two attached rings. One ring has five sides and the other has six. When combined with a sugar, any of the five bases become nucleosides. Nucleosides formed from purine bases end in "osine" and those formed from pyrimidine bases end in "idine." Adenosine and thymidine are examples of nucleosides. Bases are the most basic components, followed by nucleosides, nucleotides, and then DNA or RNA.

Ester bonds are bonds in organic compounds that are formed by alcohol and organic acids. Water is typically a product when ester bonds are formed. Fats have ester bonds formed by fatty acids and glycerol (an alcohol).

Codons

Codons are groups of three nucleotides on the messenger RNA, and can be visualized as three rungs of a ladder. A codon has the code for a single amino acid. There are 64 codons but 20 amino acids. More than one combination, or triplet, can be used to synthesize the necessary amino acids. For example, AAA (adenine-adenine-adenine) or AAG (adenine-adenine-guanine) can serve as codons for lysine. These groups of three occur in strings, and might be thought of as frames. For example, AAAUCUUCGU, if read in groups of three from the beginning, would be AAA, UCU, UCG, which are codons for lysine, serine, and serine, respectively. If the same sequence was read in groups of three starting from the second position, the groups would be AAU (asparagine), CUU (proline), and so on. The resulting amino acids would be completely different. For this reason, there are start and stop codons that indicate the beginning and ending of a sequence (or frame). AUG (methionine) is the start codon. UAA, UGA, and UAG, also known as ocher, opal, and amber, respectively, are stop codons

Mutations

Gene disorders are the result of DNA mutations. DNA mutations lead to unfavorable gene disorders, but also provide genetic variability. This diversity can lead to increased survivability of a species. Mutations can be neutral, beneficial, or harmful. Mutations can be hereditary, meaning they are passed from parent to child. Polymorphism refers to differences in humans, such as eye and hair color, that may have originally been the result of gene mutations, but are now part of the normal variation of the species. Mutations can be de novo, meaning they happen either only in sex cells or shortly after fertilization. They can also be acquired, or somatic. These are the kinds that happen as a result of DNA changes due to environmental factors or replication errors. Mosaicism is when a mutation happens in a cell during an early embryonic stage. The result is that some cells will have the mutation andsome will not.

DNA level mutation

A DNA mutation occurs when the normal gene sequence is altered. Mutations can happen when DNA is damaged as a result of environmental factors, such as chemicals, radiation, or ultraviolet rays from the sun. It can also happen when errors are made during DNA replication. The phosphate-sugar side rail of DNA can be damaged if the bonds between oxygen and phosphate groups are disassociated. Translocation happens when the broken bonds attempt to bond with other DNA. This repair can cause a mutation. The nucleotide itself can be altered. A C, for example, might look like a T. During replication, the damaged C is replicated as a T and paired with a G, which is incorrect base pairing. Another way mutations can occur is if an error is made by the DNA polymerase while replicating a base. This happens about once for every 100,000,000 bases. A repair protein proofreads the code, however, so the mistake is usually repaired.

Ribosomes and tRNA anticodons

When the DNA is unwound during transcription, the mRNA makes a complimentary copy of codons, during which T becomes A, C becomes G, etc. During translation, the rRNA interprets the code again in a complementary fashion. A becomes U (there is no T), G becomes C, etc. Ribosomes make proteins from amino acids by using the information on mRNA as a template for sequencing amino acids in a protein. Transfer RNA (tRNA) carries amino acids that have attached to it to the ribosome. The anticodons on the tRNA are a string of triplet bases that are complementary to the mRNA. For example, a codon that is

AAA on the mRNA would be associated with the anticodon UUU on the tRNA. Another example is that GGG on mRNA would be associated with the anticodon CCC on tRNA.

Translocation

Translocation is a genetic mutation in which one piece of a chromosome is transferred to another chromosome. Burkitt's lymphoma, chronic myelogenous leukemia, and Down syndrome are all examples. Trisomy 21, or Down syndrome, occurs when a copy of chromosome 21 attaches to chromosome 14. Most Down syndrome cases are caused by a pair of chromosomes (the 21st) that does not split during meiosis. Both divided cells will have an abnormal number of chromosomes. One will have 22 and the other will have 24. When this egg gets fertilized, it will have three copies of chromosome 21 instead of two. Down syndrome can also be caused by translocation between the 14th and 21st chromosomes. In these instances, genetic material is swapped. There are 200 to 250 genes on the 21st chromosome. The overexpression of the gene results in the following Down syndrome traits: premature aging, decreased immune system function, heart defects, skeletal abnormalities, disruption of DNA synthesis and repair, intellectual disabilities, and cataracts.

Mendel's laws

Mendel's laws are the law of segregation (the first law) and the law of independent assortment (the second law). The law of segregation states that there are two alleles and that half of the total number of alleles are contributed by each parent organism. The law of independent assortment states that traits are passed on randomly and are not influenced by other traits. The exception to this is linked traits. A Punnett square can illustrate how alleles combine from the contributing genes to form various phenotypes. One set of a parent's genes are put in columns, while the genes from the other parent are placed in rows. The allele combinations are shown in each cell. When two different alleles are present in a pair, the dominant one is expressed. A Punnett square can be used to predict the outcome of crosses.

Gene, genotype, phenotype, and allele

A gene is a portion of DNA that identifies how traits are expressed and passed on in an organism. A gene is part of the genetic code. Collectively, all genes form the genotype of an individual. The genotype includes genes that may not be expressed, such as recessive genes. The phenotype is the physical, visual manifestation of genes. It is determined by the basic genetic information and how genes have been affected by their environment. An allele is a variation of a gene. Also known as a trait, it determines the manifestation of a gene. This manifestation results in a specific physical appearance of some facet of an organism, such as eye color or height. For example the genetic information for eye color is a gene. The gene variations responsible for blue, green, brown, or black eyes are called alleles. Locus (pl. loci) refers to the location of a gene or alleles.

Monohybrid and hybrid crosses

Genetic crosses are the possible combinations of alleles, and can be represented using Punnett squares. A monohybrid cross refers to a cross involving only one trait. Typically, the ratio is 3:1 (DD, Dd, Dd, dd), which is the ratio of dominant gene manifestation to recessive gene manifestation. This ratio occurs when both parents have a pair of dominant and recessive genes. If one parent has a pair of dominant genes (DD) and the other has a pair of recessive (dd) genes, the recessive trait can not be expressed in the next generation because the resulting crosses all have the Dd genotype. A dihybrid cross refers to one involving more than one trait, which means more combinations are possible. The ratio of genotypes for a dihybrid cross is 9:3:3:1 when the traits are not linked. The ratio for incomplete dominance is 1:3:1:, which corresponds to dominant, mixed, and recessive phenotypes.

Dominant and recessive genes

Gene traits are represented in pairs with an upper case letter for the dominant trait (A) and a lower case letter for the recessive trait (a). Genes occur in pairs (AA, Aa, or aa). There is one gene on each chromosome half supplied by each parent organism. Since half the genetic material is from each parent, the offspring's traits are represented as a combination of these. A dominant trait only requires one gene of a gene pair for it to be expressed in a phenotype, whereas a recessive requires both genes in order to be manifested. For example, if the mother's genotype is Dd and the father's is dd, the possible combinations are Dd and dd. The dominant trait will be manifested if the genotype is DD or Dd. The recessive trait will be manifested if the genotype is dd. Both DD and dd are homozygous pairs. Dd is heterozygous.

Crossing over, gametes, pedigree analysis, and probability analysis

Crossing over: This refers to the swapping of genetic material between homologous chromosomes. This leads to different combinations of genes showing up in a phenotype. This is part of gene recombination, which is when DNA breaks down and is then reassembled.

Gametes: These are the sex cells in organisms that reproduce sexually. Each gamete contains half the genetic information of the parent. They are haploid (having 23 chromosome pairs in humans). The resulting zygote, which is formed when the two gametes become one cell, is diploid (46 chromosome pairs in humans).

Pedigree analysis: This involves isolating a trait in an organism and tracing its manifestation. Pedigree charts are often used for this type of analysis. A family pedigree shows how a trait can be seen throughout generations.

Probability analysis: This calculates the chances of a particular trait or combination of traits being expressed in an organism.

Co-dominance and incomplete dominance

Co-dominance refers to the expression of both alleles so that both traits are shown. Cows, for example, can have hair colors of red, white, or red and white (not pink). In the latter color, both traits are fully expressed. The ABO human blood typing system is also co-dominant. Incomplete dominance is when both the dominant and recessive genes are expressed, resulting in a phenotype that is a mixture of the two. The fact that snapdragons can be red, white, or pink is a good example. The dominant red gene (RR) results in a red flower because of large amounts of red pigment. White (rr) occurs because both genes call for no pigment. Pink (Rr) occurs because one gene is for red and one is for no pigment. The colors blend to produce pink flowers. A cross of pink flowers (Rr) can result in red (RR), white (rr), or pink (Rr) flowers.

Non-Mendelian terms

Polygenic inheritance: This goes beyond the simplistic Mendelian concept that one gene influences one trait. It refers to traits that are influenced by more than one gene, and takes into account environmental influences on development.

Multiple alleles: Only two alleles make up a gene, but when there are three or more possible alleles, it is known as a multiple allele. A gene where only two alleles are possible is termed polymorphic.
Complete dominance: This refers the situation in which a homozygous pair of dominant alleles (AA) and a heterozygous pair of alleles (Aa) result in the same phenotype. Dominate genes have the following characteristics: they are expressed in each generation; they are passed on to roughly half the offspring; and a parent that does not express the trait can not pass it on to offspring. The Mendelian complete dominance concept states that one gene consisting of two alleles is the only factor involved in the creation of a phenotype. Most traits, however, are more complex.

Linkage

Linkage involves characteristics that are on the same chromosome. This leads to two different traits being seen together more often than not. Linkage is the exception to independent assortment. Sex-linked traits are those that occur on a sex chromosome. Autosomal refers to non-sex chromosomes. In humans, there are 22 autosomal pairs of chromosomes and a pair of sex chromosomes. Depending on the sex, pairs are either XX (female) or XY (male). Since females don't have Y chromosomes, alleles on this gene are only manifested in males. Males can only pass on sex-linked traits on the X chromosome to their daughters since sons would not receive an X from them. Hemizygous means there is only one copy of a gene. Color blindness occurs more in males than females because it is a sex-linked trait on the X chromosome. Since it is recessive, females have a better chance of expressing the dominant characteristic of non-color blindness.

ABO blood system

Human blood typing, which uses the ABO system, is an example of co-dominance and multiple alleles. Multiple alleles means there are more than two possible alleles and therefore more than just four possible gene combinations. The types of alleles are A, B, and O. A and B are co-dominant. In co-dominance, both alleles are completely expressed. A and B both produce enzymes that produce antigens. A produces type A antigens and B produces type B antigens. Antigen molecules are located on the surfaces of red blood cells. Type O does not produce enzymes, nor does it have antigens on its surface. The antigens trigger a response in the immune system to help repel foreign substances. Matching blood types during medical procedures is important since the human immune system can detect and attack blood that is a different type. Specific blood types are used in transfusions, and blood types are determined based on the proteins (or lack of proteins) contained in the blood.

Lethal allele, pleiotropy, epistasis, and karyotype

Lethal allele: This is when a mutation in an essential gene results in the death of the organism. Cystic fibrosis and Tay-Sachs disease are examples of lethal recessive alleles.

Pleiotropy: This refers to a gene that affects more than one trait.

Epistasis: This refers to the situation in which two or more genes determine a single phenotype.

Karyotype: This is a picture of genes based on a sample of blood or skin.

The non-Mendelian concept of polygenetic inheritance takes into account environmental factors on phenotypes. For example, an individual inherits genes that help determine height, but a diet lacking in certain nutrients could limit that individual's ability to reach that height. Another example is the concept of genetic disposition, which is a propensity for a certain disease that is genetically inherited, but not necessarily manifested. For example, individuals with certain skin types are more likely to develop skin cancer. If they limit their exposure to solar radiation, however, this will not necessarily occur.

Genetic engineering, cloning, restriction enzymes, and vectors

Genetic engineering: This refers to changing or manipulating an organism's genes. Other terms that may be used to refer to genetic engineering are recombinant DNA, gene splicing, cloning, and genetic modification or manipulation. Genetic engineering is different from indirect gene manipulation, in which breeding is controlled based on observable phenotypes. Genetic engineering refers to altering the genes themselves.

Cloning: There are two definitions for cloning. The first refers to the natural cloning that occurs in nature when organisms reproduce asexually and make exact copies of them. This can happen in bacteria, plants, birds, and other organisms. The definition heard more in popular culture refers to cloning as the genetic engineering of portions of DNA, cells, or entire organisms.

Blood types

There are four possible blood types: A, B, AB, and O. These types are produced by combinations of the three alleles. AA and AO lead to type A blood. BB and BO lead to type B blood. AB leads to type AB blood because the alleles are co-dominant. AB has both A protein and antigens and B protein and antigens. The O allele is recessive. OO leads to blood type O, which lacks proteins and blood-surface antigens. Blood donors with an O blood type are known as universal donors because they do not have the type of antigens that can trigger immune system responses. Blood donors with type AB blood are known as universal recipients because they do not have the antibodies that will attack A and B antigen molecules. If parents have AB and O blood, offspring have a 50% chance of having type A blood and a 0% chance of having type O blood.

Applications of genetic engineering

Diagnostic and medical applications include treating diabetes with insulin, producing human proteins, treating hemophilia, anemia, and blood clots, and manufacturing hepatitis B vaccine. Gene therapy has been used to replace defective alleles with normal alleles. For example, if a patient has a condition caused by an enzyme deficiency, replacing the defective allele enables the person to produce that enzyme. Medical forensic applications involving DNA analysis include using it to identify individuals and solve criminal cases. Agricultural applications include crop modification to develop types of wheat, cotton, and soybeans that resist weed controlling herbicides. Plants can be altered to make them grow bigger or vaccinated to make them resistant to plant viruses and insects.

Restriction enzymes: These are proteins that can recognize portions of DNA strands and cleave them at certain points.

Vectors: Vectors deliver DNA to a cell, and can include viruses and bacterial plasmids.

Recombinant DNA and gene splicing

Recombinant DNA (rDNA) refers to manipulating sequences of DNA. One portion of DNA is removed and replaced with another. Gene splicing is a way to recombine DNA. In gene splicing, base pairs of DNA are chemically cleaved. Restriction enzymes are used to perform the cutting part of gene splicing. Once base pairs are separated, different additional genetic information can be added by a vector. DNA ligase (an enzyme) is used to put the pieces back together. The process of DNA recombination happens naturally and incrementally as a result of evolution. Use of recombinant DNA produced through genetic engineering has been used in the laboratory in diagnostic, medical forensic and agricultural applications.

Human genome project

The human genome project was an international effort by scientists in 18 countries that was undertaken to gain information about human DNA. The project set out to identify all of the genes in human DNA, which number about 20,000-25,000. Other goals included: determining the sequences of the three billion base pairs comprising human DNA, inputting information collected into databases, producing tools for data analysis and making them available, and opening a discussion about the ethical, legal, and social implications of obtaining such in-depth knowledge about the genetic makeup of humans. The completed mapping and sequencing is expected to lead to further research in the fields of molecular medicine and DNA forensics. It's also expected to spur on research in related fields, such as energy source development, bioarchaeology, human migration and evolution, agriculture improvement and production, livestock breeding, and bioprocessing.

Natural selection, gradualism, and punctuated equilibrium

Natural selection: This theory developed by Darwin states that traits that help give a species a survival advantage are passed on to subsequent generations. Members of a species that do not have the advantageous trait die before they reproduce. Darwin's four principles are: from generation to generation, there are various individuals within a species; genes determine variations; more individuals are born than survive to maturation; and specific genes enable an organism to better survive.

Gradualism: This can be contrasted with punctuationism. It is the idea that evolution proceeds at a steady pace and does not include sudden developments of new species or features from one generation to the next.

Punctuated equilibrium: This can be contrasted with gradualism. It is an idea in evolutionary biology that states that evolution involves long time periods of no change (stasis) accompanied by relatively brief periods (hundreds of thousands of years) of rapid change.

Evidence supporting theory of evolution

Scientific evidence supporting the theory of evolution can be found in biogeography, comparative anatomy and embryology, the fossil record, and molecular evidence. Biogeography studies the geographical distribution of animals and plants. Evidence of evolution related to the area of biogeography includes species that are well suited for extreme environments. The fossil record shows that species lived only for a short time period before becoming extinct. The fossil record can also show the succession of plants and animals. Living fossils are existing species that have not changed much morphologically and are very similar to ancient examples in the fossil record. Examples include the horseshoe crab and ginko. Comparative embryology studies how species are similar in the embryonic stage, but become increasingly specialized and diverse as they age. Vestigial organs are those that still exist, but become nonfunctional. Examples include the hind limbs of whales and the wings of birds that can no longer fly, such as ostriches.

Rate of evolution

The rate of evolution is affected by the variability of a population. Variability increases the likelihood of evolution. Variability in a population can be increased by mutations, immigration, sexual reproduction (as opposed to asexual reproduction), and size. Natural selection, emigration, and smaller populations can lead to decreased variability. Sexual selection affects evolution. If fewer genes are available, it will limit the number of genes passed on to subsequent generations. Some animal mating behaviors are not as successful as others. A male that does not attract a female because of a weak mating call or dull feathers, for example, will not pass on its genes. Mechanical isolation, which refers to sex organs that do not fit together very well, can also decrease successful mating.

Three types of evolution

Three types of evolution are divergent, convergent, and parallel. Divergent evolution refers to two species that become different over time. This can be caused by one of the species adapting to a different environment. Convergent evolution refers to two species that start out fairly different, but evolve to share many similar traits. Parallel evolution refers to species that are not similar and do not become more or less similar over time. Mechanisms of evolution include descent (the passing on of genetic information), mutation, migration, natural selection, and genetic variation and drift. The biological definition of species refers to a group of individuals that can mate and reproduce. Speciation refers to the evolution of a new biological species. The biological species concept (BSC) basically states that a species is a community of individuals that can reproduce and have a niche in nature.

Prezygotic barriers to reproduction

Spatial: This refers to species that are separated by a distance that prevents them from mating.

Geographical: This is when species are physically separated by a barrier. A barrier can divide a population, which is known as vicariance. If a population crosses a barrier to create two species, it is known as dispersal.
Habitat: This refers to species that live in different habitats in the same area.

Temporal: This refers to the fact that species reach sexual maturity at different times. An example is plants that flower at different times of the year.

Behavioral: This refers to the fact that mating rituals distinguish interaction between sexes. For example, many species of crickets are morphologically (structurally) the same, yet a female of one species will only respond to the mating rituals of males within her species.
Mechanical: This refers to physiological structural differences that prevent mating or the transfer of gametes.

Gametic isolation: This refers to the fact that fertilization may not occur when gametes of different species are not compatible.

Allele frequency

The gene pool refers to all alleles of a gene and their combinations. The Hardy-Weinberg principle (or Castle-Hardy Weinberg principle) postulates that the allele frequency for dominant and recessive alleles will remain the same in a population through successive generations if certain conditions exist. These conditions are: no mutations, large populations, random mating, no migration, and equal genotypes. This is an ideal and not how most population's function. Changes in the frequency and types of alleles in a gene pool can be caused by gene flow, random mutation, nonrandom mating, and genetic drift. In organisms that reproduce by sexual reproduction, reproduction isolation is defined as something that acts as a barrier to two species reproducing. These barriers are classified as prezygotic and postzygotic.

Random mutations, nonrandom mating, and gene migration

Random mutations: These are genetic changes caused by DNA errors or environmental factors such as chemicals and radiation. Mutations can be beneficial or harmful.

Nonrandom mating: This refers to the fact that the probability of two individuals mating in a population is not the same for all pairs. Nonrandom mating can be caused by geographical isolation, small populations, and other factors. Nonrandom mating can lead to inbreeding (mating with a relative), which can lead to a decline in physical fitness as seen in a phenotype and the reduction of allele frequency and occurrence.

Gene migration: Also known as gene flow, gene migration is the movement of alleles to another population. This can occur through immigration, when individuals of a species move into an area, or through emigration, when individuals of a species move out of an area.

Postzygotic barriers to reproduction

Hybrid viability: This is when a hybrid zygote does not reach maturity.

Hybrid sterility: This is also known as hybrid infertility. It occurs when two species produce a hybrid offspring that reaches maturity, but is sterile. An example of this is the mule. Mules are the result of a horse and a donkey mating. Mules, however, can not reproduce.

Hybrid breakdown: This is when the first generation is not only viable, but also reaches maturity and can reproduce. Subsequent generations, however, are neither viable nor fertile.

Hybrid zygote abnormality: This is when two species produce a zygote that does not survive to birth or germination, does not develop normally or reach sexual maturity, and cannot reproduce.

Allopatric speciation: This refers to speciation that occurs because of geographical factors, such as physical barriers or dispersal.

Sympatric speciation: This refers to speciation that happens within parent populations.

Parapatric speciation: This refers to speciation that occurs because of an extreme change in habitat.

Bottleneck and adaptive radiation

Bottleneck: This occurs when a small percentage of a population survives a disaster or when the size of a population is greatly reduced for at least one generation. It results in reduced allele diversity, and can even lead to entire alleles being eliminated in a species. This can lead to an increased inability to adapt to certain environmental factors. An example of a bottleneck is that hunting by humans reduced the northern elephant seal population to 20 individuals. Their population is now about 30,000, but the population's genes are much less varied than the genes of the southern elephant seal population. Another example is that a typhoon killed all but 30 people on an island in the South Pacific. One of the survivors had the recessive gene for color blindness. Currently, about 10% of the current population of 2,000 is color blind.

Adaptive radiation: This refers to the fact that speciation occurs through adapting to an environment through natural selection. It also refers to the fact that a species has a common ancestor.

Genetic drift and the founder's effect

Genetic drift: Easily observable in small populations, genetic drift is a change in the frequency of an allele.

Founder's effect: This occurs when a small population breaks away from a larger population and forms a smaller and isolated population. The resulting reduction in allele diversity leads to a greater expression of certain genetic traits than would be observed in a larger population. An example is the Amish in America, who are the descendants of 30 Swiss founders. The Amish are isolated by culture and breed within their population. One of the founders had Ellis-van Creveld syndrome. It is rare in larger populations, but is found at a rate of about 1 in 200 in the Amish community. It results in short stature, extra fingers and toes, and heart defects.

Earth's age, abiotic synthesis and endosymbiotic theory

Earth's age is estimated to be 4.5 billion years.

Abiotic synthesis: This is related to the commonly accepted theory that life originated from inorganic matter. It refers to the making of organic molecules outside of a living body, and is believed to have been the first step in the development of life on Earth. The theory was tested in an experiment performed by a graduate student at Stanford University in 1953. He combined the inorganic molecules water, hydrogen, methane, and ammonia in a closed, sterile flask and applied heat. To recreate the effect of lightning, he used an electric charge. His ingredients started as a clear mixture. After a week, he had a cloudy soup that contained amino acids and organic compounds.

Endosymbiotic theory: This is the belief that eukaryotes (cells with nuclei) developed from prokaryotic cells (those without nuclei). The theory is that chloroplasts in plant cells and mitochondria in animal cells evolved from smaller prokaryotes living within larger prokaryotes.

Origin of life on Earth

One theory of how life originated on Earth is that life developed from nonliving materials. The first stage of this transformation happened when abiotic (nonliving) synthesis took place, which is the formation of monomers like amino acids and nucleotides. Next, monomers joined together to create polymers such as proteins and nucleic acids. These polymers are then believed to have formed into protobionts. The last stage was the development of the process of heredity. Supporters of this theory believe that RNA was the first genetic material. Another theory postulates that hereditary systems came about before the origination of nucleic acids. Another theory is that life, or the precursors for it, were transported to Earth from a meteorite or other object from space. There is no real evidence to support this theory.

Five kingdom classification system

The groupings in the five kingdom classification system are kingdom, phylum/division, class, order, family, genus, and species. A memory aid for this is: King Phillip Came Over For Good Soup. The five kingdoms are Monera, Protista, Fungi, Plantae, and Animalia. The kingdom is the top level classification in this system. Below that are the following groupings: phylum, class, order, family, genus, and species. The Monera kingdom includes about 10,000 known species of prokaryotes, such as bacteria and cyanobacteria. Members of this kingdom can be unicellular organisms or colonies. The next four kingdoms consist of eukaryotes. The Protista kingdom includes about 250,000 species of unicellular protozoans and unicellular and multicellular algae. The Fungi kingdom includes about 100,000 species. A recently introduced system of classification includes a three domain grouping above kingdom. The domain groupings are Archaea, Bacteria (which both consist of prokaryotes), and Eukarya, which include eukaryotes. According to the five kingdom classification system, humans are: kingdom Animalia, phylum Chordata, subphylum Vertebrata, class Mammalia, order Primate, family Hominidae, genus Homo, and species Sapiens.

Protista kingdom

Organisms in the Protista kingdom are classified according to their methods of locomotion, their methods of reproduction, and how they get their nutrients. Protists can move by the use of a flagellum, cilia, or pseudopod. Flagellates have flagellum, which are long tails or whip-like structures that are rotated to help the protist move. Ciliates use cilia, which are smaller hair-like structures on the exterior of a cell that wiggle to help move the surrounding matter. Amoeboids use pseudopodia to move. Bacteria reproduce either sexually or asexually. Binary fission is a form of asexual reproduction whereby bacteria divide in half to produce two new organisms that are clones of the parent. In sexual reproduction, genetic material is exchanged. When kingdom members are categorized according to how they obtain nutrients, the three types of protists are photosynthetic, consumers, and saprophytes. Photosynthetic protists convert sunlight into energy. Organisms that use photosynthesis are considered producers. Consumers, also known as heterotrophs, eat or consume other organisms. Saprophytes consume dead or decaying substances.

Fungi kingdom

Mycology is the study of fungi. The Fungi kingdom includes about 100,000 species. They are further delineated as mushrooms, yeasts, molds, rusts, mildews, stinkhorns, puffballs, and truffles. Fungi are characterized by cell walls that have chitin, a long chain polymer carbohydrate. Fungi are different from species in the Plant kingdom, which have cell walls consisting of cellulose. Fungi are thought to have evolved from a single ancestor. Although they are often thought of as a type of plant, they are more similar to animals than plants. Fungi are typically small and numerous, and have a diverse morphology among species. They can have bright red cups and be orange jellylike masses, and their shapes can resemble golf balls, bird nests with eggs, starfish, parasols, and male genitalia. Some members of the stinkhorn family emit odors similar to dog scat to attract flies that help transport spores that are involved in reproduction. Fungi of this family are also consumed by humans.

Molecular oxygen

When the Earth was formed, the atmosphere did not contain oxygen. It is thought to have appeared in the Paleoproterozoic era about 2.5 to 1.6 billion years ago. First, oxygen combined with iron in oceans to form banded iron formations (thin layers of iron oxides and layers of iron poor rock). After that, oxygen began to "gas out" of the oceans slowly. One of the major events in Earth's geologic history is the great oxygen event, or oxygen catastrophe, during which large amounts of oxygen led to the extinction of anaerobic organisms. This, in turn, led to an increased number of aerobic organisms. Eventually, it also resulted in the development of eukaryotic cells and more complex life forms.

Organism and microbe

An organism is a living thing. A unicellular organism is an organism that has only one cell. Examples of unicellular organisms are bacteria and paramecium. A multicellular organism is one that consists of many cells. Humans are a good example. By some estimates, the human body is made up of billions of cells. Others think the human body has more than 75 trillion cells.

The term microbe refers to small organisms that are only visible through a microscope. Examples include viruses, bacteria, fungi, and protozoa. Microbes are also referred to as microorganisms, and it is these that are studied by microbiologists. Bacteria can be rod shaped, round (cocci), or spiral (spirilla). These shapes are used to differentiate among types of bacteria. Bacteria can be identified by staining them. This particular type of stain is called a gram stain. If bacteria are gram-positive, they absorb the stain and become purple. If bacteria are gram-negative, they do not absorb the stain and become a pinkish color.

Viruses

Some scientists do not consider viruses to belong to any of the five kingdoms or to be living organisms for many reasons. Viruses do not meet the definition of a cell. They cannot be classified as eukaryotic or prokaryotic. They are generally smaller than and not as complex as living cells, which are the basic units of life. Viruses do not have nuclei. They are macromolecules consisting of long chains of genetic material (either RNA or DNA) encased in protein. Viruses also lack membrane-bound organelles, ribosomes, and cytoplasm, all of which are usually found in cells. Viruses do not perform the basic cell processes involved in the ADP/ATP cycle, and they are not capable of cellular respiration or gas exchange. They reproduce by gaining control of a host cell and making it replicate the viral DNA instead of its own.

Characteristics of viruses

Viruses are microorganisms that replicate in the cells of other organisms, including plants, animals, bacteria, and other microorganisms. All viruses have a head. Some also have a tail consisting of protein. The tail is used to attach to a host cell and enter it. This is one way in which viruses introduce their genetic material to the host. The head of a virus, also called a protein capsid, contains genetic material in the form of DNA, RNA, or enzymes. The adenovirus and the herpes virus are both DNA viruses. The HIV retrovirus, influenza, and the rotavirus are RNA viruses. The number of virus types is thought to be in the millions. Virology is a branch of microbiology that is devoted to the study of viruses. Viruses can be transmitted to other organisms in a number of ways, such as by insects, by air, and through direct contact.

Vascular and nonvascular plants

Vascular plants have vascular tissue in the form of xylem and phloem. These make up the parts of the plants, such as the roots, stems, and leaves that are involved in transporting minerals and water throughout the plant. This capability enables vascular plants to grow tall. Food/energy that is converted by photosynthesis in the leaves is brought down to the roots, while water is brought to the top of the plant. Nonvascular (or avascular) plants lack true leaves, stems, and roots. Nonvascular plants do not develop vascular tissue, such as xylem and phloem. They tend to be small, and individual cells are adjacent to their environment.

Plant kingdom groupings

Only plants in the division bryophyta (mosses and liverworts) are nonvascular, which means they do not have xylem to transport water. All of the plants in the remaining divisions are vascular, meaning they have true roots, stems, leaves, and xylem. Pteridophytes are plants that use spores and not seeds to reproduce. They include the following divisions: Psilophyta (whisk fern), Lycophyta (club mosses), Sphenophyta (horsetails), and Pterophyta (ferns). Spermatophytes are plants that use seeds to reproduce. Included in this category are gymnosperms, which are flowerless plants that use naked seeds, and angiosperms, which are flowering plants that contain seeds in or on a fruit. Gymnosperms include the following divisions: cycadophyta (cycads), ginkgophyta (maidenhair tree), gnetophyta (ephedra and welwitschia), and coniferophyta (which includes pinophyta conifers). Angiosperms comprise the division anthophyta (flowering plants).

Plant phyla

Chlorophyta are green algae. Bryophyta are nonvascular mosses and liverworts. They have root-like parts called rhizoids. Since they do not have the vascular structures to transport water, they live in moist environments. Lycophyta are club mosses. They are vascular plants. They use spores and need water to reproduce. Equisetopsida (sphenophyta) are horsetails. Like lycophyta, they need water to reproduce with spores. They have rhizoids and needle-like leaves. The pteridophytes (filicopsida) are ferns. They have stems (rhizomes). Spermatopsida are the seed plants. Gymnosperms are a conifer, which means they have cones with seeds that are used in reproduction. Plants with seeds require less water. Cycadophyta are cone-bearing and look like palms. Gnetophyta are plants that live in the desert. Coniferophyta are pine trees, and have both cones and needles. Ginkgophyta are ginkos. Anthophyta is the division with the largest number of plant species, and includes flowering plants with true seeds.

Processes and systems of plants

Plants are autotrophs, which mean they make their own food. In a sense, they are self sufficient. Three major processes used by plants are photosynthesis, transpiration, and respiration. Photosynthesis involves using sunlight to make food for plants. Transpiration evaporates water out of plants. Respiration is the utilization of food that was produced during photosynthesis.

Two major systems in plants are the shoot and the root system. The shoot system includes leaves, buds, and stems. It also includes the flowers and fruits in flowering plants. The shoot system is located above the ground. The root system is the component of the plant that is underground, and includes roots, tubers, and rhizomes. Meristems form plant cells by mitosis. Cells then differentiate into cell types to form the three types of plant tissues, which are dermal, ground, and vascular. Dermal refers to tissues that form the covering or outer layer of a plant. Ground tissues consist of parenchyma, collenchyma, and/or sclerenchyma cells.

Plant transpiration

The rate of transpiration is affected by light, temperature, humidity, wind, and the saturation of the soil. Light encourages stomata to open, and water is lost more quickly than in the dark. Since water evaporates quicker in higher temperatures, the rate of transpiration increases as the temperature increases. If an area is humid, the rate of transpiration is decreased. The opposite is true for areas of lower humidity. This is explained by the principle of diffusion. The greater the difference in humidity or concentrations of substances in two regions, the greater the rate of diffusion between them will be. Water in the soil replaces water that has been lost through transpiration. If water in the soil is not replaced, the rate of transpiration decreases. Photosynthesis also slows, the stomata close, and the plant wilts when it loses turgor as water is lost from cells.

Plant alternation of generations

Alternation of generations refers to the fact that the two processes used during sexual reproduction alternate. These processes are meiosis and fertilization. In meiosis, sex cells divide and genetic material is reduced by half, which results in a gamete. Two gametes are joined during fertilization, and the resulting cell is diploid. This occurs in both plants and animals. Plants have a gametophyte and a sporophyte generation. The gametophyte generation starts with the production of a haploid spore. More haploid spores are produced through mitosis. Sexual reproduction occurs during this stage, which results in a zygote. This is the start of the second generation, which is known as the sporophyte generation. A primary difference between plant and animal sexual reproduction is that plants can undergo mitosis with haploid cells. Cells can be controlled with this single set of chromosomes.

Plant root system

Plant roots include zones where cell differentiation, elongation and division, and meristem formation occur. Primary meristems include protoderms, ground meristems, procambiums, and apical meristems. There is also a root cap. A tuber is an underground stem that is enlarged and used for food storage. A rhizome is an underground stem of sorts that sends out roots and shoots from its nodes (bulging or swelling points). Vascular tissues include xylem and phloem. Xylem can be scattered throughout a pith or formed into rings. Phloem allows for food transport down a plant. The food travels from where it was produced through photosynthesis to other structures, such as roots, that require the food. Phloem can be made up of bundles of sieve tubes. It is usually located outside the xylem.

Meristems in vegetative growth

The meristems of plants are where new cells are formed through mitosis. These cells then differentiate into specific tissue types, which may form part of the root system or increase a plant's girth, height, or length. Cambiums are meristems that are responsible for secondary growth, which increases girth. Flowering plants go through cycles of vegetative growth, or propagation. They use flowers to reproduce sexually. Vegetative propagation occurs at the apical meristems located on the tip of the stem. These start as undifferentiated cells that can form into more stems, leaves, and secondary meristems (or lateral buds), which form branches. Nodes are areas where leaves can develop. The area between nodes is termed internodal. On a stem, the apical meristem on the end is the terminal bud. Sometimes, this can become a flower bud. Lenticels allow for the diffusion of oxygen and carbon dioxide gas.

Transpiration, respiration, and phylogenetic

Transpiration is the movement of water through a vascular plant. It is also the method by which water is evaporated out of plants. Transpiration mainly happens during the process of photosynthesis, when water and minerals travel up through the xylem and are used and water is released through stomata (flattened oval-shaped openings). During transpiration, water is drawn up a plant. This process also helps cool leaves.

Respiration: This refers to the process of metabolizing sugars to provide plants with the energy they need for growth and reproduction. The chemical equation is $C_6H_{12}O_6 + 6O_2 \rightarrow 6CO_2 + 6H_2O + energy$. During the process of respiration, sugars are burned, energy is released, oxygen is used, and water and carbon dioxide are produced. Respiration can occur as a light or dark reaction.

Phylogenetic: This refers to organisms that are related because of their evolutionary history.

Reproduction in flowering plants

There are at least 230,000 species of flowering plants. They represent about 90 percent of all plants. Angiosperms have a sexual reproduction phase that includes flowering. When growing plants, one may think they develop in the following order: seeds, growth, flowers, and fruit. The reproductive cycle has the following order: flowers, fruit, and seeds. In other words, seeds are the products of successful reproduction. The colors and scents of flowers serve to attract pollinators. Flowers and other plants can also be pollinated by wind. When a pollen grain meets the ovule and is successfully fertilized, the ovule develops into a seed. A seed consists of three parts: the embryo, the endosperm, and a seed coat. The embryo is a small plant that has started to develop, but this development is paused. Germination is when the embryo starts to grow again. The endosperm consists of proteins, carbohydrates, or fats. It typically serves as a food source for the embryo. The seed coat provides protection from disease, insects, and water.

Reproduction methods

Bryophytes are seedless plants. They include liverworts, hornworts, and mosses. They use spores that form into gametophytes to reproduce. Sperm are flagellated, meaning they require at least some water to swim to the egg. Some bryophytes are plants that are one sex or the other, but other bryophytes have both sexes on the same plant. Ferns also have flagellated sperm and require water for the same reason as bryophytes. Both ferns and bryophytes undergo alternation of generations. These plants spend about half of their reproductive cycles as sporophytes, making haploid spores through meiosis during this stage. The other half of the cycle is spent as a haploid gametophyte. At this point, male and female gametes join to form one zygote. Seed plants use seeds to reproduce. Flowering plants use flowers and seeds.

Pollination in flowering plants

The anthers of the stamens (male parts) have microsporangia that form into a pollen grain, which consists of a small germ cell within a larger cell. The pollen grain is released and lands on a stigma (female) portion of the pistil. It grows a pollen tube the length of the style and ends up at the ovule. The pollen grain releases the sperm and fertilization occurs. In double fertilization, one of the sperm joins with the egg to become a diploid zygote. The other sperm becomes the endosperm nucleus. Seeds are formed. One cotyledon (monocot) or two cotyledons (dicot) also form to store food and surround the embryo. Correspondingly, monocots produce one seed leaf, while dicots produce two. The seed matures and becomes dormant, and fruits typically form.

Sexual parts of flowering plants

Flowering plants can be categorized sexually according to which organs they have. Flowers can be bisexual or unisexual. Species can be dioecious, which means male and female flowers are contained on different individual plants. Monoecious means that both male and female flowers are on one individual. Bisexual flowers are those that have all of the following: sepal, petal, stamen, and pistil. If they have all of these parts, they are considered complete. They have both the male stamen and the female counterpart, the pistil. Unisexual flowers only have a pistil or a stamen, not both. Incomplete flowers do not have all four parts. The flower rests upon a pedicel and is contained with the receptacle. The carpal is made up of the stigma at the tip, a style, and the ovary at the base. The ovary contains the ovules (eggs). Carpels are sometimes formed as a single pistil. The stamen includes the anther and the filament, and produces the male pollen.

Photoperiodism

Photoperiodism refers to the fact that plants are affected by seasons, particularly by the amount of daylight that occurs in each season. The amount of daylight triggers processes such as flowering, growth in roots and stems, and leaves falling off of trees. Long day plants, like the name implies, do not need many night time hours to instigate flowering. Short day plants have an affinity for longer nights and shorter days. Short day plants tend to flower as days get shorter. Long day plants tend to flower when days get longer. Other plants are considered to be day neutral. Examples of long day obligate (meaning long days are essential) plants are oats, clover, and carnations. Examples of long day facultative (meaning long days are desirable, but not essential) plants are turnip, lettuce, wheat, and barley. Examples of short day obligate plants are tobacco, strawberries, and coffee. Examples of short day facultative plants are cotton, sugar cane, and rice.

Fruits in flowering plants

The fruit can encase the mature seed, such as in tomatoes, cherries, and apples. The seed can also be on the outside of the fruit, such as in corn and strawberries. These are called simple fruits, and are produced by one ovary. Another classification of simple fruits is botanical fruits, which are fruits that develop out of a flower. Examples of these are tomatoes, squash, and eggplant. Simple fruits can also have fruits that are dry. Examples of this are poppies, peanuts, and walnuts. Many nuts are simple fruits formed when the ovary wall hardens. One of the seeds produced remains attached. Aggregate fruits are produced by many ovaries in one flower. Each ovary is separately fertilized and forms the aggregate fruit. Examples of these are raspberries, blackberries, and strawberries. Multiple fruits refer to many flowers on a single structure. Examples are pineapples and figs.

Monocot and dicot structures

The diversity of plants leads to an abundance of plant structures. Not all structures are found in all plants, and many plants have different structures that perform similar functions. Monocots and dicots are both flowering plants. The bark of a woody dicot (tree) is structurally very different than the exterior rind of a monocot corn stem, even though both serve as the outermost layer. Within both are the vascular tissues phloem and xylem. In a woody dicot, the tree trunk is made of xylem. When water is abundant, such as during the spring, the xylem vessels that are made are large. Those made later in the summer are narrower since there is less water. When viewed in cross section, these two layers form the ring of a tree's trunk, which is why they can be used to calculate a tree's age.

Tropism, geotropic, plagiotropic, phototropism, and thigmotropism

Tropism refers to the fact that plants grow in response to specific stimuli. Seeds are geotropic (or gravitropic), meaning they grow as a response to gravity. Roots are positively geotropic and grow towards gravity. Stems are negatively geotropic and grow away from the force of gravity. A seed planted upside down will still grow roots and stems in the right direction. Plagiotropic refers to the fact that secondary branches and roots grow at right angles to gravity. Phototropism refers to the fact that a plant bends or grows toward a light source. Thigmotropism refers to how plants respond to contact. Plant hormones are organic compounds that usually influence changes in plants. They can cause fruit to ripen or instigate plant growth. Five major groups of hormones are auxins, gibberellins, ethylenes, cytokinins, and abscisic acids. Auxins occur naturally and can be synthesized. They affect plant cell elongation, apical dominance, and rooting. Gibberellins affect plant height. Ethylenes help fruit ripen. Cytokinins are involved in cell division. Abscisic acids inhibit other hormones.

Animal kingdom subdivisions

The animal kingdom includes about one million species. Metazoans are multicellular animals. Food is ingested and enters a mesoderm-lined coelom (body cavity). Phylum porifera and coelenterate are exceptions. The taxonomy of animals involves grouping them into phyla according to body symmetry and plan, as well as the presence of or lack of segmentation. The more complex phyla that have a coelom and a digestive system are further classified as protostomes or deuterostomes according to blastula development. In protostomes, the blastula's blastopore (opening) forms a mouth. In deuterostomes, the blastopore forms an anus. Taxonomy schemes vary, but there are about 36 phyla of animals. The corresponding term for plants at this level is division. The most notable phyla include chordata, mollusca, porifera, cnidaria, platyhelminthes, nematoda, annelida, arthropoda, and echinodermata, which account for about 96 percent of all animal species.

Animal kingdom facts

The animal kingdom is comprised of more than one million species in about 30 divisions (the plant kingdom uses the term phyla). There about 800,000 species of insects alone, representing half of all animal species. The characteristics that distinguish members of the animal kingdom from members of other kingdoms are that they are multicellular, are heterotrophic, reproduce sexually (there are some exceptions), have cells that do not contain cell walls or photosynthetic pigments, can move at some stage of life, and can rapidly respond to the environment as a result of specialized tissues like nerve and muscle. Heterotrophic refers to the method of getting energy by eating food that has energy releasing substances. Plants, on the other hand, are autotrophs, which mean they make their own energy. During reproduction, animals have a diploid embryo in the blastula stage. This structure is unique to animals. The blastula resembles a fluid-filled ball.

Animal protostomic

Members of the protostomic phyla have mouths that are formed from blastopores.

Mollusca: Classes include bivalvia (organisms with two shells, such as clams, mussels, and oysters), gastropoda (snails and slugs), cephalopoda (octopus, squid, and chambered nautilus), scaphopoda, amphineura (chitons), and monoplacophora.

Annelida: This phylum includes the classes oligochaeta (earthworms), polychaeta (clam worms), and hirudinea (leeches). The have true coeloms enclosed within the mesoderm. They are segmented, have repeating units, and have a nerve trunk.

Arthropoda: The phylum is diverse and populous. Members can be found in all types of environments. They have external skeletons, jointed appendages, bilateral symmetry, and nerve cords. They also have open circulatory systems and sense organs. Subphyla include crustacea (lobster, barnacles, pill bugs, and daphnia), hexapoda (all insects, which have three body segments, six legs, and usual wings), myriapoda (centipedes and millipedes), and chelicerata (the horseshoe crab and arachnids). Pill bugs have gills. Bees, ants, and wasps belong to the order hymenoptera. Like several other insect orders, they undergo complete metamorphosis.

Animal phyla

These four animal phyla lack a coelom or have a pseudocoelom.

Porifera: These are sponges. They lack a coelom and get food as water flows through them. They are usually found in marine and sometimes in freshwater environments. They are perforated and diploblastic, meaning there are two layers of cells.

Cnidaria: Members of this phylum are hydrozoa, jellyfish, and obelia. They have radial symmetry, sac-like bodies, and a polyp or medusa (jellyfish) body plan. They are diploblastic, possessing both an ectoderm and an endoderm. Food can get in through a cavity, but members of this phylum do not have an anus.

Platyhelminthes: These are also known as flatworms. Classes include turbellaria (planarian) and trematoda (which include lung, liver, and blood fluke parasites). They have organs and bilateral symmetry. They have three layers of tissue: an ectoderm, a mesoderm, and an endoderm.

Nematoda: These are roundworms. Hookworms and many other parasites are members of this phylum. They have a pseudocoelom, which means the coelom is not completely enclosed within the mesoderm. They also have a digestive tract that runs directly from the mouth to the anus. They are nonsegmented.

Extrinsic

Extrinsic refers to homeostatic systems that are controlled from outside the body. In higher animals, the nervous system and endocrine system help regulate body functions by responding to stimuli. Hormones in animals regulate many processes, including growth, metabolism, reproduction, and fluid balance. The names of hormones tend to end in "-one." Endocrine hormones are proteins or steroids. Steroid hormones (anabolic steroids) help control the manufacture of protein in muscles and bones.

Invertebrates do not have a backbone, whereas vertebrates do. The great majority of animal species (an estimated 98 percent) are invertebrates, including worms, jellyfish, mollusks, slugs, insects, and spiders. They comprise 30 phyla in all. Vertebrates belong to the phylum chordata. The vertebrate body has two cavities. The thoracic cavity holds the heart and lungs and the abdominal cavity holds the digestive organs. Animals with exoskeletons have skeletons on the outside. Examples are crabs and turtles. Animals with endoskeletons have skeletons on the inside. Examples are humans, tigers, birds, and reptiles.

Animal deuterostomic phyla

Members of the deuterostomic phyla have anuses that are formed from blastopores.

Echinodermata: Members of this phylum have radial symmetry, are marine organisms, and have a water vascular system. Classes include echinoidea (sea urchins and sand dollars), crinoidea (sea lilies), asteroidea (starfish), ophiuroidea (brittle stars), and holothuroidea (sea cucumbers).

Chordata: This phylum includes humans and all other vertebrates, as well as a few invertebrates (urochordata and cephalochordata). Members of this phylum include agnatha (lampreys and hagfish), gnathostomata, chondrichthyes (cartilaginous fish-like sharks, skates, and rays), osteichthyes (bony fishes, including ray-finned fish that humans eat), amphibians (frogs, salamander, and newts), reptiles (lizards, snakes, crocodiles, and dinosaurs), birds, and mammals.

Animal systems and structure

Systems in animals have developed to perform various functions, including providing physical protection and obtaining food. Some animals have internal or external skeletons, shells, or skin that provide protection and support. Skin helps prevent water loss. Muscle systems enable movement. Brains and nervous systems help animals respond to external stimuli by processing incoming and outgoing signals. The main systems in animals are skeletal, muscular, nervous, digestive, respiratory, reproductive, and circulatory. The human stomach, for example, aids in the process of turning consumed food sources into energy. It has many tissue types: smooth muscle tissue, loose connective tissue, nervous tissue, blood, and columnar epithelial tissue. Many animals have a stomach or digestive chamber with two openings. These are known as metazoans.

Animal tissue types

Animals have four main tissues types: epithelial, connective, muscle, and bone. Epithelial tissue is found on body surfaces (like skin) and lining body cavities (like the stomach). Its function is to form and protect various glands. The three types of epithelial tissue are squamous (flattened), cuboidal (cube-shaped), and columnar (elongated). It can be further classified as simple (a single layer) or stratified (more than one layer). Epithelial cells move substances in, around, and out of the body. They can also have protective and secretory functions. Glands comprised of epithelial tissue can be unicellular or multicellular. Connective tissue is used to bind, support, protect, form blood, store fat, and fill space. The two kinds of connective tissue are loose and fibrous. In the human body, cartilage, bone, tendons, ligaments, blood, and protective layers on muscle, nerve, and blood vessels are types of connective tissue. The three types of muscle tissue are skeletal (striated), smooth, and cardiac.

Organ systems

The 11 major organ systems are: skeletal, muscular, nervous, digestive, respiratory, circulatory, skin, excretory, immune, endocrine, and reproductive.

Skeletal: This consists of the bones and joints. The skeletal system provides support for the body through its rigid structure, provides protection for internal organs, and works to make organisms motile. Growth hormone affects the rate of reproduction and the size of body cells, and also helps amino acids move through membranes.

Muscular: This includes the muscles. The muscular system allows the body to move and respond to its environment.

Nervous: This includes the brain, spinal cord, and nerves. The nervous system is a signaling system for intrabody communications among systems, responses to stimuli, and interaction within an environment. Signals are electrochemical. Conscious thoughts and memories and sense interpretation occur in the nervous system. It also controls involuntary muscles and functions, such as breathing and the beating of the heart.

Muscle in mammals

Skeletal muscle is strong, quick, and capable of voluntary contraction. Skeletal muscle fibers are striated and cylinder shaped. They have about 25 nuclei that are located to the side of the cell. Skeletal muscle consists of myofibrils that contain two types of filaments (myofilaments) made of proteins. The two types of filaments are actin and myosin. These filaments are aligned, giving the appearance of striation. During contraction, they slide against each other and become more overlapped. Smooth muscle is weak, slow, and usually contracts involuntarily. Examples in humans can be found in the gastrointestinal tract, blood vessels, bladder, uterus, hair follicles, and parts of the eye. Smooth muscle fibers are not striated, but spindle shaped. They are somewhat long and a little wider in the center. Each cell contains one nucleus that is centrally located. Smooth muscle cells also contain myofibrils, but they are not aligned. Cardiac muscle is strong, quick, and continuously contracts involuntarily. It is found in the myocardium of the heart.

Circulatory and skin systems

Circulatory: This includes the heart, blood, and blood vessels, such as veins, arteries, and capillaries. Blood transports oxygen and nutrients to cells and carbon dioxide to the lungs.

Skin (integumentary): This includes skin, hair, nails, sense receptors, sweat glands, and oil glands. The skin is a sense organ, provides an exterior barrier against disease, regulates body temperature through perspiration, manufactures chemicals and hormones, and provides a place for nerves from the nervous system and parts of the circulation system to travel through. Skin has three layers: epidermis, dermis, and subcutaneous. The epidermis is the thin, outermost, waterproof layer. Basal cells are located in the epidermis. The dermis contains the sweat glands, oil glands, and hair follicles. The subcutaneous layer has connective tissue, and also contains adipose (fat) tissue, nerves, arteries, and veins.

Digestive and respiratory systems

Digestive: This includes the mouth, pharynx, esophagus, stomach, intestines, rectum, anal canal, teeth, salivary glands, tongue, liver, gallbladder, pancreas, and appendix. The system helps change food into a form that the body can process and use for energy and nutrients. Food is eventually eliminated as solid waste. Digestive processes can be mechanical, such as chewing food and churning it in the stomach, and chemical, such as secreting hydrochloric acid to kill bacteria and converting protein to amino acids. The overall system converts large food particles into molecules so the body can use them. The small intestine transports the molecules to the circulatory system. The large intestine absorbs nutrients and prepares the unused portions of food for elimination.

Respiratory: This includes the nose, pharynx, larynx, trachea, bronchi, and lungs. It is involved in gas exchange, which occurs in the alveoli. Fish have gills instead of lungs.

Endocrine system

The endocrine system includes the pituitary gland, pineal gland, hypothalamus, thyroid gland, parathyroids, thymus, adrenals, pancreas, ovaries, and testes. It controls systems and processes by secreting hormones into the blood system. Exocrine glands are those that secrete fluid into ducts. Endocrine glands secrete hormones directly into the blood stream without the use of ducts. Prostaglandin (tissue hormones) diffuses only a short distance from the tissue that created it, and influences nearby cells only. Adrenal glands are located above each kidney. The cortex secretes some sex hormones, as well as mineralocorticoids and glucocorticoids involved in immune suppression and stress response. The medulla secretes epinephrine and norepinephrine. Both elevate blood sugar, increase blood pressure, and accelerate heart rate. Epinephrine also stimulates heart muscle. The islets of Langerhans are clumped within the pancreas and secrete glucagon and insulin, thereby regulating blood sugar levels. The four parathyroid glands at the rear of the thyroid secrete parathyroid hormone.

Excretory, immune, and reproductive systems

Excretory: This includes the kidneys, ureters, bladder, and urethra. The excretory system helps maintain the amount of fluids in the body. Wastes from the blood system and excess water are removed in urine. The system also helps remove solid waste.

Immune: This includes the lymphatic system, lymph nodes, lymph vessels, thymus, and spleen. Lymph fluid is moved throughout the body by lymph vessels that provide protection against disease. This system protects the body from external intrusions, such as microscopic organisms and foreign substances. It can also protect against some cancerous cells.

Reproductive: In the male, this system includes the testes, vas deferens, urethra, prostate, penis, and scrotum. In the female, this system includes the ovaries, fallopian tubes (oviduct and uterine tubes), cervix, uterus, vagina, vulva, and mammary glands. Sexual reproduction helps provide genetic diversity as gametes from each parent contribute half the DNA to the zygote offspring. The system provides a method of transporting the male gametes to the female. It also allows for the growth and development of the embryo. Hormones involved are testosterone, interstitial cell stimulating hormone (ICSH), luteinizing hormone (LH), follicle stimulating hormone (FSH), and estrogen. Estrogens secreted from the ovaries include estradiol, estrone, and estriol. They encourage growth, among other things. Progesterone helps prepare the endometrium for pregnancy.

Reproductive systems in animals

Based on whether or not and when an organism uses meiosis or mitosis, the three possible cycles of reproduction are haplontic, diplontic, and haplodiplontic. Fungi, green algae, and protozoa are haplontic. Animals and some brown algae and fungi are diplontic. Plants and some fungi are haplodiplontic. Diplontic organisms, like multicelled animals, have a dominant diploid life cycle. The haploid generation is simply the egg and sperm. Monoecious species are bisexual (hermaphroditic). In this case, the individual has both male and female organs: sperm-bearing testicles and egg-bearing ovaries. Hermaphroditic species can self fertilize. Some worms are hermaphroditic. Cross fertilization is when individuals exchange genetic information. Most animal species are dioecious, meaning individuals are distinctly male or female.

Hormones

The small cone-like pineal glands located in the brain secrete melatonin, which acts as a biological clock. The dual-lobed pituitary gland in the brain secretes growth hormone (stimulates tissue growth), thyroid stimulating hormone (signals the body to produce thyroxin), adrenocorticotropic hormone (signals the adrenal gland to produce cortisol), follicle-stimulating hormone (signals ovarian follicles to mature in females; helps regulate sperm cell production in males), luteinizing hormone (stimulates the production of estrogens and starts ovulation; stimulates production of testosterone), melanocyte-stimulating hormone (skin tone), and prolactin (stimulates milk let-down). These are all secreted by the anterior lobe. The posterior lobe secretes antidiuretic hormone and oxytocin. The thyroid in the neck secretes thyroxine, triiodothyronine, and calcitonin. These are involved with brain development, reproductive tract functions, and metabolism regulation. The thymus secretes thymosin.

Nutritional requirements

Carbohydrates are the primary source of energy as they can be easily converted to glucose. Fats (oils or lipids) are usually not very water soluble, and vitamins A, D, E, and K are fat soluble. Fats are needed to help process these vitamins and can also store energy. Fats have the highest calorie value per gram (9,000 calories). Dietary fiber, or roughage, helps the excretory system. In humans, fiber can help regulate blood sugar levels, reduce heart disease, help food pass through the digestive system, and add bulk. Dietary minerals are chemical elements that are involved with biochemical functions in the body. Proteins consist of amino acids. Proteins are broken down in the body into amino acids that are used for protein biosynthesis or fuel. Vitamins are compounds that are not made by the body, but obtained through the diet. Water is necessary to prevent dehydration since water is lost through the excretory system and perspiration.

Classifications of animals

As heterotrophs, animals can be further classified as carnivores, herbivores, omnivores, and parasites. Predation refers to a predator that feeds on another organism, which results in its death. Detritivory refers to heterotrophs that consume organic dead matter. Carnivores are animals that are meat eaters. Herbivores are plant eaters, and omnivores eat both meat and plants. A parasite's food source is its host. A parasite lives off of a host, which does not benefit from the interaction. Nutrients can be classified as carbohydrates, fats, fiber, minerals, proteins, vitamins, and water. Each supply a specific substance required for various species to survive, grow, and reproduce. A calorie is a measurement of heat energy. It can be used to represent both how much energy a food can provide and how much energy an organism needs to live.

Vitamins

Humans need dietary vitamins, which can be classified as either water soluble or fat soluble. Vitamins A, D, E, and K are fat soluble. Vitamins C and B are water soluble. Vitamin A (retinol) can be found in milk, eggs, liver, and some vegetables and fruits. It plays a role in immune system function, cell growth, and eye function.
Vitamin C (ascorbic acid) is in berries, peppers, and citrus fruits. It helps promote cell cohesiveness and healthy bones, teeth, and gums. It also improves brain function and aids in the absorption of some minerals. Other vitamins include: D (calciferol), which strengthens bones; vitamin B_2 (riboflavin), which is found in eggs; vitamin E (tocopherol); B_{12} (cyanocobalamin), which plays a role in red blood cell and nerve function; K (phylloquinone), which is found in alfalfa; B_5 (pantothenic acid); B_7 (biotin); B_6 (pyridoxine); B_3 (niacin); B_9 (folic acid); and B_1 (thiamine), which is needed to convert carbohydrates and plays a role in heart, muscle and nervous system function.

Minerals

Dietary minerals that are necessary for humans include potassium, chloride, sodium, calcium, phosphorus, magnesium, zinc, iron, manganese, copper, iodine, selenium, and molybdenum. Potassium is involved with ATP synthesis, and can be found in beans, bananas, and potatoes. Chloride, found in salt, is involved in making hydrochloric acid in the stomach. Substances like potassium and sodium are electrolytes, which mean they are conductive. Calcium is in dairy products, nuts, and green leafy vegetables. It is involved in the functions of the muscle, heart, digestive system, and bones. Magnesium is in nuts and soy beans. It is involved in ATP synthesis. Some enzymes need zinc to function. Iron is in green leafy vegetables, fish, eggs, beans, whole and enriched grains, and red meat. It is used by proteins and enzymes. Manganese and selenium are enzyme co-factors.

Early growth in humans

The zygote has genetic information from both parent organisms. After fertilization, the zygote undergoes many mitotic divisions, also called cleavage, by which the cell divides and grows into a morula and then a blastula. This hollow sphere undergoes rearrangement and differentiation. In sponges, blastula larvae swim to a new location and then form into a new individual. In humans, the blastocyst is implanted by day six or seven. It attaches to the endometrium. The blastula forms a gastrula with a digestive chamber and two germ layers: the external ectoderm and internal endoderm. In most cases, a mesoderm also develops between them. These germ layers then differentiate to form tissues and organs. Roughly two weeks after fertilization, the embryo starts to form a yolk sac that will make blood cells, an embryonic disc, and a chorion (the placenta). By week three, the beginnings of the spinal cord, brain, muscles, bones, and face appear. After that, cardiac cells begin to beat.

Process of reproduction

Individuals of a species have specialized reproductive cells. These cells are responsible for meiosis, which typically results in motile spermatozoa in the male and non-motile, food-containing ova in the female (gametogenesis). Gametogenesis refers to the production of haploid gametes. Spermatogenesis refers to sperm production, which occurs in the testes. Oogenesis refers to egg formation, which takes place in the ovaries. It also produces a polar body. Before fertilization, the oocyte continues to develop in a follicle. In the female, human luteinizing hormone (LH) causes the follicle to break open and the oocyte to slowly move down the fallopian tube. Fertilization occurs when the two gametes fuse to form a zygote, which develops into an individual. Sperm needs to be deposited within five days of ovulation for fertilization to occur. The ovaries secrete estrogen and progesterone. The testes secrete testosterone. The placenta secretes chorionic gonadotropin.

Changes that can lead to disease

Sometimes, the body's immune system attacks its own cells even when they are harmless. Faulty genes can lead to body parts and systems that do not function properly. Viruses, which can get introduced to the body in a variety of ways, can cause gastrointestinal pain and destroy immune system cells, which leave the body vulnerable to secondary bacterial infections and cancer cell growth. Cardiac dysfunction is a response (a compensatory mechanism) to the heart trying to maintain normal heart function. Eventually, this causes the cardiac system to weaken. When the heart muscle contracts to pump blood out, it is referred to as systolic blood flow. When the heart muscle relaxes and blood flows back in, it is referred to as diastolic blood flow. If there are problems related to systolic and/or diastolic blood flow, the amount of blood output can be lessened. The ventricle can become stiffer and will not completely fill. Dysfunction can cause the heart to try to compensate and maintain normalcy by pumping harder.

Asexual reproduction

Asexual reproduction occurs when only one parent is responsible for reproduction. Forms of this include budding, fragmentation, parthenogenesis, and self-fertilization.

Budding: This occurs when the offspring start as a growth on the parent organism's body. Jellyfish and some echinoderms have buds that leave the parent. Other organisms, such as corals, continue to be attached and form colonies.

Fragmentation: This is similar to budding, but after maturity the individual fragments into about eight pieces. Each fragment develops into another mature individual. Some small worms reproduce using this method.

Parthenogenesis: This is also known as virgin birth because the female produces eggs that develop without being fertilized. Specific species of fish, insects, frogs, and lizards reproduce by parthenogenesis.

Self-fertilization: Some species are considered hermaphroditic, meaning individuals have both male and female reproductive parts. Fertilization can be achieved within the individual.

Social behaviors

Territoriality: This refers to members of a species protecting areas from other members of their species and from other species. Species members claim specific areas as their own. Dominance: This refers to the species in a community that is the most populous.

Altruism: This is when a species or individual in a community exhibits behaviors that benefit another individual at a cost to itself. In biology, altruism does not have to be a conscious sacrifice.

Threat display: This refers to behavior by an organism that is intended to intimidate or frighten away members of its own or another species.

The principle of competitive exclusion (Gause's Law) states that if there are limited or insufficient resources and species are competing for them, these species will not be able to co-exist. The result is that one of the species will become extinct or be forced to undergo a behavioral or evolutionary change. Another way to say this is that "complete competitors cannot coexist."

Population

Population is a measure of how many individuals exist in a specific area. It can be used to measure the size of human, plant, or animal groups. Population growth depends on many factors. Factors that can limit the number of individuals in a population include lack of resources such as food and water, space, habitat destruction, competition, disease, and predators. Exponential growth refers to an unlimited rising growth rate. This kind of growth can be plotted on a chart in the shape of a J. Carrying capacity is the population size that can be sustained. The world's population is about 6.8 billion and growing. The human population has not yet reached its carrying capacity. Population dynamics refers to how a population changes over time and the factors that cause changes. An S-shaped curve shows that population growth has leveled off. Biotic potential refers to the maximum reproductive capacity of a population given ideal environmental conditions.

Interspecific relationships

Predation, parasitism, commensalism, and mutualism are all types of species interactions that affect species populations. Intraspecific relationships are relationships among members of a species. Interspecific relationships are relationships between members of different species.

Predation: This is a relationship in which one individual feeds on another (the prey), causing the prey to die.

Commensalism: This refers to interspecific relationships in which one of the organisms benefits. Mutualism, competition, and parasitism are all types of commensalism.

Mutualism: This is a relationship in which both organisms benefit from an interaction.

Competition: This is a relationship in which both organisms are harmed.

Parasitism: This is a relationship in which one organism benefits and the other is harmed.

Biomass: In ecology, biomass refers to the mass of one or all of the species (species biomass) in an ecosystem or area.

Community

A community is any number of species interacting within a given area. A niche is the role of a species within a community. Species diversity refers to the number of species within a community and their populations.

A biome refers to an area in which species are associated because of climate. The six major biomes in North America are desert, tropical rain forest, grassland, coniferous forest, deciduous forest, and tundra.

Biotic: Biotic factors are the living factors, such as other organisms, that affect a community or population. Abiotic factors are nonliving factors that affect a community or population, such as facets of the environment.

Ecology: Ecology is the study of plants, animals, their environments, and how they interact.

Ecosystem: An ecosystem is a community of species and all of the environment factors that affect them.

Food chains and biomagnifications

A food chain is a linking of organisms in a community that is based on how they use each other as food sources. Each link in the chain consumes the link above it and is consumed by the link below it. The exceptions are the organism at the top of the food chain and the organism at the bottom.

Biomagnification (bioamplification): This refers to an increase in concentration of a substance within a food chain. Examples are pesticides or mercury. Mercury is emitted from coal-fired power plants and gets into the water supply, where it is eaten by a fish. A larger fish eats smaller fish, and humans eat fish. The concentration of mercury in humans has now risen. Biomagnification is affected by the persistence of a chemical, whether it can be broken down and negated, food chain energetics, and whether organisms can reduce or negate the substance.

Ecoystem stability and ecologic succession

Ecosystem stability: This is a concept that states that a stable ecosystem is perfectly efficient. Seasonal changes or expected climate fluctuations are balanced by homeostasis. It also states that interspecies interactions are part of the balance of the system. Four principles of ecosystem stability are that waste disposal and nutrient replenishment by recycling is complete, the system uses sunlight as an energy source, biodiversity remains, and populations are stable in that they do not over consume resources.

Ecologic succession: This is the concept that states that there is an orderly progression of change within a community. An example of primary succession is that over hundreds of years bare rock decomposes to sand, which eventually leads to soil formation, which eventually leads to the growth of grasses and trees. Secondary succession occurs after a disturbance or major event that greatly affects a community, such as a wild fire or construction of a dam.

Biochemical cycles

Biochemical cycles are how chemical elements required by living organisms cycle between living and nonliving organisms. Elements that are frequently required are phosphorus, sulfur, oxygen, carbon, gaseous nitrogen, and water. Elements can go through gas cycles, sedimentary cycles, or both. Elements circulate through the air in a gas cycle and from land to water in a sedimentary one.

Mimicry is an adaptation developed as a response to predation. It refers to an organism that has a similar appearance to another species, which is meant to fool the predator into thinking the organism is more dangerous than it really is. Two examples are the drone fly and the io moth. The fly looks like a bee, but cannot sting. The io moth has markings on its wings that make it look like an owl. The moth can startle predators and gain time to escape. Predators can also use mimicry to lure their prey.

Food webs

A food web consists of interconnected food chains in a community. The organisms can be linked to show the direction of energy flow. Energy flow in this sense is used to refer to the actual caloric flow through a system from trophic level to trophic level. Trophic level refers to a link in a food chain or a level of nutrition. The 10% rule is that from trophic level to level, about 90% of the energy is lost (in the form of heat, for example). The lowest trophic level consists of primary producers (usually plants), then primary consumers, then secondary consumers, and finally tertiary consumers (large carnivores). The final link is decomposers, which break down the consumers at the top. Food chains usually do not contain more than six links. These links may also be referred to as ecological pyramids.

Contributing individuals to the theory of evolution

Cuvier (1744-1829)
Cuvier was a French naturalist who used the fossil record (paleontology) to compare the anatomies of extinct species and existing species to make conclusions about extinction. He believed in the catastrophism theory more strongly than the theory of evolution.

Lamarck (1769-1832)
Lamarck was a French naturalist who believed in the idea of evolution and thought it was a natural occurrence influenced by the environment. He studied medicine and botany. Lamarck put forth a theory of evolution by inheritance of acquired characteristics. He theorized that organisms became more complex by moving up a ladder of progress.

Lyell (1797-1875)
Lyell was a British geologist who believed in geographical uniformitarianism, which can be contrasted with catastrophism.

Charles Robert Darwin (1809-1882)
Darwin was an English naturalist known for his belief that evolution occurred by natural selection. He believed that species descend from common ancestors.

Alfred Russell Wallace (1823-1913)
He was a British naturalist who independently developed a theory of evolution by natural selection. He believed in the transmutation of species (that one species develops into another).

Earth and Space Science

Rocks and minerals

The physical properties (as opposed to chemical structures) used to identify minerals are hardness, luster, color, cleavage, streak, form (the external shape), and other special properties. Senses other than sight, such as touch, taste, and smell, may be used to observe physical properties. Hardness is the resistance a mineral has to scratches. The Mohs Hardness Scale is used to rate hardness from 1 to 10. Color can often not be determined definitively as some minerals can be more than one color. Luster is determined by reflected light. Luster can be described as metallic (shiny), sub-metallic (dull), non-metallic (vitreous, like glass), or earthy (like dirt or powder). Streak is the true color of the mineral in powdered form. It can be determined by rubbing the specimen across an unglazed porcelain tile. Fracture or cleavage is how a mineral reacts to stress, such as being struck with a hammer. Other properties that can be used to identify rocks and minerals include magnetism, a salty taste, or a pungent odor in a streak test.

Minerals are naturally occurring, inorganic solids with a definite chemical composition and an orderly internal crystal structure. A polymorph is two minerals with the same chemical composition, but a different crystal structure. Rocks are aggregates of one or more minerals, and may also contain mineraloids (minerals lacking a crystalline structure) and organic remains. The three types of rocks are sedimentary, igneous, and metamorphic. Rocks are classified based on their formation and the minerals they contain. Minerals are classified by their chemical composition. Geology is the study of the planet Earth as it pertains to the composition, structure, and origin of its rocks. Petrology is the study of rocks, including their composition, texture, structure, occurrence, mode of formation, and history. Mineralogy is the study of minerals.

Sedimentary rock

Sedimentary rocks are formed by the process of lithification, which involves compaction, the expulsion of liquids from pores, and the cementation of the pre-existing rock. It is pressure and temperature that are responsible for this process. Sedimentary rocks are often formed in layers in the presence of water, and may contain organic remains, such as fossils. Sedimentary rocks are organized into three groups: detrital, biogenic, and chemical. Texture refers to the size, shape, and grains of sedimentary rock. Texture can be used to determine how a particular sedimentary rock was created. Composition refers to the types of minerals present in the rock. The origin of sedimentary rock refers to the type of water that was involved in its creation. Marine deposits, for example, likely involved ocean environments, while continental deposits likely involved dry land and lakes.

Mineral classification

Minerals are classified by chemical composition and internal crystalline structure. They are organized into classes. Native elements such as gold and silver are not classified in this manner. The eight classes are sulfides, oxides\hydroxides, halides, carbonates, sulfates, phosphates, and silicates. These classes are based on the dominant anion (negatively charged ion) or anionic group. Minerals are classified in this way for three main reasons. First, minerals with the same anion have unmistakable resemblances. Second, minerals with the same anion are often found in the same geologic environment. For example, calcite and dolomite, which belong to the same group, are often found together. Last, this method is similar to the naming convention used to identify inorganic compounds in chemistry. Minerals can be further separated into groups on the basis of internal structure.

Metamorphic rock

Metamorphic rock is that which has been changed by great heat and pressure. This results in a variety of outcomes, including deformation, compaction, destruction of the characteristics of the original rock, bending, folding, and formation of new minerals because of chemical reactions, and changes in the size and shape of the mineral grain. For example, the igneous rock ferromagnesian can be changed into schist and gneiss. The sedimentary rock carbonaceous can be changed into marble. The texture of metamorphic rocks can be classified as foliated and unfoliated. Foliation, or layering, occurs when rock is compressed along one axis during recrystallization. This can be seen in schist and shale. Unfoliated rock does not include this banding. Rocks that are compressed equally from all sides or lack specific minerals will be unfoliated. An example is marble.

Igneous rock

Igneous rock is formed from magma, which is molten material originating from beneath the Earth's surface. Depending upon where magma cools, the resulting igneous rock can be classified as intrusive, plutonic, hypabyssal, extrusive, or volcanic. Magma that solidifies at a depth is intrusive, cools slowly, and has a coarse grain as a result. An example is granite. Magma that solidifies at or near the surface is extrusive, cools quickly, and usually has a fine grain. An example is basalt. Magma that actually flows out of the Earth's surface is called lava. Some extrusive rock cools so quickly that crystals do not have time to form. These rocks have a glassy appearance. An example is obsidian. Hypabyssal rock is igneous rock that is formed at medium depths.

Earth's structure

The Earth is ellipsoid, not perfectly spherical. This means the diameter is different through the poles and at the equator. Through the poles, the Earth is about 12,715 km in diameter. The approximate center of the Earth is at a depth of 6,378 km. The Earth is divided into a crust, mantle, and core. The core consists of a solid inner portion. Moving outward, the molten outer core occupies the space from about a depth of 5,150 km to a depth of 2,890 km. The mantle consists of a lower and upper layer. The lower layer includes the D' (D prime) and D" (D double-prime) layers. The solid portion of the upper mantle and crust together form the lithosphere, or rocky sphere. Below this, but still within the mantle, is the asthenosphere, or weak sphere. These layers are distinguishable because the lithosphere is relatively rigid, while the asthenosphere resembles a thick liquid.

Maps

Traditional maps represent land in two dimensions, while topographic maps represent elevation through the use of contour lines. Contour lines help show changes to elevations above the surface of the Earth and on the ocean floor. They also help show the shape of

Earth's surface features. The United States Geological Survey (USGS) produces frequently used quadrangle maps in various scales. A quadrangle topographic map is bounded by two lines of latitude and two lines of longitude. A 7.5-minute map shows an area that spans 7.5 minutes of latitude and 7.5 minutes of longitude. The name of the quadrangle map appears at the top, and usually indicates the name of a prominent feature. Topographic maps that show much less detail are also available. They might show a much larger area, such as a country or state. USGS quad maps also refer to adjacent quad maps. Other information contained on quad maps includes the projection and grid used, scale, contour intervals, and magnetic declination, which is the difference between true north and magnetic north.

Earth's chemical composition

The Earth's core consists of hot iron and forms of nickel. The mantle consists of different materials, including iron, magnesium, and calcium. The crust covers the mantle, consists of a thin layer of much lighter rocks, and is further subdivided into continental and oceanic portions. The continental portion consists mainly of silicates, such as granite. The oceanic portion consists of heavier, volcanic rocks, such as basalt. The upper 10 miles of the lithosphere layer (the crust and part of the mantle) is made up of 95% igneous rock (or its metamorphic equivalent), 4% shale, 0.75% sandstone, and 0.25% limestone. There are over 4,000 known minerals, but only about 20 make up some 95% of all rocks. There are, however, more than 3,000 individual kinds of minerals in the Earth's crust. Silicates are the largest group of minerals.

Mountains

Orogeny refers to the formation of mountains, particularly the processes of folding and faulting caused by plate tectonics. Folding is when layers of sedimentary rock are pressed together by continental plate movements. Sections of rock that are folded upward are called anticlines. Sections of rock that are folded downward are called synclines. Examples of folded mountains are the Alps and the Himalayans. Fault-block mountains are created when tectonic plate movement produces tension that results in displacement. Mountains in the Southwest United States are examples of fault-blocking mountains. Mountains can also be caused by volcanic activity and erosion.

Tectonic Convection

Heat is transferred through the process of convection, which is a cycle. Hot material rises and spreads, cooling as it spreads. The cool material then sinks, where it is heated again. The process of convection can be seen in a pot of boiling water. It is believed this same process is happening deep within the Earth. Greater depths are associated with more pressure and heat. The weight of all the rocks causes the increase in pressure, while the decay of heavy radioactive elements such as uranium produces heat. This creates hot areas of molten material that find their way upward and to the surface in an effort to equalize, which means pressure and temperature are reduced. This causes the processes involved in plate tectonics.

Plate tectonic theory

The theory of plate tectonics states that the lithosphere, the solid portion of the mantle and Earth's crust, consists of major and minor plates. These plates are on top of and move with the viscous upper mantle, which is heated because of the convection cycle that occurs in the interior of the Earth. There are different estimates as to the exact number of major and minor plates. The number of major plates is believed to be between 9 and 15, and it is thought that there may be as many as 40 minor plates. The United States is atop the North American plate. The Pacific Ocean is atop the Pacific plate. The point at which these two plates slide horizontally along the San Andreas fault is an example of a transform plate boundary. The other two types of boundaries are divergent (plates that are spreading apart and forming new crust) and convergent (the process of subduction causes one plate to go under another). The movement of plates is what causes other features of the Earth's crust, such as mountains, volcanoes, and earthquakes.

Volcanic activities and plate tectonics

Volcanoes can occur along any type of tectonic plate boundary. At a divergent boundary, as plates move apart, magma rises to the surface, cools, and forms a ridge. An example of this is the mid-Atlantic ridge. Convergent boundaries, where one plate slides under another, are often areas with a lot of volcanic activity. The subduction process creates magma. When it rises to the surface, volcanoes can be created. Volcanoes can also be created in the middle of a plate over hot spots. Hot spots are locations where narrow plumes of magma rise through the mantle in a fixed place over a long period of time. The Hawaiian Islands and Midway are examples. The plate shifts and the island moves. Magma continues to rise through the mantle, however, which produces another island. Volcanoes can be active, dormant, or extinct. Active volcanoes are those that are erupting or about to erupt. Dormant volcanoes are those that might erupt in the future and still have internal volcanic activity. Extinct volcanoes are those that will not erupt.

Types of volcanoes

The three types of volcanoes are shield, cinder cone, and composite. A shield volcano is created by a long-term, relatively gentle eruption. This type of volcanic mountain is created by each progressive lava flow that occurs over time. A cinder cone volcano is created by explosive eruptions. Lava is spewed out of a vent into the air. As it falls to the ground, the lava cools into cinders and ash, which build up around the volcano in a cone shape. A composite volcano is a combination of the other two types of volcanoes. In this type, there are layers of lava flows and layers of ash and cinder.

Seismic deformation and seismic waves

There are two types of deformations created by an earthquake fault rupture: static and dynamic. Static deformation permanently displaces the ground. Examples are when a road or railroad track becomes distorted by an earthquake. Plate tectonics stresses the fault by creating tension with slow plate movements. An earthquake releases the tension. Plate tectonics also cause a second type of deformation. This type results in dynamic motions that take the form of seismic waves. These sound waves can be compressional waves, also known as primary or P waves, or shear waves, also known as secondary or S waves. P waves travel fastest, with speeds ranging between 1.5 and 8 kilometers per second. Shear waves are slower. P waves shake the ground in the direction they are propagating. S waves shake perpendicularly or transverse to the direction of propagation. Seismographs use a simple pendulum to record earthquake movement in a record called a seismogram. A seismogram can help seismologists estimate the distance, direction, Richter magnitude, and type of faulting of an earthquake.

Earthquakes plate tectonics

Most earthquakes are caused by tectonic plate movement. They occur along fractures called faults or fault zones. Friction in the faults prevents smooth movement. Tension builds up over time, and the release of that tension results in earthquakes. Faults are grouped based on the type of slippage that occurs. The types of faults are dip-slip, strike-slip, and oblique-slip. A dip-slip fault involves vertical movement along the fault plane. In a normal dip-slip fault, the wall that is above the fault plane moves down. In a reverse dip-slip fault, the wall above the fault plane moves up. A strike-slip fault involves horizontal movement along the fault plane. Oblique-slip faults involve both vertical and horizontal movement. The Richter magnitude scale measures how much seismic energy was released by an earthquake.

Erosion

Erosion is the wearing away of rock materials from the Earth's surface. Erosion can be classified as natural geologic erosion and erosion due to human activity. Natural geologic erosion occurs due to weathering and gravity. Factors involved in natural geologic erosion are typically long term forces. Human activity such as development, farming, and deforestation occurs over shorter periods of time. Soil, which supports plant growth, is the topmost layer of organic material. One type of erosion is sheet erosion, which is the gradual and somewhat uniform removal of surface soil. Rills are small rivulets that cut into soil. Gullies are rills that have become enlarged due to extended water run-off. Sandblows are caused by wind blowing away particles. Negative effects of erosion include sedimentation in rivers, which can pollute water and damage ecosystems. Erosion can also result in the removal of topsoil, which destroys crops and prevents plants from growing. This reduces food production and alters ecosystems.

Hydrologic cycle

The hydrologic, or water, cycle refers to water movement on, above, and in the Earth. Water can be in any one of its three states during different phases of the cycle. The three states of water are liquid water, frozen ice, and water vapor. Processes involved in the hydrologic cycle include precipitation, canopy interception, snow melt, runoff, infiltration, subsurface flow, evaporation, sublimation, advection, condensation, and transpiration. Precipitation is when condensed water vapor falls to Earth. Examples include rain, fog drip, and various forms of snow, hail, and sleet. Canopy interception is when precipitation lands on plant foliage instead of falling to the ground and evaporating. Snow melt is runoff produced by melting snow. Infiltration occurs when water flows from the surface into the ground. Subsurface flow refers to water that flows underground. Evaporation is when water in a liquid state changes to a gas. Sublimation is when water in a solid state (such as snow or ice) changes to water vapor without going through a liquid phase. Advection is the movement of water through the atmosphere. Condensation is when water vapor changes to liquid water. Transpiration is when water vapor is released from plants into the air.

Deposition

Deposition, or sedimentation, is the geological process in which previously eroded material is transported or added to a land form or land mass. Erosion and sedimentation are complementary geological processes. Running water causes a substantial amount of deposition of transported materials in both fresh water and coastal areas. Examples include gravity transporting material down the slope of a mountain and depositing it at the base of the slope. Another example is when sandstorms deposit particles in other locations. When glaciers melt and retreat, it can result in the deposition of sediments. Evaporation is also considered to cause deposition since dissolved materials are left behind when water evaporates. Deposition can include the build up of organic materials. For example, chalk is partially made up of the small calcium carbonate skeletons of marine plankton, which helps create more calcium carbonate from chemical processes.

Weathering

There are two basic types of weathering: mechanical and chemical. Weathering is a very prominent process on the Earth's surface. Materials weather at different rates, which are known as differential weathering. Mechanical and chemical weathering is interdependent. For example, chemical weathering can loosen the bonds between molecules and allow mechanical weathering to take place. Mechanical weathering can expose the surfaces of land masses and allow chemical weathering to take place. Impact, abrasion, frost wedging, root wedging, salt wedging, and uploading are types of mechanical weathering. Types of chemical weathering are dissolution, hydration, hydrolysis, oxidation, biological, and carbonation. The primary type of chemical weathering is caused by water dissolving a mineral. The more acidic water is, the more effective it is at weathering. Carbonic and sulfuric acids can enter rain when they are present in the atmosphere. This lowers the pH value of rain, making it more acidic. Normal rain water has a pH value of 5.5. Acid rain has a pH value of 4 or less.

Radioactive dating

Radioactive dating, also known as radiometric dating, is a technique that can be used to determine the age of rocks and even the Earth itself. The process compares the amount of radioactive material in a rock to the amount of material that has "decayed." Decay refers to the fact that the nuclide of an element loses subatomic particles over time. The process includes a parent element that undergoes changes to create a daughter element, also known as the decay product. The daughter element can also be unstable and lose particles, creating another daughter element. This is known as a decay chain. Decay occurs until all the elements are stable. Three types of dating techniques are radiocarbon dating, potassium-argon dating, and uranium-lead dating. These techniques can be used to date a variety of natural and manmade materials, including archaeological artifacts.

Mass extinction

Mass extinction, also known as an extinction event, is a decrease in the number of species over a short period of time. While there are many theories as to the causes of mass extinction, it occurs when a relatively large number of species die off or when fewer species evolve than expected. Extinction events are classified as major and minor. It is generally accepted that there have been five major extinction events in Earth's history. The five most significant mass extinction events are Ordovician-Silurian, Permian-Triassic, Late Devonian, Triassic-Jurassic, and Cretaceous-Tertiary.

Uniformitarianism, catastrophism, and superposition

Uniformitarianism: Also known as gradualism, uniformitarianism is the belief among modern geologists that the forces, processes, and laws that we see today have existed throughout geologic time. It involves the belief that the present is the key to the past, and that relatively slow processes have shaped the geological features of Earth. Catastrophism: This is the belief that the Earth was shaped by sudden, short-term catastrophic events.

Superposition: In geology, and in the field of stratigraphy in particular, the law of superposition is that underground layers closer to the surface were deposited more recently.

Geologic time scale

One year is 365.25 days long. The International System of Units (SI) suggests the symbol "a" for a standard year or annum. The prefixes "M" for mega and "G" for giga are used to refer to one million and one billion years, respectively. Ma stands for a megannum (10^6 years) and Ga stands for a gigannum (10^9 years). For example, it can be said that the Earth was formed 4.5 billion years ago, or 4.5 Ga. The term "ago" is understood. Use of the abbreviation "mya" for millions of years (ago) is discouraged, but it is still occasionally used. The abbreviation "BP" stands for "before present." The "present" is defined as January 1, 1950, since present changes from year to year. Another abbreviation used is BCE, which stands for "Before the Common Era." Christian and current can also be used in place of common.

Geologists use the geologic time scale when discussing Earth's chronology and the formation of rocks and minerals. Age is calculated in millions of years before the present time. Units of time are often delineated by geologic or paleontologic events. Smaller units of time such as eras are distinguished by the abundance and/or extinction of certain plant and animal life. For example, the extinction of the dinosaurs marks the end of the Mesozoic era and the beginning of the Cenozoic, the present, era. We are in the Holocene epoch. The supereon encompasses the greatest amount of time. It is composed of eons. Eons are divided into eras, eras into periods, and periods into epochs. Layers of rock also correspond to periods of time in geochronology. Current theory holds that the Earth was formed 4.5 billion years ago.

Development of geologic time scale

The first known observations of stratigraphy were made by Aristotle, who lived before the time of Christ. He observed seashells in ancient rock formations and on the beach, and concluded that the fossilized seashells were similar to current seashells. Avicenna, a Persian scholar from the 11th century, also made early advances in the development of stratigraphy with the concept of superposition. Nicolas Steno, a Danish scientist from the 17th century, expounded upon this with the belief that layers of rock are piled on top of each other. In the 18th century, Abraham Werner categorized rocks from four different periods: the Primary, Secondary, Tertiary, and Quaternary periods. This fell out of use when the belief emerged that rock layers containing the same fossils had been deposited at the same time, and were therefore from the same age. British geologists created the names for many of the time divisions in use today. For example, the Devonian period was named after the county of Devon, and the Permian period was named after Perm, Russia.

Relative and absolute time

A numerical, or "absolute," age is a specific number of years, such as 150 million years ago. A "relative" age refers to a time range, such as the Mesozoic era. It is used to determine whether one rock formation is older or younger than another formation. Radioactive dating is a form of absolute dating and stratigraphy is a form of relative dating. Radioactive dating techniques have provided the most information about the absolute age of rocks and other geological features. Together, geochronologists have created a geologic time scale. Biostratigraphy uses plant and animal fossils within rock to determine its relative age.

Stratigraphy

Stratigraphy is a branch of geology that involves the study of rock layers and layering. Sedimentary rocks are the primary focus of stratigraphy. Subfields include lithostratigraphy, which is the study of the vertical layering of rock types, and biostratigraphy, which is the study of fossil evidence in rock layers. Magnetostratigraphy is the study of changes in detrital remnant magnetism (DRM), which is used to measure the polarity of Earth's magnetic field at the time a stratum was deposited. Chronostratigraphy focuses on the relative dating of rock strata based on the time of rock formation. Unconformity refers to missing layers of rock.

Fossils

Fossils provide a wealth of information about the past, particularly about the flora and fauna that once occupied the Earth, but also about the geologic history of the Earth itself and how Earth and its inhabitants came to be. Some fossilized remains in the geohistorical record exemplify ongoing processes in the Earth's environment, such as weathering, glaciation, and volcanism. These have all led to evolutionary changes in plants and animals. Other fossils support the theory that catastrophic events caused drastic changes in the Earth and its living creatures. One example of this type of theory is that a meteor struck the Earth and caused dinosaurs to become extinct. Both types of fossils provide scientists with a way to hypothesize whether these types of events will happen again.

Fossils are preservations of plants, animals, their remains, or their traces that date back to about 10,000 years ago. Fossils and where they are found in rock strata makes up the fossil record. Fossils are formed under a very specific set of conditions. The fossil must not be damaged by predators and scavengers after death, and the fossil must not decompose. Usually, this happens when the organism is quickly covered with sediment. This sediment builds up and molecules in the organism's body are replaced by minerals. Fossils come in an array of sizes, from single-celled organisms to large dinosaurs.

Atmospheric layers

Earth's atmosphere has five main layers. From lowest to highest, these are the troposphere, the stratosphere, the mesosphere, the thermosphere, and the exosphere. Between each pair of layers is a transition layer called a pause. The troposphere includes the tropopause, which is the transitional layer of the stratosphere. Energy from Earth's surface is transferred to the troposphere. Temperature decreases with altitude in this layer. In the stratosphere, the temperature is inverted, meaning that it increases with altitude. The stratosphere includes the ozone layer, which helps block ultraviolet light from the Sun. The stratopause is the transitional layer to the mesosphere. The temperature of the mesosphere decreases with height. It is considered the coldest place on Earth, and has an average temperature of -85 degrees Celsius. Temperature increases with altitude in the thermosphere, which includes the thermopause. Just past the thermosphere is the exobase, the base layer of the exosphere. Beyond the five main layers are the ionosphere, homosphere, heterosphere, and magnetosphere.

Earth's atmosphere

The atmosphere consists of 78% nitrogen, 21% oxygen, and 1% argon. It also includes traces of water vapor, carbon dioxide and other gases, dust particles, and chemicals from Earth. The atmosphere becomes thinner the farther it is from the Earth's surface. It becomes difficult to breathe at about 3 km above sea level. The atmosphere gradually fades into space. The lowest layer of the atmosphere is called the troposphere. Its thickness varies at the poles and the equator, varying from about 7 to 17 km. This is where most weather occurs. The stratosphere is next, and continues to an elevation of about 51 km. The mesosphere extends from the stratosphere to an elevation of about 81 km. It is the coldest layer and is where meteors tend to ablate. The next layer is the thermosphere. It is where the International Space Station orbits. The exosphere is the outermost layer, extends to 10,000 km, and mainly consists of hydrogen and helium.

Tropospheric circulation

Most weather takes place in the troposphere. Air circulates in the atmosphere by convection and in various types of "cells." Air near the equator is warmed by the Sun and rises. Cool air rushes under it, and the higher, warmer air flows toward Earth's poles. At the poles, it cools and descends to the surface. It is now under the hot air, and flows back to the equator. Air currents coupled with ocean currents move heat around the planet, creating winds, weather, and climate. Winds can change direction with the seasons. For example, in Southeast Asia and India, summer monsoons are caused by air being heated by the Sun. This air rises, draws moisture from the ocean, and causes daily rains. In winter, the air cools, sinks, pushes the moist air away, and creates dry weather.

Layers above Earth's surface

The ozone layer, although contained within the stratosphere, is determined by ozone (O_3) concentrations. It absorbs the majority of ultraviolet light from the Sun. The ionosphere is part of both the exosphere and the thermosphere. It is characterized by the fact that it is a plasma, a partially ionized gas in which free electrons and positive ions are attracted to each other, but are too energetic to remain fixed as a molecule. It starts at about 50 km above Earth's surface and goes to 1,000 km. It affects radio wave transmission and auroras. The ionosphere pushes against the inner edge of the Earth's magnetosphere, which is the highly magnetized, non-spherical region around the Earth. The homosphere encompasses the troposphere, stratosphere, and mesosphere. Gases in the homosphere are considered well mixed. In the heterosphere, the distance that particles can move without colliding is large. As a result, gases are stratified according to their molecular weights. Heavier gases such as oxygen and nitrogen occur near the bottom of the heterosphere, while hydrogen, the lightest element, is found at the top.

Hydrosphere

Much of Earth is covered by a layer of water or ice called the hydrosphere. Most of the hydrosphere consists of ocean water. The water cycle and the many processes involved in it take place in the hydrosphere. There are several theories regarding how the Earth's hydrosphere was formed. Earth contains more surface water than other planets in the inner solar system. Outgassing, the slow release of trapped water vapor from the Earth's interior, is one theory used to explain the existence of water on Earth. This does not really account for the quantity of water on Earth, however. Another hypothesis is that the early Earth was subjected to a period of bombardment by comets and water-rich asteroids, which resulted in the release of water into the Earth's environment. If this is true, much of the water on the surface of the Earth today originated from the outer parts of the solar system beyond Neptune.

Formation of Earth's atmosphere

It is generally believed that the Earth's atmosphere evolved into its present state. Some believe Earth's early atmosphere contained hydrogen, helium, methane, ammonia, and some water vapor. These elements also played a role in planet formation. Earth's early atmosphere was developed before the emergence of living organisms as we know them today. Eventually, the hot hydrogen and helium escaped Earth's gravity and drifted off. Others believe the early atmosphere contained a large amount of carbon dioxide. Either way, there was probably little oxygen at the time. One theory is that a second stage of the atmosphere evolved over several hundred million years through a process during which methane, ammonia, and water vapor broke down and reformed into nitrogen, hydrogen, and carbon dioxide. About two billion years ago, higher levels of oxygen were found in the atmosphere, which is indicated by large deposits of iron ore. At the same time, iron ores created in oxygen-poor environments stopped forming. The oxygen in the atmosphere today comes mainly from plants and microorganisms such as algae.

Paleozoic era

The Paleozoic era began about 542 Ma and lasted until 251 Ma. It is further divided into six periods. The Paleozoic era began after the supercontinent Pannotia started to break up and at the end of a global ice age. By the end of the era, the supercontinent Pangaea had formed. The beginning of the Paleozoic era is marked by Cambrian Explosion, a time when there were abundant life forms according to the fossil record. The end of the era is marked by one of the major extinction events, the Permian extinction, during which almost 90 percent of the species living at the time became extinct. Many plant and animal forms appeared on the land and in the sea during this era. It is also when large land plants first appeared in the fossil record. There are many invertebrates found in the fossil record of the Paleozoic era, and fish, amphibians, and reptiles also first appeared in the fossil record during this era. There were also large swamps and forests, some of which were formed into coal deposits that exist today.

Earth's formation

Earth's early development began after a supernova exploded. This led to the formation of the Sun out of hydrogen gas and interstellar dust. These same elements swirled around the newly-formed Sun and formed the planets, including Earth. Scientists theorize that about 4.5 billion years ago, Earth was a chunk of rock surrounded by a cloud of gas. It is believed it lacked water and the type of atmosphere that exists today. Heat from radioactive materials in the rock and pressure in the Earth's interior melted the interior. This caused the heavier materials, such as iron, to sink. Lighter silicate-type rocks rose to the Earth's surface. These rocks formed the Earth's earliest crust. Other chemicals also rose to the Earth's surface, helping to form the water and atmosphere. There is one material that has been dated by scientists and found to be 4.4 billion years old. The material is zircon, which consists of zirconium, silicon, and oxygen. Zircon is a mineral that has a high resistance to weathering.

Cenozoic era

The Cenozoic era began about 65.5 Ma and continues to the present. It is marked by the Cretaceous-Tertiary extinction event (extinction of the dinosaurs as well as many invertebrates and plants). The Cenozoic era is further divided into the Paleogene, Neogene, and Quaternary periods. During the Cenozoic era, Pangaea continued to drift, and the plates eventually moved into their present positions. The Pleistocene Ice Age, also known as Quaternary glaciation or the current ice age began about 2.58 Ma and includes the glaciation occurring today. Mammals continued to evolve and other plants and animals came into existence during this era. The fossil record includes the ancestors of the horse, rhinoceros, and camel. It also includes the first dogs and cats and the first humanlike creatures. The first humans appeared less than 200,000 years ago.

Mesozoic era

The Mesozoic era is known as the Age of the Dinosaurs. It is also the era during which the dinosaurs became extinct. The fossil record also shows the appearance of mammals and birds. Trees that existed included gymnosperms, which have uncovered seeds and are mostly cone bearing, and angiosperms, which have covered seeds and are flowering plants. The angiosperm group is currently the dominant plant group. It was also during this era that the supercontinent Pangaea divided into the continental pieces that exist today. During the Cretaceous period, sea levels rose until one-third of the Earth's present land mass was underwater, and then receded. This period created huge marine deposits and chalk. The extinction of the dinosaurs happened about 65 Ma, and was believed to have been triggered by the impact of an asteroid.

Ocean

The ocean is the salty body of water that encompasses the Earth. It has a mass of 1.4×10^{24} grams. Geographically, the ocean is divided into three large oceans: the Pacific Ocean, the Atlantic Ocean, and the Indian Ocean. There are also other divisions, such as gulfs, bays, and various types of seas, including Mediterranean and marginal seas. Ocean distances can be measured by latitude, longitude, degrees, meters, miles, and nautical miles. The ocean accounts for 70.8% of the surface of the Earth, amounting to 361,254,000 km². The ocean's depth is greatest at Challenger Deep in the Mariana Trench. The ocean floor here is 10,924 meters below sea level. The depths of the ocean are mapped by echo sounders and satellite altimeter systems. Echo sounders emit a sound pulse from the surface and record the time it takes to return. Satellite altimeters provide better maps of the ocean floor.

Ocean's importance

The ocean covers 71 percent of the Earth's surface and contains 97 percent of the planet's water. The ocean is an important part of the biosphere, the hydrologic cycle, and tropospheric circulation. It also plays a key role in Earth's weather and climate, which influence the daily lives of humans. The main uses of the ocean and coastal areas for humans are food, transport, oil, gas, and recreation. It is estimated that the ocean provides a means of support for almost 50 percent of all species on Earth. Roughly 20 percent of the animal protein in human diets comes from the ocean.

Seawater

Salinity is a measure of the amount of dissolved salts in ocean water. It is defined in terms of conductivity. Salinity is influenced by the geologic formations in the area, with igneous formations leading to lower salinity and sedimentary formations leading to higher salinity. Dryer areas with greater rates of evaporation also have higher salt concentrations. Areas where fresh water mixes with ocean water have lower salt concentrations. Hydrogen and oxygen make up about 96.5% of sea water. The major constituents of the dissolved solids of sea water at an atomic level are chlorine (55.3%), sodium (30.8%), magnesium (3.7%), sulfur (2.6%), calcium (1.2%), and potassium (1.1%). The salinity of ocean water is fairly constant, ranging from 34.60 to 34.80 parts per thousand, which is 200 parts per million. Measuring variation on this small of a scale requires instruments that are accurate to about one part per million.

Ocean floor

The ocean floor includes features similar to those found on land, such as mountains, ridges, plains, and canyons. The oceanic crust is a thin, dense layer that is about 10 km thick. The greatest volume of water is contained in the basins with lesser volumes that occupy the low-lying areas of the continents, which are known as the continental shelves. The continental slope connects the shelf to the ocean floor of the basin. The continental rise is a slightly sloping area between the slope and the basin. A seamount is an undersea volcanic peak that rises to a height of at least 1,000 meters. A guyot is a seamount with a flat top. A mid-ocean ridge is a continuous undersea mountain chain. Sills are low parts of ridges separating ocean basins or other seas. Trenches are long, narrow troughs. Many isolated peaks and seamounts are scattered throughout the ocean basins, and interrupt ocean currents.

Gyres and the Coriolis effect

Gyres are surface ocean currents that form large circular patterns. In the Northern Hemisphere, they flow clockwise. In the Southern Hemisphere, they flow counterclockwise. These directions are caused by the Coriolis effect. The Coriolis effect occurs due to the fact that the Earth is a rotating object. In the Northern Hemisphere, currents appear to be curving to the right. In the Southern Hemisphere, currents appear to be curving to the left. This is because the Earth is rotating. Gyres tend to flow in the opposite direction near the Earth's poles. In the portion of the Pacific Ocean north of the equator, the major currents are

North Pacific, California, North Equatorial, and Kuroshio. In the South Pacific, they are South Equatorial, East Australia, South Pacific, and Peru. In the North Atlantic, they are the North Atlantic Drift, Canary, North Equatorial, and Gulf Stream. In the South Atlantic, they are South Equatorial, Brazil, South Atlantic, and Benguela.

Ocean currents

Surface currents are caused by winds. Subsurface currents, which occur deep beneath the ocean's surface, are caused by land masses and the Earth's rotation. The density of ocean water can also affect currents. Sea water with a higher salinity is denser than sea water with a lower salinity. Water from denser areas flows to areas with water that is less dense. Currents are classified by temperature. Colder polar sea water flows south towards warmer water, forming cold currents. Warm water currents swirl around the basins and equator. In turn, heat lost and gained by the ocean creates winds. Ocean currents play a significant role in transferring this heat toward the poles, which aids in the development of many types of weather phenomena.

Upwelling and Ekman transport

Upwelling occurs where wind blows parallel to a coast. This causes the ocean surface to move away from the coast. Deep-sea water, which is usually cold and rich in nutrients, rises to takes its place. Ekman transport refers to the impact of the Coriolis effect when wind moves water. Wind blowing in one direction tries to move the surface layer of water in a straight line, but the rotation of the Earth causes water to move in a curved direction. The wind continues to blow the surface of the water and the surface water turns slightly. Below the surface, the water turns even more, eventually creating a spiral. This creates water movement at a right angle to the wind direction. The importance of upwelling is that it brings the nutrient-rich dead and rotting sea creatures closer to the ocean's surface. Here, they are consumed by phytoplankton, which is in turn eaten by zooplankton. Fish eat the zooplankton, and larger creatures and humans eat the fish. Downwelling is the opposite of upwelling.

Deep sea currents

Deep sea currents are often likened to a conveyor belt because they circumnavigate the entire ocean, albeit weakly, and slowly mix deeper and shallower water. In the winter, deep circulation carries cold water from high latitudes to lower latitudes throughout the world. This takes place in areas where most water is at a depth of between 4 and 5 km. This water mass can be as cold as or colder than 4°C. Surface ocean temperatures average about 17°C, but can vary from -2°C to 36°C. The vast cold mass of sea water is also dense and has a high saline content, which forces it to sink at high latitudes. It spreads out, stratifies, and fills the ocean basins. Deep mixing occurs and then the water upwells. The manner in which deep sea currents move can be described as abyssal circulation.

Ocean waves

Most waves in the ocean are formed by winds. The stronger the winds are, the larger the waves will be. The highest point of a wave is the crest. The lowest point of a wave is the trough. The wavelength is measured from crest to crest. The wave height is measured from the trailing trough to the peak of the crest. The wave frequency refers to the number of wave crests passing a designated point each second. A wave period is the time it takes for a wave crest to reach the point of the wave crest of the previous wave. The energy in the wave runs into the shallow sea floor. This causes the wave to become steeper and then fall over, or break.

Other types of waves

Waves that reach the shore are not all the same size. They can be larger or smaller than average. About once an hour, there is usually a wave that is twice the size of others. There are even larger, but rare, rogue waves, which often travel alone and in a direction different than other waves. Swells are waves that have traveled a great distance. These types of waves are usually large waves with flatter crests. They are very regular in shape and size. The sea level slowly rises and falls over the period of a day. These types of waves on the sea surface are known as tides. Tides have wavelengths of thousands of kilometers. They differ from other wave types in that they are created by slow and very small changes in gravity due to the motion of the Sun and the Moon relative to Earth.

Tsunamis

Seismic sea waves or tsunamis (sometimes mistakenly called tidal waves) are formed by seismic activity. A tsunami is a series of waves with long wavelengths and long periods. Far out at sea, the heights of these waves are typically less than one meter. The wavelength may be 100 km and the wave period may range from five minutes to one hour. However, as seismic sea waves approach the shoreline, the bottom of the wave is slowed down by the shallower sea floor. The top is not slowed as much, and wave height increases to as much as 20 meters. These waves can hit the shore at speeds of up to 30 miles per hour. Tsunamis are caused by earthquakes, submarine landslides, and volcanic eruptions.

Beaufort wind scale

The Beaufort wind scale assigns a numerical value to wind conditions and the appearance of the sea. Zero represents a calm, mirror-like sea with no measurable wind. Twelve is the maximum on the Beaufort scale, and represents hurricane force winds with speeds of 35.2 meters per second (m/s). Visibility is greatly reduced, the sea air is filled with foam, and the sea is completely white with driving spray. The scale is as follows: 1 is light wind with a speed of 1.2 m/s; 2 is a light breeze of 2.8 m/s; 3 is a gentle breeze of 4.9 m/s; 4 is a moderate breeze of 7.7 m/s; and 5 is a fresh breeze of 10.5 m/s. At 5, there are moderate waves, many white caps, and some spray. Six is a strong breeze of 13.1 m/s; 7 is a near gale with wind speeds of 15.8 m/s; 8 is gale force winds of 18.8 m/s; 9 is strong gales of 22.1 m/s; 10 is considered a storm with wind speeds of 25.9 m/s; and 11 is a violent storm.

Shoreline

The area where land meets the sea is called the shoreline. This marks the average position of the ocean. Longshore currents create longshore drift or transport (also called beach drift). This is when ocean waves move toward a beach at an angle, which moves water along the coast. Sediment is eroded from some areas and deposited in others. In this way, it is moved along the beach. Rip currents are strong, fast currents that occur when part of longshore current moves away from the beach. Hard, man-made structures built perpendicular to the beach tend to trap sand on the up-current side. Erosion occurs on the down-current side. Features formed by the sediment deposited by waves include spits, bay-mouth bars, tombolos, barrier islands, and buildups. Sand is composed of weather-resistant, granular materials like quartz and orthoclase. In some locations, it is composed of rock and basalt.

Tides

The gravitational pull of the Sun and Moon causes the oceans to rise and fall each day, creating high and low tides. Most areas have two high tides and two low tides per day. Because the Moon is closer to the Earth than the Sun, its gravitational pull is much greater. The water on the side of the Earth that is closest to the Moon and the water on the opposite side experience high tide. The two low tides occur on the other sides. This changes as the Moon revolves around the Earth. Tidal range is the measurement of the height difference between low and high tide. Tidal range also changes with the location of the Sun and Moon throughout the year, creating spring and neap tides. When all these bodies are aligned, the combined gravitational pull is greater and the tidal range is also greater. This is what creates the spring tide. The neap tide is when the tidal range is at its lowest, which occurs when the Sun and Moon are not at right angles.

Black smokers

Black smokers are a relatively recently discovered feature of the ocean floor. They were first identified in 1977. A black smoker is a type of hydrothermal vent formed when superheated water from below Earth's crust emerges from the ocean floor. This hot water is also rich in sulfides and other minerals from the Earth's crust. When the hot water comes in contact with the cold ocean water, it creates a black chimney-like structure around the vent. Water temperatures around black smokers have been recorded at 400°C. However, water pressure is too great on the sea floor to allow for boiling. The water is also very acidic (twice that of vinegar). It is estimated that the yearly volume of water passing through black smokers is 1.4×10^{14} kg.

Carbon cycle

The carbon and nutrient cycles of the ocean are processes that are due in part to the deep currents, mixing, and upwelling that occur in the ocean. Carbon dioxide (CO_2) from the atmosphere is dissolved into the ocean at higher latitudes and distributed to the denser deep water. Where upwelling occurs, CO_2 is brought back to the surface and emitted into the tropical air. Phytoplankton are typically single-celled organisms that are nourished by the Sun. They are photosynthetic autotrophs, meaning they convert water, carbon dioxide, and solar energy into food. They drift with the currents, produce oxygen as a byproduct, and serve as a food source. Zooplankton feed on phytoplankton. Zooplankton are heterotrophic organisms, meaning they do not synthesize their own food. Zooplankton can be single-celled creatures or much larger organisms, such as jellyfish, mollusks, and crustaceans.

El Niño-Southern Oscillation (ENSO)

The El Niño-Southern Oscillation (ENSO) is a climate pattern of the Pacific Ocean area that lasts 6 to 18 months and causes weather that is different from the expected seasonal patterns and variations. There are two sets of events associated with ENSO: El Niño and La Niña. The usual weather patterns for the Pacific Ocean involve the movement of sea water by winds from the eastern part of the tropical Pacific to the western part of the Pacific Ocean. This pattern causes cold deep water upwells in the eastern Pacific. This creates wet weather and is considered a low-pressure system. Conversely, the eastern Pacific is a dry, high-pressure system. El Niño weakens upwelling because equalization in air pressure leads to less wind, which leads to more water staying in the eastern Pacific. La Niña increases upwelling because winds grow stronger because of higher air pressures across the Pacific. Both El Niño and La Niña cause extreme weather events such as droughts, heavy rain, and flooding.

Rift valley

Rift valleys occur both on land and in the ocean. They are a result of plate tectonics, and occur when plates are spreading apart. In the ocean, this is part of the crust development cycle in which new crust is created at mid-ocean ridges and old crust is lost at the trenches. The Mid-Atlantic Ridge is an example of this. It occurs at divergent Eurasian and North American plates and in the South Atlantic, African, and South American plates. The East Pacific Rise is also a mid-oceanic ridge. The most extensive rift valley is located along the crest of the mid-ocean ridge system. It is a result of sea floor spreading.

Beaches

Weathering erodes the parent material of beaches, rock and soil, into sand, which is typically quartz. Other parts of the soil such as clay and silt are deposited in areas of the continental shelf. The larger sand particles get deposited in the form of a beach. This includes a near shore, which is underwater, a fore shore, the area typically considered the beach, and a back shore. The offshore starts about 5 meters from the shoreline and extends to about 20 meters. The beach also includes wet and dry parts and a fore dune and rear dune. Waves typically move sand from the sea to the beach, and gravity and wave action move it back again. Wind gradually pushes sand particles uphill in a jumping motion called saltation. Sand stays deposited in the form of dunes and the dunes appear as if they roll backward. Storms can both erode a beach and provide additional deposition.

North Atlantic Oscillation (NAO)

The North Atlantic Oscillation is a climatic occurrence that affects winter weather in the Northern Hemisphere, particularly in the east coast regions of the United States, Europe, and North Africa. Atmospheric pressure over the North Atlantic caused by the Icelandic Low and the high pressure Azores leads to the North Atlantic Oscillation. There is both a "positive" and "negative" phase of the NAO. The positive phase is when strong winds caused by a large difference in air pressure send wet winter storms from eastern North America to northern Europe. Weaker winds associated with a smaller difference in air pressure cause eastern North America and northern Europe to have fewer winter storms. Instead, the weather is rainy in southern Europe and North Africa.

Weather, climate, and meteorology

Meteorology is the study of the atmosphere, particularly as it pertains to forecasting the weather and understanding its processes. Weather is the condition of the atmosphere at any given moment. Most weather occurs in the troposphere. Weather includes changing events such as clouds, storms, and temperature, as well as more extreme events such as tornadoes, hurricanes, and blizzards. Climate refers to the average weather for a particular area over time, typically at least 30 years. Latitude is an indicator of climate. Changes in climate occur over long time periods.

Weather phenomena

Common atmospheric conditions that are frequently measured are temperature, precipitation, wind, and humidity. These weather conditions are often measured at permanently fixed weather stations so weather data can be collected and compared over time and by region. Measurements may also be taken by ships, buoys, and underwater instruments. Measurements may also be taken under special circumstances. The measurements taken include temperature, barometric pressure, humidity, wind speed, wind direction, and precipitation. Usually, the following instruments are used: A thermometer is used for measuring temperature; a barometer is used for measuring barometric/air pressure; a hygrometer is used for measuring humidity; an anemometer is used for measuring wind speed; a weather vane is used for measuring wind direction; and a rain gauge is used for measuring precipitation.

Latitudinal variation of solar radiation

Latitude is a measurement of the distance from the equator. The distance from the equator indicates how much solar radiation a particular area receives. The equator receives more sunlight, while polar areas receive less. The Earth tilts slightly on its rotational axis. This tilt determines the seasons and affects weather. There are eight biomes or ecosystems with particular climates that are associated with latitude. Those in the high latitudes, which get the least sunlight, are tundra and taiga. Those in the mid latitudes are grassland, temperate forest, and chaparral. Those in latitudes closest to the equator are the warmest. The biomes are desert and tropical rain forest. The eighth biome is the ocean, which is unique because it consists of water and spans the entire globe. Insolation refers to incoming solar radiation. Diurnal variations refer to the daily changes in insolation. The greatest insolation occurs at noon.

Tilt of the Earth

The tilt of the Earth on its axis is 23.5°. This tilt causes the seasons and affects the temperature because it affects the amount of Sun the area receives. When the Northern or Southern Hemispheres are tilted toward the Sun, the hemisphere tilted toward the sun experiences summer and the other hemisphere experiences winter. This reverses as the Earth revolves around the Sun. Fall and spring occur between the two extremes. The equator gets the same amount of sunlight every day of the year, about 12 hours, and doesn't experience seasons. Both poles have days during the winter when they are tilted away from the Sun and receive no daylight. The opposite effect occurs during the summer. There are 24 hours of daylight and no night. The summer solstice, the day with the most amount of sunlight, occurs on June 21st in the Northern Hemisphere and on December 21st in the Southern Hemisphere. The winter solstice, the day with the least amount of sunlight, occurs on December 21st in the Northern Hemisphere and on June 21st in the Southern Hemisphere.

Breezes

Sea breezes and land breezes help influence an area's prevailing winds, particularly in areas where the wind flow is light. Sea breezes, also called onshore breezes, are the result of the different capacities for absorbing heat of the ocean and the land. The sea can be warmed to a greater depth than the land. It warms up more slowly than the land's surface. Land heats air above it as its temperature increases. This heated; warmer is less dense and rises as a result. The cooler air above the sea and higher sea level pressure create a wind flow in the direction of the land. Coastal areas often receive these cooler breezes. Land cools slower at night than the ocean, and coastal breezes weaken at this time. When the land becomes so cool that it is cooler than the sea surface, the pressure over the ocean is lower than the land. This creates a land breeze. This can cause rain and thunderstorms over the ocean.

Wind

Winds are the result of air moving by convection. Masses of warm air rise, and cold air sweeps into their place. The warm air also moves, cools, and sinks. The term "prevailing wind" refers to the wind that usually blows in an area in a single direction. Dominant winds are the winds with the highest speeds. Belts or bands that run latitudinal and blow in a specific direction are associated with convection cells. Hadley cells are formed directly north and south of the equator. The Farrell cells occur at about 30° to 60°. The jet stream runs between the Farrell cells and the polar cells. At the higher and lower latitudes, the direction is easterly. At mid latitudes, the direction is westerly. From the North Pole to the south, the surface winds are Polar High Easterlies, Subpolar Low Westerlies, Subtropical High or Horse Latitudes, North-East Trade winds, Equatorial Low or Doldrums, South-East Trades, Subtropical High or Horse Latitudes, Subpolar Low Easterlies, and Polar High.

Thunderstorms

A thunderstorm is one of the many weather phenomena that can be created during the ongoing process of heat moving through Earth's atmosphere. Thunderstorms form when there is moisture to form rain clouds, unstable air, and lift. Unstable air is usually caused by warm air rising quickly through cold air. Lift can be caused by fronts, sea breezes, and elevated terrain, such as mountains. Single cell thunderstorms have one main draft. Multicell clusters have clusters of storms. Multicell lines have severe thunderstorms along a squall line. Supercell thunderstorms are large and severe, and have the capacity to produce destructive tornadoes. Thunder is a sonic shock wave caused by the rapid expansion of air around lightning. Lightning is the discharge of electricity during a thunderstorm. Lightning can also occur during volcanic eruptions or dust storms.

Atmospheric variations

Terrain affects several local atmospheric conditions, including temperature, wind speed, and wind direction. When there are land forms, heating of the ground can be greater than the heating of the surrounding air than it would be at the same altitude above sea level. This creates a thermal low in the region and amplifies any existing thermal lows. It also changes the wind circulation. Terrain such as hills and valleys increase friction between the air and the land, which disturbs the air flow. This physical block deflects the wind, and the resulting air flow is called a barrier jet. Just as the heating of the land and air affect sea and land

- 123 -

breezes along the coast, rugged terrain affects the wind circulation between mountains and valleys.

Cyclones

Cyclones generally refer to large air masses rotating in the same direction as the Earth. They are formed in low pressure areas. Cyclones vary in size. Some are mesoscale systems, which vary in size from about 5 km to hundreds of kilometers. Some are synoptic scale systems, which are about 1,000 km in size. The size of subtropical cyclones is somewhere in between. Cold-core polar and extratropical cyclones are synoptic scale systems. Warm-core tropical, polar low and mesocyclones are mesoscale systems. Extratropical cyclones, sometimes called mid-latitude cyclones or wave cyclones, occur in the middle latitudes. They have neither tropical nor polar characteristics. Extratropical cyclones are everyday phenomena which, along with anticyclones, drive the weather over much of the Earth. They can produce cloudiness, mild showers, heavy gales, and thunderstorms. Anticyclones occur when there is a descending pocket of air of higher than average pressure. Anticyclones are usually associated with clearing skies and drier, cooler air.

Tornados

During a tornado, wind speeds can be upward of 300 miles per hour. Tornados are rotating funnel-like clouds. They have a very high energy density, which means they are very destructive to a small area. They are also short-lived. About 75% of the world's tornadoes occur in the United States, mostly in an area of the Great Plains known as Tornado Alley. If there are two or more columns of air, it is referred to as a multiple vortex tornado. A satellite tornado is a weak tornado that forms near a larger one within the same mesocyclone. A waterspout is a tornado over water. The severity of tornadoes is measured using the Enhanced Fujita Scale. An EF-0 rating is associated with a 3-second wind gust between 65 and 85 miles per hour, while an EF-5 is associated with wind speeds of greater than 200 mph.

Humidity

Humidity refers to water vapor contained in the air. The amount of moisture contained in air depends upon its temperature. The higher the air temperature, the more moisture it can hold. These higher levels of moisture are associated with higher humidity. Absolute humidity refers to the total amount of moisture air is capable of holding at a certain temperature. Relative humidity is the ratio of water vapor in the air compared to the amount the air is capable of holding at its current temperature. As temperature decreases, absolute humidity stays the same and relative humidity increases. A hygrometer is a device used to measure humidity. The dew point is the temperature at which water vapor condenses into water at a particular humidity.

Hurricanes

A hurricane is one of the three weather phenomena that can occur as a result of a tropical cyclone. A tropical cyclone is a warm-core, low-pressure condition that circles in the same direction as the Earth. A tropical depression has sustained winds of up to 30 miles per hour (mph), with rotational winds around a center. A tropical storm appears more circular and has more rotation than a tropical depression. Its winds range from 39 to 73 mph. A

- 124 -

hurricane appears well-organized and sometimes has a recognizable eye with strong rotation. Its wind speed is more than 73 mph. Hurricanes are classified using the Saffir-Simpson Scale, which ranges from category 1 to category 5. A category 5 hurricane has wind speeds greater than 155 mph. Hurricanes are named alphabetically through the season starting with "A." The letters "Q," "U," and "Z" are not used. There are six lists of names that are used from year to year. The names of devastating hurricanes are retired from the list.

Precipitation

After clouds reach the dew point, precipitation occurs. Precipitation can take the form of a liquid or a solid. It is known by many names, including rain, snow, ice, dew, and frost. Liquid forms of precipitation include rain and drizzle. Rain or drizzle that freezes on contact is known as freezing rain or freezing drizzle. Solid or frozen forms of precipitation include snow, ice needles or diamond dust, sleet or ice pellets, hail, and graupel or snow pellets. Virga is a form of precipitation that evaporates before reaching the ground. It usually looks like sheets or shafts falling from a cloud. The amount of rainfall is measured with a rain gauge. Intensity can be measured according to how fast precipitation is falling or by how severely it limits visibility. Precipitation plays a major role in the water cycle since it is responsible for depositing much of the Earth's fresh water.

Heat waves

A heat wave is a stretch of hotter than normal weather. Some heat waves may involve high humidity and last longer than a week. Heat waves can form if a warm high-pressure weather system stalls in an area. The jet stream is a flow that moves air through the middle latitudes. When this shifts, it can bring a pattern of unusually warm weather into a region, creating a heat wave. Heat can be trapped by cities. If there is no rain or clouds to help cool the weather, the heat wave can linger. In humans, heat waves can lead to heat stroke, heat exhaustion, cramps, dehydration, and even death. Plants can dry up and crops can fail. There is also a greater threat of fires during a heat wave in dry areas.

Cloud types

Most clouds can be classified according to the altitude of their base above Earth's surface. High clouds occur at altitudes between 5,000 and 13,000 meters. Middle clouds occur at altitudes between 2,000 and 7,000 meters. Low clouds occur from the Earth's surface to altitudes of 2,000 meters. Types of high clouds include cirrus (Ci), thin wispy mare's tails that consist of ice; cirrocumulus (Cc), small, pillow-like puffs that often appear in rows; and cirrostratus (Cs), thin, sheetlike clouds that often cover the entire sky. Types of middle clouds include altocumulus (Ac), gray-white clouds that consist of liquid water; and altostratus (As), grayish or blue-gray clouds that span the sky. Types of low clouds include stratus (St), gray and fog-like clouds consisting of water droplets that take up the whole sky; stratocumulus (Sc), low-lying, lumpy gray clouds; and nimbostratus (Ns), dark gray clouds with uneven bases that indicate rain or snow. Two types of clouds, cumulus (Cu) and cumulonimbus (Cb), are capable of great vertical growth. They can start at a wide range of altitudes, from the Earth's surface to altitudes of 13,000 meters.

Cloud formation

Clouds form when air cools and warm air is forced to give up some of its water vapor because it can no longer hold it. This vapor condenses and forms tiny droplets of water or ice crystals called clouds. Particles, or aerosols, are needed for water vapor to form water droplets. These are called condensation nuclei. Clouds are created by surface heating, mountains and terrain, rising air masses, and weather fronts. Clouds precipitate, returning the water they contain to Earth. Clouds can also create atmospheric optics. They can scatter light, creating colorful phenomena such as rainbows, colorful sunsets, and the green flash phenomenon.

Air masses and weather fronts

Air masses are large volumes of air in the troposphere of the Earth. They are categorized by their temperature and by the amount of water vapor they contain. Arctic and Antarctic air masses are cold, polar air masses are cool, and tropical and equatorial air masses are hot. Other types of air masses include maritime and monsoon, both of which are moist and unstable. There are also continental and superior air masses, which are dry. A weather front separates two masses of air of different densities. It is the principal cause of meteorological phenomena. Air masses are quickly and easily affected by the land they are above. They can have certain characteristics, and then develop new ones when they get blown over a different area.

Nonstandard cloud types

Contrails, or condensation trails, are thin white streaks caused by jets. These are created from water vapor condensing and freezing the jet's exhaust particles. Contrails can be further classified as short-lived, persistent non-spreading, and persistent. Lenticular or lee wave, clouds are created by an air current over an obstacle, such as a mountain. They appear to be stationary, but are actually forming, dissipating, and reforming in the same place. Kelvin-Helmholtz clouds are formed by winds with different speeds or directions. They look like ocean waves. Mammatus clouds hang down from the base of a cloud, usually a cumulonimbus cloud. They often occur during the warmer months.

Pressure systems

The concept of atmospheric pressure involves the idea that air exerts a force. An imaginary column of air 1 square inch in size rising through the atmosphere would exert a force of 14.7 pounds per square inch (psi). Both temperature and altitude affect atmospheric pressure. Low and high pressure systems tend to want to equalize. Air tends to move from areas of high pressure to areas of low pressure. When air moves into a low pressure system, the air that was there gets pushed up, creating lower temperatures and pressures. Water vapor condenses and forms clouds and possibly rain and snow. A barometer is used to measure air pressure.

Bergeron system

The Bergeron classification system uses three sets of letters to identify the following characteristics of air masses: moisture content, thermal characteristics from where they originated, and the stability of the atmosphere. The first, moisture content, uses the following letters: "c" represents the dry continental air masses and "m" stands for the moist maritime air masses. The second set of abbreviations are as follows: "T" indicates the air mass is tropical in origin; "P" indicates the air mass is polar in origin; "A" indicates the air mass is Antarctic in origin; "M" stands for monsoon; "E" indicates the air mass is equatorial in origin; and "S" is used to represent superior air, which is dry air formed by a downward motion. The last set of symbols provides an indicator of the stability of the mass. "K" indicates the mass is colder than the ground below it, while "w" indicates the mass is warmer than the ground. For example, cP is a continental polar air mass, while cPk is a polar air mass blowing over the Gulf Stream, which is warmer than the mass.

Frontal systems

A cold front is a mass of cold air, usually fast moving and dense, that moves into a warm air front, producing clouds. This often produces a temperature drop and rain, hail (frozen rain), thunder, and lightning. A warm front is pushed up by a fast moving cold front. It is often associated with high wispy clouds, such as cirrus and cirrostratus clouds. A stationary front forms when a warm and cold front meet, but neither is strong enough to move the other. Winds blowing parallel to the fronts keep the front stationary. The front may remain in the same place for days until the wind direction changes and both fronts become a single warm or cold front. In other cases, the entire front dissipates. An occluded front is when a cold front pushes into a warm front. The warm air rises and the two masses of cool air join. These types of fronts often occur in areas of low atmospheric pressure.

Weather fronts and maps

A weather front is the area between two differing masses of air that affects weather. Frontal movements are influenced by the jet stream and other high winds. Movements are determined by the type of front. Cold fronts move up to twice as fast as warm ones. It is in the turbulent frontal area that commonplace and dramatic weather events take place. This area also creates temperature changes. Weather phenomena include rain, thunderstorms, high winds, tornadoes, cloudiness, clear skies, and hurricanes. Different fronts can be plotted on weather maps using a set of designated symbols. Surface weather maps can also include symbols representing clouds, rain, temperature, air pressure, and fair weather.

Cold fronts are represented on weather maps as a blue line. Solid blue triangles are used to indicate the direction of movement. Warm fronts are represented with a red line. Solid red semi-circles are used to indicate the direction of the front. The cold and warm front symbols are merged and alternated to point in opposite directions to indicate a stationary front. An occluded front is represented by a purple line with alternating solid purple triangles and semi-circles. A surface trough is represented by an orange dashed line. A squall or shear line is represented by a red line. Two dots and a dash are alternated to form the line. A dry line is represented by an orange line with semi-circles in outline form. A tropical wave is represented by a straight orange line. An "L" is used to indicate an area of low atmospheric pressure and an "H" is used to indicate an area of high atmospheric pressure.

Weather phenomena

Shearline: This evolves from a stationary front that has gotten smaller. Wind direction shifts over a short distance.

Dry line or dew point line: This separates two warm air masses of differing moisture content. At lower altitudes, the moist air mass wedges under the drier air. At higher altitudes, the dry air wedges under the moist air. This is a frequent occurrence in the Midwest and Canada, where the dry air of the Southwest and the moister air of the Gulf of Mexico meet. This can lead to extreme weather events, including tornadoes and thunderstorms.

Squall line: Severe thunderstorms can form at the front of or ahead of a cold front. In some cases, severe thunderstorms can also outrun cold fronts. A squall line can produce extreme weather in the form of heavy rain, hail, lightning, strong winds, tornadoes, and waterspouts.

Tropical waves or easterly waves: These are atmospheric troughs or areas of low air pressure that travel westward in the tropics, causing clouds and thunderstorms.

Astronomy

Astronomy is the scientific study of celestial objects and their positions, movements, and structures. Celestial does not refer to the Earth in particular, but does include its motions as it moves through space. Other objects include the Sun, the Moon, planets, satellites, asteroids, meteors, comets, stars, galaxies, the universe, and other space phenomena. The term astronomy has its roots in the Greek words "astro" and "nomos," which means "laws of the stars."

Weather forecasting

Short and long-term weather forecasting is important because the day-to-day weather greatly affects humans and human activity. Severe weather and natural events can cause devastating harm to humans, property, and sources of livelihood, such as crops. The persistence method of forecasting can be used to create both short and long-term forecasts in areas that change very little or change slowly. It assumes that the weather tomorrow will be similar to the weather today. Barometric pressure is measured because a change in air pressure can indicate the arrival of a cold front that could lead to precipitation. Long-term forecasts based on climate data are useful to help people prepare for seasonal changes and severe events such as hurricanes.

Universe structure

What can be seen of the universe is believed to be at least 93 billion light years across. To put this into perspective, the Milky Way galaxy is about 100,000 light years across. Our view of matter in the universe is that it forms into clumps. Matter is organized into stars, galaxies, clusters of galaxies, superclusters, and the Great Wall of galaxies. Galaxies consist of stars, some with planetary systems. Some estimates state that the universe is about 13 billion years old. It is not considered dense, and is believed to consist of 73 percent dark energy, 23 percent cold dark matter, and 4 percent regular matter. Cosmology is the study of the universe. Interstellar medium (ISM) is the gas and dust in the interstellar space between a galaxy's stars.

Universe origin

The universe can be said to consist of everything and nothing. The universe is the source of everything we know about space, matter, energy, and time. There are likely still phenomena that have yet to be discovered. The universe can also be thought of as nothing, since a vast portion of the known universe is empty space. It is believed that the universe is expanding. The Big Bang theory, which is widely accepted among astronomers, was developed to explain the origin of the universe. There are other theories regarding the origin of the universe, such as the Steady-State theory and the Creationist theory. The Big Bang theory states that all the matter in the universe was once in one place. This matter underwent a huge explosion that spread the matter into space. Galaxies formed from this material and the universe is still expanding.

Stars

Black hole: A black hole is a space where the gravitational field is so powerful that everything, including light, is pulled into it. Once objects enter the surface, the event horizon, they cannot escape.

Quasar: Quasar stands for quasi-stellar radio source, which is an energetic galaxy with an active galactic nucleus. Quasars were first identified by their emissions of large amounts of electromagnetic energy, such as radio waves and visible light. These emissions differed from those associated with other galaxies.

Blazar: A blazar is a very violent phenomenon in galaxies with supermassive black holes.

Dark matter: Although its existence has not yet been proven, dark matter may account for a large proportion of the universe's mass. It is undetectable because it does not emit any radiation, but is believed to exist because of gravitational forces exerted on visible objects.

Galaxies

Galaxies consist of stars, stellar remnants, and dark matter. Dwarf galaxies contain as few as 10 million stars, while giant galaxies contain as many as 1 trillion stars. Galaxies are gravitationally bound, meaning the stars, star systems, other gases, and dust orbits the galaxy's center. The Earth exists in the Milky Way galaxy and the nearest galaxy to ours is the Andromeda galaxy. Galaxies can be classified by their visual shape into elliptical, spiral, irregular, and starburst galaxies. It is estimated that there are more than 100 billion galaxies in the universe ranging from 1,000 to 100,000 parsecs in diameter. Galaxies can be megaparsecs apart. Intergalactic space consists of a gas with an average density of less than one atom per cubic meter. Galaxies are organized into clusters which form superclusters. Dark matter may account for up to 90% of the mass of galaxies. Dark matter is still not well understood.

Time measurements

A sidereal day is four minutes shorter than a solar day. A solar day is the time it takes the Earth to complete one revolution and face the Sun again. From noon to noon is 24 hours. A sidereal day is measured against a distant "fixed" star. As the Earth completes one rotation, it has also completed part of its revolution around the Sun, so it completes a sidereal rotation in reference to the fixed star before it completes a solar rotation. The Sun travels along the ecliptic in 365.25 days. This can be tracked day after day before dawn. After one year, the stars appear back in their original positions. As a result, different constellations are viewable at different times of the year. Sidereal years are slightly longer than tropical years. The difference is caused by the precession of the equinoxes. A calendar based on the sidereal year will be out of sync with the seasons at a rate of about one day every 71 years.

Large units of distance

An astronomical unit, also known as AU, is a widely used measurement in astronomy. One AU is equal to the distance from the Earth to the Sun, which is 150 million km, or 93 million miles. These distances can also be expressed as 149.60×10^9 m or 92.956×10^6 mi. A light year (ly) is the distance that light travels in a vacuum in one year. A light year is equal to about 10 trillion km, or 64,341 AU, and is used to measure large astronomical units. Also used for measuring large distances is the parsec (pc), which is the preferred unit since it is better suited for recording observational data. A parsec is the parallax of one arcsecond, and is about 31 trillion km (about 19 trillion miles), or about 3.26 light years. It is used to calculate distances by triangulation. The AU distance from the Earth to the Sun is used to form the side of a right triangle.

Star life cycle

There are different life cycle possibilities for stars after they initially form and enter into the main sequence stage. Small, relatively cold red dwarfs with relatively low masses burn hydrogen slowly, and will remain in the main sequence for hundreds of billions of years. Massive, hot supergiants will leave the main sequence after just a few million years. The Sun is a mid-sized star that may be in the main sequence for 10 billion years. After the main sequence, the star expands to become a red giant. Depending upon the initial mass of the star, it can become a black dwarf (from a medium-sized star), and then a small, cooling white dwarf. Massive stars become red supergiants (and sometimes blue supergiants), explode in a supernova, and then become neutron stars. The largest stars can become black holes.

Star birth

A nebula is a cloud of dust and gas that is composed primarily of hydrogen (97%) and helium (3%). Gravity causes parts of the nebula to clump together. This accretion continues adding atoms to the center of an unstable protostar. Equilibrium between gravity pulling atoms and gas pressure pushing heat and light away from the center is achieved. A star dies when it is no longer able to maintain equilibrium. A protostar may never become a star if it does not reach a critical core temperature. It may become a brown dwarf or a gas giant instead. If nuclear fusion of hydrogen into helium begins, a star is born. The "main sequence" of a star's life involves nuclear fusion reactions. During this time, the star contracts over billions of years to compensate for the heat and light energy lost. In the star's core, temperature, density, and pressure increase as the star contracts and the cycle continues.

Hertzsprung-Russell diagram

A Hertzsprung-Russell diagram (H-R diagram or HRD) is a plot or scattergraph depicting stars' temperatures and comparing them with stars' luminosities or magnitudes. This can help determine the age and evolutionary state of a star. A Hertzsprung-Russell diagram is also known as a color-magnitude diagram (CMD). It helps represent the life cycles of stars. In these plots, temperatures are plotted from highest to lowest, which aids in the comparison of H-R diagrams and observations. Hertzsprung-Russell diagrams can have many variations. Most of the stars in these diagrams lie along the line called main sequence, which contains stars that are fusing hydrogen. Other groupings include white dwarfs, subgiants, giants, and supergiants.

Spectral classification

Stars use the Morgan-Keenan classification system, which is based on spectral traits that indicate the ionization of the chromosphere. The following letter designations are used to indicate temperature, from hottest to coolest: O, B, A, F, G, K, and M. The phrase "Oh, be a fine girl/guy, kiss me" can be used as a memory aid. Different types of stars also have different corresponding colors. O stars are blue; A stars are white; G stars are yellow; and M stars are red. The numbers 0 to 9 are used to indicate tenths between two star classes. Zero indicates 0/10 and 9 indicates 9/10. Luminosity output is an indicator of size, and is expressed with the Roman numerals I, II, III, IV, and V. Supergiants are included in class I, giants are included in class III, and main sequence stars are included in class V. Using the Sun as an example, the spectral type G2V could be expressed as "a yellow two-tenths towards an orange main sequence star."

Sun

The Sun is at the center of the solar system. It is composed of 70% hydrogen (H) and 28% helium (He). The remaining 2% is made up of metals. The Sun is one of 100 billion stars in the Milky Way galaxy. Its diameter is 1,390,000 km, its mass is 1.989×10^{30} kg, its surface temperature is 5,800 K, and its core temperature is 15,600,000 K. The Sun represents more than 99.8% of the total mass of the solar system. At the core, the temperature is 15.6 million K, the pressure is 250 billion atmospheres, and the density is more than 150 times that of water. The surface is called the photosphere. The chromosphere lies above this, and the corona, which extends millions of kilometers into space, is next. Sunspots are relatively cool regions on the surface with a temperature of 3,800 K. Temperatures in the corona are over 1,000,000 K. Its magnetosphere, or heliosphere, extends far beyond Pluto.

Solar system formation

A planetary system consists of the various non-stellar objects orbiting a star, such as planets, dwarf planets, moons, asteroids, meteoroids, comets, and cosmic dust. The Sun, together with its planetary system, which includes Earth, is known as the solar system. The theory of how the solar system was created is that it started with the collapse of a cloud of interstellar gas and dust, which formed the solar nebula. This collapse is believed to have occurred because the cloud was disturbed. As it collapsed, it heated up and compressed at the center, forming a flatter protoplanetary disk with a protostar at the center. Planets formed as a result of accretion from the disk. Gas cooled and condensed into tiny particles of rock, metal, and ice. These particles collided and formed into larger particles, and then into object the size of small asteroids. Eventually, some became large enough to have significant gravity.

Solar system components

The solar system is a planetary system of objects that exist in an ecliptic plane. Objects orbit around and are bound by gravity to a star called the Sun. Objects that orbit around the Sun include: planets, dwarf planets, moons, asteroids, meteoroids, cosmic dust, and comets. The definition of planets has changed. At one time, there were nine planets in the solar system. There are now eight. Planetary objects in the solar system include four inner, terrestrial planets: Mercury, Venus, Earth, and Mars. They are relatively small, dense, rocky, lack rings, and have few or no moons. The four outer, or Jovian, planets are Jupiter, Saturn, Uranus, and Neptune, which are large and have low densities, rings, and moons. They are also known as gas giants. Between the inner and outer planets is the asteroid belt. Beyond Neptune is the Kuiper belt. Within these belts are five dwarf planets: Ceres, Pluto, Haumea, Makemake, and Eris.

Sun's energy

The Sun's energy is produced by nuclear fusion reactions. Each second, about 700,000,000 tons of hydrogen are converted (or fused) to about 695,000,000 tons of helium and 5,000,000 tons of energy in the form of gamma rays. In nuclear fusion, four hydrogen nuclei are fused into one helium nucleus, resulting in the release of energy. In the Sun, the energy proceeds towards the surface and is absorbed and re-emitted at lower and lower temperatures. Energy is mostly in the form of visible light when it reaches the surface. It is estimated that the Sun has used up about half of the hydrogen at its core since its birth. It is expected to radiate in this fashion for another 5 billion years. Eventually, it will deplete its hydrogen fuel, grow brighter, expand to about 260 times its diameter, and become a red giant. The outer layers will ablate and become a dense white dwarf the size of the Earth.

Inner terrestrial planets

Mercury: Mercury is the closest to the Sun and is also the smallest planet. It orbits the Sun every 88 days, has no satellites or atmosphere, has a Moon-like surface with craters, appears bright, and is dense and rocky with a large iron core.

Venus: Venus is the second planet from the Sun. It orbits the Sun every 225 days, is very bright, and is similar to Earth in size, gravity, and bulk composition. It has a dense atmosphere composed of carbon dioxide and some sulfur. It is covered with reflective clouds made of sulfuric acid and exhibits signs of volcanism. Lightning and thunder have been recorded on Venus's surface.

Earth: Earth is the third planet from the Sun. It orbits the Sun every 365 days. Approximately 71% of its surface is salt-water oceans. The Earth is rocky, has an atmosphere composed mainly of oxygen and nitrogen, has one moon, and supports millions of species. It contains the only known life in the solar system.

Mars: Mars it the fourth planet from the Sun. It appears reddish due to iron oxide on the surface, has a thin atmosphere, has a rotational period similar to Earth's, and has seasonal cycles. Surface features of Mars include volcanoes, valleys, deserts, and polar ice caps. Mars has impact craters and the tallest mountain, largest canyon, and perhaps the largest impact crater yet discovered.

Solar system size

The Earth is about 12,765 km (7,934 miles) in diameter. The Moon is about 3,476 km (2,160 mi) in diameter. The distance between the Earth and the Moon is about 384,401 km (238,910 mi). The diameter of the Sun is approximately 1,390,000 km (866,000 mi). The distance from the Earth to the Sun is 149,598,000 km, also known as 1 Astronomical Unit (AU). The star that is nearest to the solar system is Proxima Centauri. It is about 270,000 AU away. Some distant galaxies are so far away that their light takes several billion years to reach the Earth. In other words, people on Earth see them as they looked billions of years ago.

Oort Cloud, asteroid belt, and Kuiper Belt.

The asteroid belt is between Mars and Jupiter. The many objects contained within are composed of rock and metal similar to those found on the terrestrial planets. The Kuiper Belt is beyond Neptune's orbit, but the influence of the gas giants may cause objects from the Kuiper Belt to cross Neptune's orbit. Objects in the Kuiper Belt are still being discovered. They are thought to be composed of the frozen forms of water, ammonia, and methane, and may be the source of short-period comets. It is estimated that there are 35,000 Kuiper Belt objects greater than 100 km in diameter and perhaps 100 million objects about 20 km in diameter. There is also a hypothetical Oort Cloud that may exist far beyond the Kuiper Belt and act as a source for long-period comets.

Outer planets

Jupiter: Jupiter is the fifth planet from the Sun and the largest planet in the solar system. It consists mainly of hydrogen, and 25% of its mass is made up of helium. It has a fast rotation and has clouds in the tropopause composed of ammonia crystals that are arranged into bands sub-divided into lighter-hued zones and darker belts causing storms and turbulence. Jupiter has wind speeds of 100 m/s, a planetary ring, 63 moons, and a Great Red Spot, which is an anticyclonic storm.

Saturn: Saturn is the sixth planet from the Sun and the second largest planet in the solar system. It is composed of hydrogen, some helium, and trace elements. Saturn has a small core of rock and ice, a thick layer of metallic hydrogen, a gaseous outer layer, wind speeds of up to 1,800 km/h, a system of rings, and 61 moons.

Uranus: Uranus is the seventh planet from the Sun. Its atmosphere is composed mainly of hydrogen and helium, and also contains water, ammonia, methane, and traces of hydrocarbons. With a minimum temperature of 49 K, Uranus has the coldest atmosphere. Uranus has a ring system, a magnetosphere, and 13 moons.

Neptune: Neptune is the eighth planet from the Sun and is the planet with the third largest mass. It has 12 moons, an atmosphere similar to Uranus, a Great Dark Spot, and the strongest sustained winds of any planet (wind speeds can be as high as 2,100 km/h). Neptune is cold (about 55 K) and has a fragmented ring system.

Meteors, meteoroids, and meteorites

A meteoroid is the name for a rock from space before it enters the Earth's atmosphere. Most meteoroids burn up in the atmosphere before reaching altitudes of 80 km. A meteor is the streak of light from a meteoroid in the Earth's atmosphere, and is also known as a shooting star. Meteor showers are associated with comets, happen when the Earth passes through the debris of a comet, and are associated with a higher than normal number of meteors. Meteorites are rocks that reach the Earth's surface from space. Fireballs are very bright meteors with trails that can last as long as 30 minutes. A bolide is a fireball that burns up when it enters Earth's atmosphere. There are many types of meteorites, and they are known to be composed of various materials. Iron meteorites consist of iron and nickel with a criss-cross, or Widmanstatten, internal metallic crystalline structure. Stony iron meteorites are composed of iron, nickel, and silicate materials. Stony meteorites consist mainly of silicate and also contain iron and nickel.

Comets

A comet consists of frozen gases and rocky and metallic materials. Comets are usually small and typically have long tails. A comet's tail is made of ionized gases. It points away from the Sun and follows the comet as it approaches the Sun. The tail precedes the head as the comet moves away from the Sun. It is believed that as many as 100 billion comets exist. About 12 new ones are discovered each year. Their orbits are elliptical, not round. Some scientists theorize that short-period comets originate from the Kuiper Belt and long-period comets originate from the Oort Cloud, which is thought to be 100,000 AU away. Comets orbit the Sun in time periods varying from a few years to hundreds of thousands of years. A well-known comet, Halley's Comet, has an orbit of 76 years. It is 80 percent water, and consists of frozen water, carbon dioxide (dry ice), ammonia, and methane.

Earth-Moon-Sun system

The Earth-Moon-Sun system is responsible for eclipses. From Earth, the Sun and the Moon appear to be about the same size. An eclipse of the Sun occurs during a new Moon, when the side of the Moon facing the Earth is not illuminated. The Moon passes in front of the Sun and blocks its view from Earth. Eclipses do not occur every month because the orbit of the Moon is at about a 5° angle to the plane of Earth's orbit. An eclipse of the Moon happens during the full Moon phase. The Moon passes through the shadow of the Earth and blocks sunlight from reaching it, which temporarily causes darkness. During a lunar eclipse, there are two parts to the shadow. The umbra is the dark, inner region. The sun is completely blocked in this area. The penumbra is a partially lighted area around the umbra. Earth's shadow is four times longer than the Moon's shadow.

Natural satellites

There are about 335 moons, or satellites, that orbit the planets and objects in the solar system. Many of these satellites have been recently discovered, a few are theoretical, some are asteroid moons (moons orbiting asteroids), some are moonlets (small moons), and some are moons of dwarf planets and objects that have not been definitively categorized, such as trans-Neptunian objects. Mercury and Venus do not have any moons. There are several moons larger than the dwarf planet Pluto and two larger than Mercury. Some consider the Earth and Moon a pair of double planets rather than a planet and a satellite. Some satellites may have started out as asteroids. They were eventually captured by a planet's gravity and became moons.

Remote sensing

Remote sensing refers to the gathering of data about an object or phenomenon without physical or intimate contact with the object being studied. The data can be viewed or recorded and stored in many forms (visually with a camera, audibly, or in the form of data). Gathering weather data from a ship, satellite, or buoy might be thought of as remote sensing. The monitoring of a fetus through the use of ultrasound technology provides a remote image. Listening to the heartbeat of a fetus is another example of remote sensing. Methods for remote sensing can be grouped as radiometric, geodetic, or acoustic. Examples of radiometric remote sensing include radar, laser altimeters, light detection and ranging (LIDAR) used to determine the concentration of chemicals in the air, and radiometers used to detect various frequencies of radiation. Geodetic remote sensing involves measuring the small fluctuations in Earth's gravitational field. Examples of acoustic remote sensing include underwater sonar and seismographs.

Phases of the Moon

It takes about one month for the Moon to go through all its phases. Waxing refers to the two weeks during which the Moon goes from a new moon to a full moon. About two weeks is spent waning, going from a full moon to a new moon. The lit part of the Moon always faces the Sun. The phases of waxing are: new moon, during which the Moon is not illuminated and rises and sets with the Sun; crescent moon, during which a tiny sliver is lit; first quarter, during which half the Moon is lit and the phase of the Moon is due south on the meridian; gibbous, during which more than half of the Moon is lit and has a shape similar to a football; right side, during which the Moon is lit; and full moon, during which the Moon is fully illuminated, rises at sunset, and sets at sunrise. After a full moon, the Moon is waning. The phases of waning are: gibbous, during which the left side is lit and the Moon rises after sunset and sets after sunrise; third quarter, during which the Moon is half lit and rises at midnight and sets at noon; crescent, during which a tiny sliver is lit; and new moon, during which the Moon is not illuminated and rises and sets with the Sun.

Tropic of Cancer, Tropic of Capricorn; Antarctic and Arctic Circles

Tropic of Cancer: This is located at 23.5 degrees north. The Sun is directly overhead at noon on June 21st in the Tropic of Cancer, which marks the beginning of summer in the Northern Hemisphere.

Tropic of Capricorn: This is located at 23.5 degrees south. The Sun is directly overhead at noon on December 21st in the Tropic of Capricorn, which marks the beginning of winter in the Northern Hemisphere.

Arctic Circle: This is located at 66.5 degrees north, and marks the start of when the Sun is not visible above the horizon. This occurs on December 21st, the same day the Sun is directly over the Tropic of Capricorn.

Antarctic Circle: This is located at 66.5 degrees south, and marks the start of when the Sun is not visible above the horizon. This occurs on June 21st, which marks the beginning of winter in the Southern Hemisphere and is when the Sun is directly over the Tropic of Cancer.

Latitude, longitude, and equator

For the purposes of tracking time and location, the Earth is divided into sections with imaginary lines. Lines that run vertically around the globe through the poles are lines of longitude, sometimes called meridians. The Prime Meridian is the longitudinal reference point of 0. Longitude is measured in 15-degree increments toward the east or west. Degrees are further divided into 60 minutes, and each minute is divided into 60 seconds. Lines of latitude run horizontally around the Earth parallel to the equator, which is the 0 reference point and the widest point of the Earth. Latitude is the distance north or south from the equator, and is also measured in degrees, minutes, and seconds.

Geosynchronous and geostationary orbits

A geosynchronous orbit around the Earth has an orbital period matching the Earth's sidereal rotation period. Sidereal rotation is based on the position of a fixed star, not the Sun, so a sidereal day is slightly shorter than a 24-hour solar day. A satellite in a geosynchronous orbit appears in the same place in the sky at the same time each day. Technically, any object with an orbit time period equal to the Earth's rotational period is geosynchronous. A geostationary orbit is a geosynchronous orbit that is circular and at zero inclination, which means the object is located directly above the equator. Geostationary orbits are useful for communications satellites because they are fixed in the same spot relative to the Earth. A semisynchronous orbit has an orbital period of half a sidereal day.

Equinox, solstice, perihelion, and aphelion

Equinox: This occurs twice each year when the Sun crosses the plane of the Earth's celestial equator. During an equinox, Earth is not tilted away from or towards the Sun. The length of day and night are roughly equal. The two equinoxes are the March equinox and the September equinox.

Solstice: The summer solstice, the day with the most amount of sunlight, occurs on June 21st in the Northern Hemisphere and on December 21st in the Southern Hemisphere. The winter solstice, the day with the least amount of sunlight, occurs on December 21st in the Northern Hemisphere and on June 21st in the Southern Hemisphere.

Perihelion: This is the point in an object's orbit when it is closest to the Sun.

Aphelion: This is the point in an object's orbit when it is farthest from the Sun.

Piloted space missions

The Soviet space program successfully completed the first space flight by orbiting Yuri Gagarin in 1961 on Vostok 1. His orbit lasted 1 hour, 48 minutes. Later in 1961, the U.S. completed its first piloted space flight by launching Alan Shepard into space in the Mercury-Redstone 3. This space mission was suborbital. The first woman in space was Valentina Tereshkova, who orbited the Earth 48 times aboard Vostok 6 in 1963. The first space flight with more than one person and also the first that didn't involve space suits took place on the Voskhod in 1964. The first person on the Moon was American Neil Armstrong. In 1969, he traveled to the Moon on Apollo 11, which was the 11th manned space flight completed in the Apollo program, which was conducted from 1968 to 1972. In 2003, Yang Liwei became the first person from China to go into space. He traveled onboard the Shenzhou 5. The Space Shuttle Orbiter has included piloted space shuttles from 1981 until the present. The program was suspended after two space shuttle disasters: Challenger in 1986 and Columbia in 2003.

Notable satellites

The first satellite to orbit the Earth was the Soviet Union's Sputnik 1 in 1957. Its two radio transmitters emitted beeps that were received by radios around the world. Analysis of the radio signals was used to gather information about the electron density of the ionosphere. Soviet success escalated the American space program. In 1958, the U.S. put Explorer 1 into orbit. The Osumi was the first Japanese satellite, which was put into orbit in 1970. The Vanguard 1 is the satellite that has orbited the Earth the longest. It was put into orbit in 1958 and was still in orbit in June, 2009. The Mir Space Station orbited Earth for 11 years, and was assembled in space starting in 1986. It was almost continuously occupied until 1999. The International Space Station began being assembled in orbit in 1998. At 43,000 cubic feet, it is the largest manned object sent into space. It circles the Earth every 90 minutes.

Limitations of space exploration

There are many limitations of space exploration. The main limitation is knowledge. Space exploration is currently time-consuming, dangerous, and costly. Manned and unmanned missions, even within the solar system, take years of planning and years to complete. The associated financial costs are great. Interstellar travel and intergalactic is not yet realistically feasible. Technological advances are needed before these types of missions can be carried out. By some estimates, it would take more than 70 years to travel to Proxima Centauri (the nearest star) using the fastest rocket technology available. It would take much longer using less advanced technologies. Space travel is dangerous for many reasons. Rocket fuel is highly explosive. Non-Earth environments are uninhabitable for humans. Finally, astronauts are exposed to larger than usual amounts of radiation.

Unpiloted space missions

The first artificial object to reach another space object was Luna 2. It crashed on the Moon in 1959. The first automatic landing was by Luna 9. It landed on the Moon in 1966. Mariner 2's flyby of Venus in 1962 was the first successful interplanetary flyby. Venera 7 landing on and transmitting data from Venus was the first interplanetary surface landing, which took place in 1970. The first soft landing on Mars was in 1971. Unpiloted spacecraft have also made successful soft landings on the asteroids Eros and Itokawa, as well as Titan, a moon of Saturn. The first flyby of Jupiter was in 1973 by Pioneer 10. Pioneer 10 was also the first craft of its kind to leave the solar system. The first flyby of Mercury was in 1974 by Mariner. The first flyby of Saturn was in 1979 by Pioneer 11. The first flyby of Uranus was in 1986 by Voyager 2, which also flew by Neptune in 1989.

Granite and basalt

Both granite and basalt are plentiful igneous rocks, but granite is intrusive and basalt is extrusive. Intrusive rocks come from magma within the Earth's crust and cool slowly. Extrusive rocks are formed from lava on the Earth's surface and cool more quickly than intrusive rocks. Granite is an igneous rock with a medium to coarse texture that is formed from magma. It can be a variety of colors. It is intrusive, massive, hard, and coarse grained. It forms a major part of continental crust. It can be composed of potassium feldspar, plagioclase feldspar, and quartz, as well as various amounts of muscovite, biotite, and hornblende-type amphiboles. Basalt is extrusive and usually colored gray to black. It has a fine grain due to quicker cooling. Basalt is porphyritic, meaning it contains larger crystals in a fine matrix. Basalt is usually composed of amphibole and pyroxene, and sometimes of plagioclase, feldspathoids, and olivine.

Moon facts

The Moon is the fifth largest satellite in the solar system. It orbits the Earth about every 27.3 days. The changes of the Earth, Sun, and Moon in relation to each other cause the phases of the Moon, which repeat every 29.5 days. The Moon's gravitational pull (along with the Sun's) is responsible for the tides on Earth. Its diameter is about 3,474 km and its gravity is about 17% of Earth's. The lunar maria (plural of mare) on the Moon's surface is dark thin layers composed of dark basalt. They were formed by ancient volcanoes. There are many impact craters on the Moon. There were numerous impact craters on Earth at one time, but they have been transformed by erosion
over time. Very few are still visible.

Greenhouse effect

The greenhouse effect refers to a naturally occurring and necessary process. Greenhouse gasses, which are ozone, carbon dioxide, water vapor, and methane, trap infrared radiation that is reflected toward the atmosphere. This is actually beneficial in that warm air is trapped. Without the greenhouse effect, it is estimated that the temperature on Earth would be 30 degrees less on average. The problem occurs because human activity generates more greenhouse gases than necessary. The practices that increase the amount of greenhouse gases are the burning of natural gas and oil, farming practices that result in the release of methane and nitrous oxide, factory operations that produce gases, and deforestation practices that decrease the amount of oxygen available to offset greenhouse gases. Population growth also increases the volume of gases released. Excess greenhouse gases cause more infrared radiation to become trapped, which increases the temperature at the Earth's surface.

Ecosystems

Human impacts on ecosystems take many forms and have many causes. They include widespread disruptions and specific niche disturbances. Humans practice many forms of environmental manipulation that affect plants and animals in many biomes and ecosystems. Many human practices involve the consumption of natural resources for food and energy production, the changing of the environment to produce food and energy, and the intrusion on ecosystems to provide shelter. These general behaviors include a multitude of specific behaviors, including the use and overuse of pesticides, the encroachment upon habitat, over hunting and over fishing, the introduction of plant and animal species into non-native ecosystems, not recycling, and the introduction of hazardous wastes and chemical byproducts into the environment. These behaviors have led to a number of consequences, such as acid rain, ozone depletion, deforestation, urbanization, accelerated species loss, genetic abnormalities, endocrine disruption in populations, and harm to individual animals.

Human affairs and the environment

Since the industrial revolution, science and technology has had a profound impact on human affairs. There has been a rapid increase in the number of discoveries in many fields. Many major and minor discoveries have led to a great improvement in the quality of life of many people. This includes longer life spans because of better nutrition, access to medical care, and a decrease in workplace health hazards. Not all of these problems have been solved, and many still exist in one form or another. For example, even though there are means to recycle, not every business does so because of economic factors. These advances, while improving the lives of many humans, have also taken their toll on the environment. A possible solution may arise when the carrying capacity for humans on Earth is reached. The population will decline, and solutions will have to be found. Otherwise, an immediate halt or decrease in the human behaviors that are causing environmental damage will need to happen.

Global warming

Rising temperatures may lead to an increase in sea levels as polar ice melts, lower amounts of available fresh water as coastal areas flood, species extinction because of changes in habitat, increases in certain diseases, and a decreased standard of living for humans. Less fresh water and losses of habitat for humans and other species can also lead to decreased agricultural production and food supply shortages. Increased desertification leads to habitat loss for humans and certain other species. Decreases in animal populations from losses of habitat and increased hunting by other species can lead to extinction. Increases in severe weather, such as huge sustained snowstorms, may also occur at unlikely latitudes. Even though global warming results in weather that is drier and warmer overall, it still gets cold enough to snow. There may be more moisture in the atmosphere due to evaporation. Global warming may cause the permanent loss of glaciers and permafrost. There might also be increases in air pollution and acid rain.

Waste disposal methods

Landfills: Methane (CH_4) is a greenhouse gas emitted from landfills. Some is used to generate electricity and some gets into the atmosphere. CO_2 is also emitted, and landfill gas can contain nitrogen, oxygen, water vapor, sulfur, mercury, and radioactive contaminants such as tritium. Landfill leachate contains acids from car batteries, solvents, heavy metals, pesticides, motor oil, paint, household cleaning supplies, plastics, and many other potentially harmful substances. Some of these are dangerous when they get into the ecosystem. Lead, mercury, and others are toxic.

Incinerators: These contribute to air pollution in that they can release nitric and sulfuric oxides, which cause acid rain.

Sewage: When dumped in raw form into oceans, sewage can introduce fecal contaminants and pathogenic organisms, which can harm ocean life and cause disease in humans.

Price of consumerism

The economics of capitalism and even of communism with an increased tendency to a market economy are such that economic growth and quality of living are associated with a wasteful cycle of production. Goods are produced as cheaply as possible with little or no regard for the ecological effects. The ultimate goal is profitability. The production process is wasteful, and often introduces hazardous byproducts into the environment. Furthermore, after the product (which is not necessary for survival) has been consumed, it may be dumped into a landfill instead of recycled. When consumer products get dumped in landfills, they can leach contamination into groundwater. Landfills can also leach gases. These are or have been dumping grounds for illegal substances, business and government waste, construction industry waste, and medical waste. These items also get dumped at illegal dump sites in urban and remote areas.

Ethical and moral issues

Ethical and moral concerns related to genetic engineering arise in the scientific community and in smaller communities within society. Religious and moral beliefs can conflict with the economic interests of businesses, and with research methods used by the scientific community. For example, the United States government allows genes to be patented. A company has patented the gene for breast and ovarian cancer and will only make it available to researchers for a fee. This leads to a decrease in research, a decrease in medical solutions, and possibly an increase in the occurrence of breast and ovarian cancers. The possibility of lateral or incidental discoveries as a result of research is also limited. For example, a researcher working on a genetic solution to treat breast cancer might accidentally discover a cure for prostate cancer. This, however, would not occur if the researcher could not use the patented gene in the first place.

Types of energy production

Coal-fired power plants: These generate electricity, and are the largest source of greenhouse gases, including sulfur oxides responsible for acid rain, carbon dioxide, mercury, and nitrogen oxides.

Nuclear power plants: Spent nuclear waste (fuel rods) is incredibly toxic to humans, causing burns, sickness, and hair loss at low levels. Higher levels result in death. Storage facilities tend to be placed on Native American lands and in communities of color. Dirty bombs can be made with uranium. The process of uranium mining (as well as the processes used to mine other precious metals) pollutes, introducing chemicals into the surrounding area and drastically changing its natural balance and beauty. Tailings can contaminate ground, surface, and well water. Some nuclear waste can remain harmful for billions of years. Strontium-90 is one radioactive pollutant. Other radioactive isotopes are also released. A huge amount of water is necessary for cooling.

Gasoline: The burning of gas and other fossil fuels releases carbon dioxide (a greenhouse gas) into the atmosphere.

Secret Key #1 - Time is Your Greatest Enemy

Pace Yourself

Wear a watch. At the beginning of the test, check the time (or start a chronometer on your watch to count the minutes), and check the time after every few questions to make sure you are "on schedule."

If you are forced to speed up, do it efficiently. Usually one or more answer choices can be eliminated without too much difficulty. Above all, don't panic. Don't speed up and just begin guessing at random choices. By pacing yourself, and continually monitoring your progress against your watch, you will always know exactly how far ahead or behind you are with your available time. If you find that you are one minute behind on the test, don't skip one question without spending any time on it, just to catch back up. Take 15 fewer seconds on the next four questions, and after four questions you'll have caught back up. Once you catch back up, you can continue working each problem at your normal pace.

Furthermore, don't dwell on the problems that you were rushed on. If a problem was taking up too much time and you made a hurried guess, it must be difficult. The difficult questions are the ones you are most likely to miss anyway, so it isn't a big loss. It is better to end with more time than you need than to run out of time.

Lastly, sometimes it is beneficial to slow down if you are constantly getting ahead of time. You are always more likely to catch a careless mistake by working more slowly than quickly, and among very high-scoring test takers (those who are likely to have lots of time left over), careless errors affect the score more than mastery of material.

Secret Key #2 - Guessing is not Guesswork

You probably know that guessing is a good idea - unlike other standardized tests, there is no penalty for getting a wrong answer. Even if you have no idea about a question, you still have a 20-25% chance of getting it right.

Most test takers do not understand the impact that proper guessing can have on their score. Unless you score extremely high, guessing will significantly contribute to your final score.

Monkeys Take the Test

What most test takers don't realize is that to insure that 20-25% chance, you have to guess randomly. If you put 20 monkeys in a room to take this test, assuming they answered once per question and behaved themselves, on average they would get 20-25% of the questions correct. Put 20 test takers in the room, and the average will be much lower among guessed questions. Why?

1. The test writers intentionally write deceptive answer choices that "look" right. A test taker has no idea about a question, so picks the "best looking" answer, which is often wrong. The monkey has no idea what looks good and what doesn't, so will consistently be lucky about 20-25% of the time.
2. Test takers will eliminate answer choices from the guessing pool based on a hunch or intuition. Simple but correct answers often get excluded, leaving a 0% chance of being correct. The monkey has no clue, and often gets lucky with the best choice.

This is why the process of elimination endorsed by most test courses is flawed and detrimental to your performance- test takers don't guess, they make an ignorant stab in the dark that is usually worse than random.

$5 Challenge

Let me introduce one of the most valuable ideas of this course- the $5 challenge:

You only mark your "best guess" if you are willing to bet $5 on it.
You only eliminate choices from guessing if you are willing to bet $5 on it.

Why $5? Five dollars is an amount of money that is small yet not insignificant, and can really add up fast (20 questions could cost you $100). Likewise, each answer choice on one question of the test will have a small impact on your overall score, but it can really add up to a lot of points in the end.

The process of elimination IS valuable. The following shows your chance of guessing it right:

If you eliminate wrong answer choices until only this many remain:	Chance of getting it correct:
1	100%
2	50%
3	33%

However, if you accidentally eliminate the right answer or go on a hunch for an incorrect answer, your chances drop dramatically: to 0%. By guessing among all the answer choices, you are GUARANTEED to have a shot at the right answer.
That's why the $5 test is so valuable- if you give up the advantage and safety of a pure guess, it had better be worth the risk.

What we still haven't covered is how to be sure that whatever guess you make is truly random. Here's the easiest way:

Always pick the first answer choice among those remaining.

Such a technique means that you have decided, **before you see a single test question**, exactly how you are going to guess- and since the order of choices tells you nothing about which one is correct, this guessing technique is perfectly random.

This section is not meant to scare you away from making educated guesses or eliminating choices- you just need to define when a choice is worth eliminating. The $5 test, along with a pre-defined random guessing strategy, is the best way to make sure you reap all of the benefits of guessing.

Secret Key #3 - Practice Smarter, Not Harder

Many test takers delay the test preparation process because they dread the awful amounts of practice time they think necessary to succeed on the test. We have refined an effective method that will take you only a fraction of the time.

There are a number of "obstacles" in your way to succeed. Among these are answering questions, finishing in time, and mastering test-taking strategies. All must be executed on the day of the test at peak performance, or your score will suffer. The test is a mental marathon that has a large impact on your future.

Just like a marathon runner, it is important to work your way up to the full challenge. So first you just worry about questions, and then time, and finally strategy:

Success Strategy

1. Find a good source for practice tests.
2. If you are willing to make a larger time investment, consider using more than one study guide- often the different approaches of multiple authors will help you "get" difficult concepts.
3. Take a practice test with no time constraints, with all study helps "open book." Take your time with questions and focus on applying strategies.
4. Take a practice test with time constraints, with all guides "open book."
5. Take a final practice test with no open material and time limits

If you have time to take more practice tests, just repeat step 5. By gradually exposing yourself to the full rigors of the test environment, you will condition your mind to the stress of test day and maximize your success.

Secret Key #4 - Prepare, Don't Procrastinate

Let me state an obvious fact: if you take the test three times, you will get three different scores. This is due to the way you feel on test day, the level of preparedness you have, and, despite the test writers' claims to the contrary, some tests WILL be easier for you than others.

Since your future depends so much on your score, you should maximize your chances of success. In order to maximize the likelihood of success, you've got to prepare in advance. This means taking practice tests and spending time learning the information and test taking strategies you will need to succeed.

Never take the test as a "practice" test, expecting that you can just take it again if you need to. Feel free to take sample tests on your own, but when you go to take the official test, be prepared, be focused, and do your best the first time!

Secret Key #5 - Test Yourself

Everyone knows that time is money. There is no need to spend too much of your time or too little of your time preparing for the test. You should only spend as much of your precious time preparing as is necessary for you to get the score you need.

Once you have taken a practice test under real conditions of time constraints, then you will know if you are ready for the test or not.

If you have scored extremely high the first time that you take the practice test, then there is not much point in spending countless hours studying. You are already there.

Benchmark your abilities by retaking practice tests and seeing how much you have improved. Once you score high enough to guarantee success, then you are ready.

If you have scored well below where you need, then knuckle down and begin studying in earnest. Check your improvement regularly through the use of practice tests under real conditions. Above all, don't worry, panic, or give up. The key is perseverance!

Then, when you go to take the test, remain confident and remember how well you did on the practice tests. If you can score high enough on a practice test, then you can do the same on the real thing.

General Strategies

The most important thing you can do is to ignore your fears and jump into the test immediately- do not be overwhelmed by any strange-sounding terms. You have to jump into the test like jumping into a pool- all at once is the easiest way.

Make Predictions

As you read and understand the question, try to guess what the answer will be. Remember that several of the answer choices are wrong, and once you begin reading them, your mind will immediately become cluttered with answer choices designed to throw you off. Your mind is typically the most focused immediately after you have read the question and digested its contents. If you can, try to predict what the correct answer will be. You may be surprised at what you can predict.

Quickly scan the choices and see if your prediction is in the listed answer choices. If it is, then you can be quite confident that you have the right answer. It still won't hurt to check the other answer choices, but most of the time, you've got it!

Answer the Question

It may seem obvious to only pick answer choices that answer the question, but the test writers can create some excellent answer choices that are wrong. Don't pick an answer just because it sounds right, or you believe it to be true. It MUST answer the question. Once you've made your selection, always go back and check it against the question and make sure that you didn't misread the question, and the answer choice does answer the question posed.

Benchmark

After you read the first answer choice, decide if you think it sounds correct or not. If it doesn't, move on to the next answer choice. If it does, mentally mark that answer choice. This doesn't mean that you've definitely selected it as your answer choice, it just means that it's the best you've seen thus far. Go ahead and read the next choice. If the next choice is worse than the one you've already selected, keep going to the next answer choice. If the next choice is better than the choice you've already selected, mentally mark the new answer choice as your best guess.

The first answer choice that you select becomes your standard. Every other answer choice must be benchmarked against that standard. That choice is correct until proven otherwise by another answer choice beating it out. Once you've decided that no other answer choice seems as good, do one final check to ensure that your answer choice answers the question posed.

Valid Information

Don't discount any of the information provided in the question. Every piece of information may be necessary to determine the correct answer. None of the information in the question is there to throw you off (while the answer choices will certainly have information to throw you off). If two seemingly unrelated topics are discussed, don't ignore either. You can be confident there is a relationship, or it wouldn't be included in the question, and you are probably going to have to determine what is that relationship to find the answer.

Avoid "Fact Traps"

Don't get distracted by a choice that is factually true. Your search is for the answer that answers the question. Stay focused and don't fall for an answer that is true but incorrect. Always go back to the question and make sure you're choosing an answer that actually answers the question and is not just a true statement. An answer can be factually correct, but it MUST answer the question asked. Additionally, two answers can both be seemingly correct, so be sure to read all of the answer choices, and make sure that you get the one that BEST answers the question.

Milk the Question

Some of the questions may throw you completely off. They might deal with a subject you have not been exposed to, or one that you haven't reviewed in years. While your lack of knowledge about the subject will be a hindrance, the question itself can give you many clues that will help you find the correct answer. Read the question carefully and look for clues. Watch particularly for adjectives and nouns describing difficult terms or words that you don't recognize. Regardless of if you completely understand a word or not, replacing it with a synonym either provided or one you more familiar with may help you to understand what the questions are asking. Rather than wracking your mind about specific detailed information concerning a difficult term or word, try to use mental substitutes that are easier to understand.

The Trap of Familiarity

Don't just choose a word because you recognize it. On difficult questions, you may not recognize a number of words in the answer choices. The test writers don't put "make-believe" words on the test; so don't think that just because you only recognize all the words in one answer choice means that answer choice must be correct. If you only recognize words in one answer choice, then focus on that one. Is it correct? Try your best to determine if it is correct. If it is, that is great, but if it doesn't, eliminate it. Each word and answer choice you eliminate increases your chances of getting the question correct, even if you then have to guess among the unfamiliar choices.

Eliminate Answers

Eliminate choices as soon as you realize they are wrong. But be careful! Make sure you consider all of the possible answer choices. Just because one appears right, doesn't mean that the next one won't be even better! The test writers will usually put more than one good answer choice for every question, so read all of them. Don't worry if you are stuck between two that seem right. By getting down to just two remaining possible choices, your odds are now 50/50. Rather than wasting too much time, play the odds. You are guessing, but guessing wisely, because you've been able to knock out some of the answer choices that you know are wrong. If you are eliminating choices and realize that the last answer choice you are left with is also obviously wrong, don't panic. Start over and consider each choice again. There may easily be something that you missed the first time and will realize on the second pass.

Tough Questions

If you are stumped on a problem or it appears too hard or too difficult, don't waste time. Move on! Remember though, if you can quickly check for obviously incorrect answer choices, your chances of guessing correctly are greatly improved. Before you completely give up, at least try to knock out a couple of possible answers. Eliminate what you can and then guess at the remaining answer choices before moving on.

Brainstorm

If you get stuck on a difficult question, spend a few seconds quickly brainstorming. Run through the complete list of possible answer choices. Look at each choice and ask yourself, "Could this answer the question satisfactorily?" Go through each answer choice and consider it independently of the other. By systematically going through all possibilities, you may find something that you would otherwise overlook. Remember that when you get stuck, it's important to try to keep moving.

Read Carefully

Understand the problem. Read the question and answer choices carefully. Don't miss the question because you misread the terms. You have plenty of time to read each question thoroughly and make sure you understand what is being asked. Yet a happy medium must be attained, so don't waste too much time. You must read carefully, but efficiently.

Face Value

When in doubt, use common sense. Always accept the situation in the problem at face value. Don't read too much into it. These problems will not require you to make huge leaps of logic. The test writers aren't trying to throw you off with a cheap trick. If you have to go beyond creativity and make a leap of logic in order to have an answer choice answer the question, then you should look at the other answer choices. Don't overcomplicate the problem by creating theoretical relationships or explanations that will warp time or space. These are normal problems rooted in reality. It's just that the applicable relationship or explanation may not be readily apparent and you have to figure things out. Use your common sense to interpret anything that isn't clear.

Prefixes

If you're having trouble with a word in the question or answer choices, try dissecting it. Take advantage of every clue that the word might include. Prefixes and suffixes can be a huge help. Usually they allow you to determine a basic meaning. Pre- means before, post- means after, pro - is positive, de- is negative. From these prefixes and suffixes, you can get an idea of the general meaning of the word and try to put it into context. Beware though of any traps. Just because con is the opposite of pro, doesn't necessarily mean congress is the opposite of progress!

Hedge Phrases

Watch out for critical "hedge" phrases, such as likely, may, can, will often, sometimes, often, almost, mostly, usually, generally, rarely, sometimes. Question writers insert these hedge phrases to cover every possibility. Often an answer choice will be wrong simply because it leaves no room for exception. Avoid answer choices that have definitive words like "exactly," and "always".

Switchback Words

Stay alert for "switchbacks". These are the words and phrases frequently used to alert you to shifts in thought. The most common switchback word is "but". Others include although, however, nevertheless, on the other hand, even though, while, in spite of, despite, regardless of.

New Information

Correct answer choices will rarely have completely new information included. Answer choices typically are straightforward reflections of the material asked about and will directly relate to the question. If a new piece of information is included in an answer choice that doesn't even seem to relate to the topic being asked about, then that answer choice is likely incorrect. All of the information needed to answer the question is usually provided for you, and so you should not have to make guesses that are unsupported or choose answer choices that require unknown information that cannot be reasoned on its own.

Time Management

On technical questions, don't get lost on the technical terms. Don't spend too much time on any one question. If you don't know what a term means, then since you don't have a dictionary, odds are you aren't going to get much further. You should immediately recognize terms as whether or not you know them. If you don't, work with the other clues that you have, the other answer choices and terms provided, but don't waste too much time trying to figure out a difficult term.

Contextual Clues

Look for contextual clues. An answer can be right but not correct. The contextual clues will help you find the answer that is most right and is correct. Understand the context in which a phrase or statement is made. This will help you make important distinctions.

Don't Panic

Panicking will not answer any questions for you. Therefore, it isn't helpful. When you first see the question, if your mind goes blank, take a deep breath. Force yourself to mechanically go through the steps of solving the problem and using the strategies you've learned.

Pace Yourself

Don't get clock fever. It's easy to be overwhelmed when you're looking at a page full of questions, your mind is full of random thoughts and feeling confused, and the clock is ticking down faster than you would like. Calm down and maintain the pace that you have set for yourself. As long as you are on track by monitoring your pace, you are guaranteed to have enough time for yourself. When you get to the last few minutes of the test, it may seem like you won't have enough time left, but if you only have as many questions as you should have left at that point, then you're right on track!

Answer Selection

The best way to pick an answer choice is to eliminate all of those that are wrong, until only one is left and confirm that is the correct answer. Sometimes though, an answer choice may immediately look right. Be careful! Take a second to make sure that the other choices are not equally obvious. Don't make a hasty mistake. There are only two times that you should stop before checking other answers. First is when you are positive that the answer choice you have selected is correct. Second is when time is almost out and you have to make a quick guess!

Check Your Work

Since you will probably not know every term listed and the answer to every question, it is important that you get credit for the ones that you do know. Don't miss any questions through careless mistakes. If at all possible, try to take a second to look back over your answer selection and make sure you've selected the correct answer choice and haven't made a costly careless mistake (such as marking an answer choice that you didn't mean to mark). This quick double check should more than pay for itself in caught mistakes for the time it costs.

Beware of Directly Quoted Answers

Sometimes an answer choice will repeat word for word a portion of the question or reference section. However, beware of such exact duplication – it may be a trap! More than likely, the correct choice will paraphrase or summarize a point, rather than being exactly the same wording.

Slang

Scientific sounding answers are better than slang ones. An answer choice that begins "To compare the outcomes..." is much more likely to be correct than one that begins "Because some people insisted..."

Extreme Statements

Avoid wild answers that throw out highly controversial ideas that are proclaimed as established fact. An answer choice that states the "process should be used in certain situations, if..." is much more likely to be correct than one that states the "process should be discontinued completely." The first is a calm rational statement and doesn't even make a definitive, uncompromising stance, using a hedge word "if" to provide wiggle room, whereas the second choice is a radical idea and far more extreme.

Answer Choice Families

When you have two or more answer choices that are direct opposites or parallels, one of them is usually the correct answer. For instance, if one answer choice states "x increases" and another answer choice states "x decreases" or "y increases," then those two or three answer choices are very similar in construction and fall into the same family of answer choices. A family of answer choices is when two or three answer choices are very similar in construction, and yet often have a directly opposite meaning. Usually the correct answer choice will be in that family of answer choices. The "odd man out" or answer choice that doesn't seem to fit the parallel construction of the other answer choices is more likely to be incorrect.

Special Report: How to Overcome Test Anxiety

The very nature of tests caters to some level of anxiety, nervousness or tension, just as we feel for any important event that occurs in our lives. A little bit of anxiety or nervousness can be a good thing. It helps us with motivation, and makes achievement just that much sweeter. However, too much anxiety can be a problem; especially if it hinders our ability to function and perform.

"Test anxiety," is the term that refers to the emotional reactions that some test-takers experience when faced with a test or exam. Having a fear of testing and exams is based upon a rational fear, since the test-taker's performance can shape the course of an academic career. Nevertheless, experiencing excessive fear of examinations will only interfere with the test-takers ability to perform, and his/her chances to be successful.

There are a large variety of causes that can contribute to the development and sensation of test anxiety. These include, but are not limited to lack of performance and worrying about issues surrounding the test.

Lack of Preparation

Lack of preparation can be identified by the following behaviors or situations:

Not scheduling enough time to study, and therefore cramming the night before the test or exam
Managing time poorly, to create the sensation that there is not enough time to do everything
Failing to organize the text information in advance, so that the study material consists of the entire text and not simply the pertinent information
Poor overall studying habits

Worrying, on the other hand, can be related to both the test taker, or many other factors around him/her that will be affected by the results of the test. These include worrying about:

Previous performances on similar exams, or exams in general
How friends and other students are achieving
The negative consequences that will result from a poor grade or failure

There are three primary elements to test anxiety. Physical components, which involve the same typical bodily reactions as those to acute anxiety (to be discussed below). Emotional factors have to do with fear or panic. Mental or cognitive issues concerning attention spans and memory abilities.

Physical Signals

There are many different symptoms of test anxiety, and these are not limited to mental and emotional strain. Frequently there are a range of physical signals that will let a test taker know that he/she is suffering from test anxiety. These bodily changes can include the following:

Perspiring
Sweaty palms
Wet, trembling hands
Nausea
Dry mouth
A knot in the stomach
Headache
Faintness
Muscle tension
Aching shoulders, back and neck
Rapid heart beat
Feeling too hot/cold

To recognize the sensation of test anxiety, a test-taker should monitor him/herself for the following sensations:

The physical distress symptoms as listed above
Emotional sensitivity, expressing emotional feelings such as the need to cry or laugh too much, or a sensation of anger or helplessness
A decreased ability to think, causing the test-taker to blank out or have racing thoughts that are hard to organize or control.

Though most students will feel some level of anxiety when faced with a test or exam, the majority can cope with that anxiety and maintain it at a manageable level. However, those who cannot are faced with a very real and very serious condition, which can and should be controlled for the immeasurable benefit of this sufferer.

Naturally, these sensations lead to negative results for the testing experience. The most common effects of test anxiety have to do with nervousness and mental blocking.

Nervousness

Nervousness can appear in several different levels:

The test-taker's difficulty, or even inability to read and understand the questions on the test
The difficulty or inability to organize thoughts to a coherent form
The difficulty or inability to recall key words and concepts relating to the testing questions (especially essays)
The receipt of poor grades on a test, though the test material was well known by the test taker

Conversely, a person may also experience mental blocking, which involves:

Blanking out on test questions
Only remembering the correct answers to the questions when the test has already finished.

Fortunately for test anxiety sufferers, beating these feelings, to a large degree, has to do with proper preparation. When a test taker has a feeling of preparedness, then anxiety will be dramatically lessened.

The first step to resolving anxiety issues is to distinguish which of the two types of anxiety are being suffered. If the anxiety is a direct result of a lack of preparation, this should be considered a normal reaction, and the anxiety level (as opposed to the test results) shouldn't be anything to worry about. However, if, when adequately prepared, the test-taker still panics, blanks out, or seems to overreact, this is not a fully rational reaction. While this can be considered normal too, there are many ways to combat and overcome these effects.

Remember that anxiety cannot be entirely eliminated, however, there are ways to minimize it, to make the anxiety easier to manage. Preparation is one of the best ways to minimize test anxiety. Therefore the following techniques are wise in order to best fight off any anxiety that may want to build.

To begin with, try to avoid cramming before a test, whenever it is possible. By trying to memorize an entire term's worth of information in one day, you'll be shocking your system, and not giving yourself a very good chance to absorb the information. This is an easy path to anxiety, so for those who suffer from test anxiety, cramming should not even be considered an option.

Instead of cramming, work throughout the semester to combine all of the material which is presented throughout the semester, and work on it gradually as the course goes by, making sure to master the main concepts first, leaving minor details for a week or so before the test.

To study for the upcoming exam, be sure to pose questions that may be on the examination, to gauge the ability to answer them by integrating the ideas from your texts, notes and lectures, as well as any supplementary readings.

If it is truly impossible to cover all of the information that was covered in that particular term, concentrate on the most important portions, that can be covered very well. Learn these concepts as best as possible, so that when the test comes, a goal can be made to use these concepts as presentations of your knowledge.

In addition to study habits, changes in attitude are critical to beating a struggle with test anxiety. In fact, an improvement of the perspective over the entire test-taking experience can actually help a test taker to enjoy studying and therefore improve the overall experience. Be certain not to overemphasize the significance of the grade - know that the result of the test is neither a reflection of self worth, nor is it a measure of intelligence; one grade will not predict a person's future success.

To improve an overall testing outlook, the following steps should be tried:

Keeping in mind that the most reasonable expectation for taking a test is to expect to try to demonstrate as much of what you know as you possibly can.
Reminding ourselves that a test is only one test; this is not the only one, and there will be others.
The thought of thinking of oneself in an irrational, all-or-nothing term should be avoided at all costs.
A reward should be designated for after the test, so there's something to look forward to. Whether it be going to a movie, going out to eat, or simply visiting friends, schedule it in advance, and do it no matter what result is expected on the exam.

Test-takers should also keep in mind that the basics are some of the most important things, even beyond anti-anxiety techniques and studying. Never neglect the basic social, emotional and biological needs, in order to try to absorb information. In order to best achieve, these three factors must be held as just as important as the studying itself.

Study Steps

Remember the following important steps for studying:

Maintain healthy nutrition and exercise habits. Continue both your recreational activities and social pass times. These both contribute to your physical and emotional well being.
Be certain to get a good amount of sleep, especially the night before the test, because when you're overtired you are not able to perform to the best of your best ability.
Keep the studying pace to a moderate level by taking breaks when they are needed, and varying the work whenever possible, to keep the mind fresh instead of getting bored. When enough studying has been done that all the material that can be learned has been learned, and the test taker is prepared for the test, stop studying and do something relaxing such as listening to music, watching a movie, or taking a warm bubble bath.

There are also many other techniques to minimize the uneasiness or apprehension that is experienced along with test anxiety before, during, or even after the examination. In fact, there are a great deal of things that can be done to stop anxiety from interfering with lifestyle and performance. Again, remember that anxiety will not be eliminated entirely, and it shouldn't be. Otherwise that "up" feeling for exams would not exist, and most of us depend on that sensation to perform better than usual. However, this anxiety has to be at a level that is manageable.

Of course, as we have just discussed, being prepared for the exam is half the battle right away. Attending all classes, finding out what knowledge will be expected on the exam, and knowing the exam schedules are easy steps to lowering anxiety. Keeping up with work will remove the need to cram, and efficient study habits will eliminate wasted time. Studying should be done in an ideal location for concentration, so that it is simple to become interested in the material and give it complete attention. A method such as SQ3R (Survey, Question, Read, Recite, Review) is a wonderful key to follow to make sure that the study habits are as effective as possible, especially in the case of learning from a textbook. Flashcards are great techniques for memorization. Learning to take good notes will mean that notes will be full of useful information, so that less sifting will need to be done to seek out what is pertinent for studying. Reviewing notes after class and then again on occasion will keep the information fresh in the mind. From notes that have been taken summary sheets and outlines can be made for simpler reviewing.

A study group can also be a very motivational and helpful place to study, as there will be a sharing of ideas, all of the minds can work together, to make sure that everyone understands, and the studying will be made more interesting because it will be a social occasion.

Basically, though, as long as the test-taker remains organized and self confident, with efficient study habits, less time will need to be spent studying, and higher grades will be achieved.

To become self confident, there are many useful steps. The first of these is "self talk." It has been shown through extensive research, that self-talk for students who suffer from test anxiety, should be well monitored, in order to make sure that it contributes to self confidence as opposed to sinking the student. Frequently the self talk of test-anxious students is negative or self-defeating, thinking that everyone else is smarter and faster, that they always mess up, and that if they don't do well, they'll fail the entire course. It is important to decreasing anxiety that awareness is made of self talk. Try writing any negative self thoughts and then disputing them with a positive statement instead. Begin self-encouragement as though it was a friend speaking. Repeat positive statements to help reprogram the mind to believing in successes instead of failures.

Helpful Techniques

Other extremely helpful techniques include:

Self-visualization of doing well and reaching goals
While aiming for an "A" level of understanding, don't try to "overprotect" by setting your expectations lower. This will only convince the mind to stop studying in order to meet the lower expectations.
Don't make comparisons with the results or habits of other students. These are individual factors, and different things work for different people, causing different results.
Strive to become an expert in learning what works well, and what can be done in order to improve. Consider collecting this data in a journal.
Create rewards for after studying instead of doing things before studying that will only turn into avoidance behaviors.
Make a practice of relaxing - by using methods such as progressive relaxation, self-hypnosis, guided imagery, etc - in order to make relaxation an automatic sensation.
Work on creating a state of relaxed concentration so that concentrating will take on the focus of the mind, so that none will be wasted on worrying.
Take good care of the physical self by eating well and getting enough sleep.
Plan in time for exercise and stick to this plan.

Beyond these techniques, there are other methods to be used before, during and after the test that will help the test-taker perform well in addition to overcoming anxiety. Before the exam comes the academic preparation. This involves establishing a study schedule and beginning at least one week before the actual date of the test. By doing this, the anxiety of not having enough time to study for the test will be automatically eliminated. Moreover, this will make the studying a much more effective experience, ensuring that the learning will be an easier process. This relieves much undue pressure on the test-taker.

Summary sheets, note cards, and flash cards with the main concepts and examples of these main concepts should be prepared in advance of the actual studying time. A topic should never be eliminated from this process. By omitting a topic because it isn't expected to be on the test is only setting up the test-taker for anxiety should it actually appear on the exam. Utilize the course syllabus for laying out the topics that should be studied. Carefully go over the notes that were made in class, paying special attention to any of the issues that the professor took special care to emphasize while lecturing in class. In the textbooks, use the chapter review, or if possible, the chapter tests, to begin your review.

It may even be possible to ask the instructor what information will be covered on the exam, or what the format of the exam will be (for example, multiple choice, essay, free form, true-false). Additionally, see if it is possible to find out how many questions will be on the test. If a review sheet or sample test has been offered by the professor, make good use of it, above anything else, for the preparation for the test. Another great resource for getting to know the examination is reviewing tests from previous semesters. Use these tests to review, and aim to achieve a 100% score on each of the possible topics. With a few exceptions, the goal that you set for yourself is the highest one that you will reach.

Take all of the questions that were assigned as homework, and rework them to any other possible course material. The more problems reworked, the more skill and confidence will form as a result. When forming the solution to a problem, write out each of the steps. Don't simply do head work. By doing as many steps on paper as possible, much clarification and therefore confidence will be formed. Do this with as many homework problems as possible, before checking the answers. By checking the answer after each problem, a reinforcement will exist, that will not be on the exam. Study situations should be as exam-like as possible, to prime the test-taker's system for the experience. By waiting to check the answers at the end, a psychological advantage will be formed, to decrease the stress factor.

Another fantastic reason for not cramming is the avoidance of confusion in concepts, especially when it comes to mathematics. 8-10 hours of study will become one hundred percent more effective if it is spread out over a week or at least several days, instead of doing it all in one sitting. Recognize that the human brain requires time in order to assimilate new material, so frequent breaks and a span of study time over several days will be much more beneficial.

Additionally, don't study right up until the point of the exam. Studying should stop a minimum of one hour before the exam begins. This allows the brain to rest and put things in their proper order. This will also provide the time to become as relaxed as possible when going into the examination room. The test-taker will also have time to eat well and eat sensibly. Know that the brain needs food as much as the rest of the body. With enough food and enough sleep, as well as a relaxed attitude, the body and the mind are primed for success.

Avoid any anxious classmates who are talking about the exam. These students only spread anxiety, and are not worth sharing the anxious sentimentalities.

Before the test also involves creating a positive attitude, so mental preparation should also be a point of concentration. There are many keys to creating a positive attitude. Should fears become rushing in, make a visualization of taking the exam, doing well, and seeing an A written on the paper. Write out a list of affirmations that will bring a feeling of confidence, such as "I am doing well in my English class," "I studied well and know my material," "I enjoy this class." Even if the affirmations aren't believed at first, it sends a positive message to the subconscious which will result in an alteration of the overall belief system, which is the system that creates reality.

If a sensation of panic begins, work with the fear and imagine the very worst! Work through the entire scenario of not passing the test, failing the entire course, and dropping out of school, followed by not getting a job, and pushing a shopping cart through the dark alley where you'll live. This will place things into perspective! Then, practice deep breathing and create a visualization of the opposite situation - achieving an "A" on the exam, passing the entire course, receiving the degree at a graduation ceremony.

On the day of the test, there are many things to be done to ensure the best results, as well as the most calm outlook. The following stages are suggested in order to maximize test-taking potential:

Begin the examination day with a moderate breakfast, and avoid any coffee or beverages with caffeine if the test taker is prone to jitters. Even people who are used to managing caffeine can feel jittery or light-headed when it is taken on a test day.
Attempt to do something that is relaxing before the examination begins. As last minute cramming clouds the mastering of overall concepts, it is better to use this time to create a calming outlook.
Be certain to arrive at the test location well in advance, in order to provide time to select a location that is away from doors, windows and other distractions, as well as giving enough time to relax before the test begins.
Keep away from anxiety generating classmates who will upset the sensation of stability and relaxation that is being attempted before the exam.
Should the waiting period before the exam begins cause anxiety, create a self-distraction by reading a light magazine or something else that is relaxing and simple.

During the exam itself, read the entire exam from beginning to end, and find out how much time should be allotted to each individual problem. Once writing the exam, should more time be taken for a problem, it should be abandoned, in order to begin another problem. If there is time at the end, the unfinished problem can always be returned to and completed.

Read the instructions very carefully - twice - so that unpleasant surprises won't follow during or after the exam has ended.

When writing the exam, pretend that the situation is actually simply the completion of homework within a library, or at home. This will assist in forming a relaxed atmosphere, and will allow the brain extra focus for the complex thinking function.

Begin the exam with all of the questions with which the most confidence is felt. This will build the confidence level regarding the entire exam and will begin a quality momentum. This will also create encouragement for trying the problems where uncertainty resides.

Going with the "gut instinct" is always the way to go when solving a problem. Second guessing should be avoided at all costs. Have confidence in the ability to do well.

For essay questions, create an outline in advance that will keep the mind organized and make certain that all of the points are remembered. For multiple choice, read every answer, even if the correct one has been spotted - a better one may exist.

Continue at a pace that is reasonable and not rushed, in order to be able to work carefully. Provide enough time to go over the answers at the end, to check for small errors that can be corrected.

Should a feeling of panic begin, breathe deeply, and think of the feeling of the body releasing sand through its pores. Visualize a calm, peaceful place, and include all of the sights, sounds and sensations of this image. Continue the deep breathing, and take a few minutes to continue this with closed eyes. When all is well again, return to the test.

If a "blanking" occurs for a certain question, skip it and move on to the next question. There will be time to return to the other question later. Get everything done that can be done, first, to guarantee all the grades that can be compiled, and to build all of the confidence possible. Then return to the weaker questions to build the marks from there.

Remember, one's own reality can be created, so as long as the belief is there, success will follow. And remember: anxiety can happen later, right now, there's an exam to be written!

After the examination is complete, whether there is a feeling for a good grade or a bad grade, don't dwell on the exam, and be certain to follow through on the reward that was promised...and enjoy it! Don't dwell on any mistakes that have been made, as there is nothing that can be done at this point anyway.

Additionally, don't begin to study for the next test right away. Do something relaxing for a while, and let the mind relax and prepare itself to begin absorbing information again.

From the results of the exam - both the grade and the entire experience, be certain to learn from what has gone on. Perfect studying habits and work some more on confidence in order to make the next examination experience even better than the last one.

Learn to avoid places where openings occurred for laziness, procrastination and day dreaming.

Use the time between this exam and the next one to better learn to relax, even learning to relax on cue, so that any anxiety can be controlled during the next exam. Learn how to relax the body. Slouch in your chair if that helps. Tighten and then relax all of the different muscle groups, one group at a time, beginning with the feet and then working all the way up to the neck and face. This will ultimately relax the muscles more than they were to begin with. Learn how to breathe deeply and comfortably, and focus on this breathing going in and out as a relaxing thought. With every exhale, repeat the word "relax."

As common as test anxiety is, it is very possible to overcome it. Make yourself one of the test-takers who overcome this frustrating hindrance.